SCHOLASTIC

100

2014 CURRICULUM

COMPUTING
LESSONS

Terms and conditions

IMPORTANT – PERMITTED USE AND WARNINGS – READ CAREFULLY BEFORE USING

IF YOU ACCEPT THE ABOVE CONDITIONS YOU MAY PROCEED TO USE THE CD-ROM.

Recommended system requirements:

- Windows: XP (Service Pack 3), Vista (Service Pack 2), Windows 7 or Windows 8 with 2.33GHz processor
- Mac: OS 10.6 to 10.8 with Intel Core™ Duo processor
- 1GB RAM (recommended)
- 1024 x 768 Screen resolution
- CD-ROM drive (24x speed recommended)
- 16-bit sound card
- Adobe Reader (version 9 recommended for Mac users)
- Broadband internet connections (for installation and updates)

For all technical support queries, please phone Scholastic Customer Services on 0845 6039091.

SCHOLASTIC

Book End, Range Road, Witney, Oxfordshire, OX29 0YD
www.scholastic.co.uk

© 2014, Scholastic Ltd

1 2 3 4 5 6 7 8 9   4 5 6 7 8 9 0 1 2 3

British Library Cataloguing-in-Publication Data
A catalogue record for this book is available from the
British Library.

ISBN 978-1407-12856-6
Printed by Bell & Bain Ltd, Glasgow

Due to the nature of the web we cannot guarantee
the content or links of any site mentioned. We strongly
recommend that teachers check websites before using
them in the classroom.

Extracts from *The National Curriculum in England,
Computing Programme of Study* © Crown Copyright.
Reproduced under the terms of the Open Government
Licence (OGL). http://www.nationalarchives.gov.uk/doc/
open-government-licence/open-government-licence.htm

Authors
Zoe Ross and Steve Bunce

Editorial team
Mark Walker, Jenny Wilcox, Kim Vernon, Lucy Tritton,
Sarah Sodhi, Suzanne Adams

Cover Design
Andrea Lewis

Design
Sarah Garbett @ Sg Creative Services

CD-ROM development
Hannah Barnett, Phil Crothers, MWA Technologies
Private Ltd

Illustrations
Tomek.gr

Acknowledgements
The publishers gratefully acknowledge permission
to reproduce the following copyright material:

Walker Books for the use of illustrations from
Handa's Surprise by Eileen Browne. Copyright ©
1994 Eileen Browne From HANDA'S SURPRISE
by Eileen Browne. Reproduced by permission of
Walker Books Ltd, London SE11 5HJ www.walker.
co.uk (1994, Walker Books Ltd).

Penguin Books Ltd. for the use of an illustration
and an extract from Funnybones by Janet and Allan
Ahlberg. Copyright © 1980 Allan Ahlberg and Jane
Ahlberg.Reproduced by permission of Penguin
Books Ltd. (1980, William Heinemann Ltd)

Every effort has been made to trace copyright
holders for the works reproduced in this book,
and the publishers apologise for any inadvertent
omissions.

SCHOLASTIC

Contents

Introduction

About the series

The *100 Computing Lessons* series is designed to meet the requirements of the 2014 Curriculum, Computing Programmes of Study. There are three books in the series, Years 1–2, 3–4 and 5–6, and each book contains lesson plans, resources and ideas matched to the new curriculum. It can be a complex task to ensure that a progressive and appropriate curriculum is followed in all year groups; this series has been carefully structured to ensure that a progressive and appropriate curriculum is followed throughout.

About the new curriculum

Computing is a subject full of opportunities for children to develop their thinking, with practical programming skills, focused on real world examples. The new 'Computing' curriculum replaces the old 'ICT' curriculum.

> *The National Curriculum for Computing aims to ensure that all pupils:*
> - *can understand and apply the fundamental principles and concepts of computer science, including abstraction, logic, algorithms and data representation*
> - *can analyse problems in computational terms, and have repeated practical experience of writing computer programs in order to solve such problems*
> - *can evaluate and apply information technology, including new or unfamiliar technologies, analytically to solve problems*
> - *are responsible, competent, confident and creative users of information and communication technology.*

> The National Curriculum Programme of Study for Computing contains guidance for Key Stages 1 and 2. The subject focuses on computational thinking with an emphasis on programming. In addition, there are other areas of computing which have equal importance. In this series, the National Curriculum has been divided into four key subject areas:
> - Algorithms and programming
> - Data and information
> - How computers work
> - Communication and e-safety
>
> The 'Algorithms and programming' parts of the Programme of Study have been combined into one block, as they are closely related and there is a progression over the key stages. Each year there are two 'Algorithms and programming' blocks and one each for 'Data and information', 'How computers work', 'Communication' and 'E-safety'.

Terminology

In this guide, the main terms used are:

Subject areas: the area of the subject, for computing, we will use 'Algorithms and programming', 'Data and information', 'How computers work' and 'Communication and e-safety'.

Objectives: by the end of Key Stage 1 and Key Stage 2, children are expected to know, apply and understand the matters, skills and processes detailed in the relevant programme of study.

■SCHOLASTIC

About the book

This book is divided into twelve chapters; six for each year group. Each chapter contains a half-term's work and is based around a topic or theme. Each chapter follows the same structure:

Chapter introduction

At the start of each chapter there is a summary of what is covered. This includes:

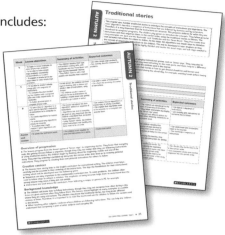

- **Introduction:** A description of what is covered in the chapter.
- **Expected prior learning:** What the children are expected to know before starting the work in the chapter.
- **Chapter at a glance:** This is a table that summarises the content of each lesson, including: the curriculum objectives, lesson objectives, a summary of the activities and the outcome.
- **Overview of progression:** A brief explanation of how the children progress through the chapter.
- **Creative context:** How the chapter could link to other curriculum areas.
- **Background knowledge:** A section explaining grammatical terms and suchlike to enhance your subject knowledge, where required.

Lessons

Each chapter contains six weeks' of lessons. At the start of each week there is an introduction about what is covered. The lesson plans then include the relevant combination of headings from below.

- **Curriculum objectives:** The relevant objectives from the Programme of Study.
- **Lesson objectives:** Objectives that are based upon the Curriculum objectives, but are more specific broken-down steps to achieve them.
- **Expected outcomes:** What you should expect all, most and some children to know by the end of the lesson.
- **Resources:** What you require to teach the lesson.
- **Introduction:** A short and engaging activity to begin the lesson.
- **Whole-class work:** Working together as a class.
- **Group/Paired/Independent work:** Children working independently of the teacher in pairs, groups or alone.
- **Differentiation:** Ideas for how to support children who are struggling with a concept or how to extend those children who understand a concept without taking them onto new work.
- **Review:** A chance to review the children's learning and ensure the outcomes of the lesson have been achieved.

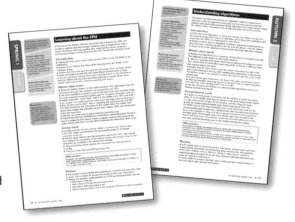

Assess and review

At the end of each chapter are activities for assessing and reviewing the children's understanding. These can be conducted during the course of the chapter's work or saved until the end of the chapter or done at a later date. They are set out the same as lesson plans with an underlying assessment focus.

Photocopiable pages

At the end of each chapter are some photocopiable pages that will have been referred to in the lesson plans. These sheets are for the children to use. There is generally a title, an instruction, an activity and an 'I can' statement at the bottom. The children should be encouraged to complete the 'I can' statements by colouring in the traffic lights to say how they think they have done (red – not very well, amber – ok, green – very well).

These sheets are also provided on the CD-ROM alongside additional pages as referenced in the lessons (see page 7 About the CD-ROM).

Tablet appendix

At the end of the book are 16 additional lessons which have been written with a specific focus on tablet computers and other touch-screen devices.

■ SCHOLASTIC

About the CD-ROM

The CD-ROM contains:

- Printable versions of the photocopiable sheets from the book and additional photocopiable sheets as referenced in the lesson plans.
- Interactive activities for children to complete or to use on the whiteboard.
- Media resources to display.
- Printable versions of the lesson plans.
- Digital versions of the lesson plans with the relevant resources linked to them.

Getting started

- Put the CD-ROM into your CD-ROM drive.
  - For Windows users, the install wizard should autorun, if it fails to do so then navigate to your CD-ROM drive. Then follow the installation process.
  - For Mac users, copy the disk image file to your hard drive. After it has finished copying double-click it to mount the disk image. Navigate to the mounted disk image and run the installer. After installation the disk image can be unmounted and the DMG can be deleted from the hard drive.
- To complete the installation of the program you need to open the program and click 'Update' in the pop-up. Please note – this CD-ROM is web-enabled and the content will be downloaded from the internet to your hard-drive to populate the CD-ROM with the relevant resources. This only needs to be done on first use, after this you will be able to use the CD-ROM without an internet connection. If at any point any content is updated you will receive another pop-up upon start up with an internet connection.

Navigating the CD-ROM

There are two options to navigate the CD-ROM either as a Child or as a Teacher.

Child

- Click on the 'Child' button on the first menu screen.
- In the second menu click on the relevant class (please note only the books installed on the machine or network will be accessible. You can also rename year groups to match your school's naming conventions via the Teacher > Settings > Rename books area).
- A list of interactive activities will be displayed, children need to locate the correct one and click 'Go' to launch it.
- There is the opportunity to print or save a PDF of the activity at the end.

Teacher

- Click on the Teacher button on the first menu screen and you will be taken to a screen showing which of the *100 Computing* books you have purchased. From here, you can also access information about getting started and the credits.
- To enter the product click 'Next' in the bottom right.
- You then need to enter a password (the password is: login).
  - On first use: Enter as a Guest by clicking on the 'Guest' button.
  - If desired, create a profile for yourself by adding your name to the list of users. Profiles allow you to save favourites and to specify which year group(s) you wish to be able to view.
  - Go to 'Settings' to create a profile for yourself – click 'Add user' and enter your name. Then choose the year groups you wish to have access to (you can return to this screen to change this at any time). Click on 'Login' at the top of the screen to re-enter the disk under your new profile.
- On subsequent uses you can choose your name from the drop-down list. The 'Guest' option will always be available if you, or a colleague, wish to use this.
- You can search the CD-ROM using the tools or save favourites.

For more information about how to use the CD-ROM, please refer to the help file which can be found in the teacher area of the CD-ROM. It is a red button with a question mark on it on the right-hand side of the screen just underneath the 'Settings' tab.

Dinosaurs

The first chapter of the year engages the children in a dinosaurs theme. They are introduced to the names of the dinosaurs and consider their physical properties, in order to sort them. The main aim is to get the children thinking about the different ways the dinosaurs can be organised, in order to introduce sorting data, in different ways. They sort the dinosaurs alphabetically, by size from smallest to largest and from largest to smallest. After this, the children prepare to display their data, considering its format, for example as an image, text, audio or video. Finally, they begin to represent the data in pictograms, which shows that data can tell a story.

Expected prior learning

● The children will have experience of naming objects and simple facts relating to their size, for example, *Which one is the largest? Which one is the smallest?* They will be starting to understand that names can be sorted alphabetically, for example, linking this idea to their names on a school register.
● They may know different types of data, such as text, images, audio and video, but have not begun to name them using these terms.

Chapter at a glance

Subject area
• Data and information

National Curriculum objective
• To use technology purposefully to create and organise digital content.

Week	Lesson objectives	Summary of activities	Expected outcomes
1	• To identify the name of the dinosaur. • To identify the size of the dinosaur. • To identify the characteristics of a dinosaur, for example, scales, tail, teeth.	• The children are introduced to the 'Dinosaurs' topic and begin to recognise the properties of dinosaurs. • They play 'Odd one out' games to develop their understanding that dinosaurs have different properties.	• Can identify the names of dinosaurs. • Can describe the different characteristics of dinosaurs.
2	• To sort the names alphabetically. • To sort the dinosaurs in order of size, from largest to smallest and from smallest to largest. • To group by characteristics, for example, horns, wings.	• The children begin to sort the dinosaurs alphabetically. • They then begin to sort the dinosaurs based on their physical features.	• Can sort the dinosaurs in simple ways. • Can categorise the dinosaurs into groups.
3	• To identify the basic data types of image, video, audio and text. • To match images and audio data types using a simple drag and drop activity.	• The children are introduced to different types of data, such as image, video, audio and text. • They then begin to combine them together.	• Can describe and use basic types of data. • Can combine images and audio data types in simple ways.
4	• To draw their favourite dinosaur, add a text name and simple text description.	• Building on the previous lesson, the children think about the data types of text and image.	• Can combine text and image data for a particular purpose.
5	• To collect data using a tally sheet.	• The children begin to organise their data, using tally charts and by using simple criteria, such as which dinosaur is the most popular?	• Can collect and organise data.
6	• To display data using simple pictograms.	• The children represent the data using simple pictograms. They reinforce the learning about data types, by labelling the pictograms.	• Can manipulate data in graphical formats.
Assess and review	• To assess the half-term's work.	• To consolidate the learning, the children are given a new activity to sort the data and represent it as a pictogram.	• Assess and review

■SCHOLASTIC

Overview of progression

● Throughout the lessons, the children build upon their knowledge of names of dinosaurs and their physical properties. They begin by ordering the data alphabetically and draw analogies with organising their class. By then naming the types of data, such as text, image or video, they lay the foundations for the following years, where they will learn about data file formats.

● Organising the data, using tally charts and pictograms, introduces the children to representing data in different ways, in order to tell a story. In the following years, they will develop these skills to represent data in different ways, to meet the needs of their audience.

Creative context

● The lessons have strong links to the mathematics curriculum, with children representing data using pictograms and other charts. The computing lessons should also draw upon the children's learning in English, especially in the phonetic reading of the names and ordering them alphabetically.

● Linking to science, the 'Dinosaurs' topic enables the children to compare and order physical characteristics, as well as identify the physical features of the dinosaurs.

Background knowledge

● The children may not have knowledge of dinosaurs. However, they will be familiar with the concepts of objects having names and being different sizes. For example, they could organise their class from smallest to tallest. Children will know the difference between a picture and text, but may not have used these terms, so you will need to introduce the vocabulary with concrete examples.

● Organising the data using tally charts and pictograms may be new to the children. You will need to assess the children's capability in understanding the pictograms and allow them to describe what they mean.

Curriculum objectives
● To use technology purposefully to create and organise digital content.

Lesson objectives
● To identify the name of the dinosaur.
● To identify the size of the dinosaur.
● To identify the characteristics of a dinosaur, for example, scales, tail, teeth.

Expected outcomes
● Can identify the names of dinosaurs.
● Can describe the different characteristics of dinosaurs.

Resources
Photocopiable page 17 'Naming dinosaurs (1)'; photocopiable page 18 'Naming dinosaurs (2)'; media resource 'Odd one out' on the CD-ROM; media resource 'Which dinosaur?' on the CD-ROM

An introduction to digital content: data and information

This lesson offers an introduction to digital content, in particular to data and information. The children will get used to identifying, naming and describing differing dinosaur characteristics. By doing so, they will be starting to label and characterise data. This prepares them for the following lessons, which consider how data can be organised and sorted.

Introduction
● Start by showing the children the media resource 'Odd one out' on the CD-ROM. As a class, work through the screens asking the children:
  ● *What animals can you see?*
  ● *Which animal is the odd one out?*
  ● *Why is it the odd one out?*
  ● *What do all the odd ones out from all the slides have in common?* (They are all dinosaurs.)

Whole-class work
● Explain to the children that today we are going to find out how much they know about dinosaurs.
● Display the media resource 'Which dinosaur?' on the CD-ROM on the whiteboard. Ask the children to identify each of the dinosaurs and then reveal the correct names. Prompt them for suggestions using books and other reference resources as necessary. Encourage the children to share any facts they know about the dinosaurs.

Group/paired work
● Allocate a dinosaur to each pair using the photocopiable pages 17 and 18 'Naming dinosaurs (1) and (2)'.
● Ask the children to work in pairs to name their dinosaur, giving it the correct size label and adding characteristics of the dinosaur, for example, if it has scales, horns or wings.

Differentiation
● Mixed-ability pairings may be useful or less confident learners could work in a small group with adult support.
● Support: Less confident learners may also be supported with dinosaur-specific vocabulary (for example, scales, horns) to enable them to label their dinosaur's features or characteristics.
● Challenge: More confident learners can consider how their dinosaur is similar to, or different from, other dinosaurs. Ask them to look at each others' dinosaurs and compare and contrast them as necessary.

Review
● As a class, encourage the children to demonstrate what they have found out about their dinosaur.
● Start to encourage thinking around how the dinosaurs are similar or different with suitable questions, such as:
  ● *Which of the dinosaurs are very large?*
  ● *Which are very small?*
  ● *Which have scales?*
  ● *Which have horns?*
● Review children's progress through their discussions and through the outcomes of the 'Naming dinosaurs' activity.

Curriculum objectives
● To use technology purposefully to create and organise digital content.

Lesson objectives
● To sort the names alphabetically.
● To sort the dinosaurs in order of size, from largest to smallest and from smallest to largest.
● To group by characteristics, for example, horns, wings.

Expected outcomes
● Can sort the dinosaurs in simple ways.
● Can categorise the dinosaurs into groups.

Resources
Photocopiable page 19 'Dinosaur cards (1)'; photocopiable page 20 'Dinosaur cards (2)'; photocopiable page 21 'Sort the dinosaurs'; interactive activity 'Names of dinosaurs' on the CD-ROM; interactive activity 'Dinosaur differences' on the CD-ROM

Sorting and categorising data and information

In this lesson, the children will discover that data and information can be sorted in different ways. They will sort dinosaurs in alphabetical order and according to size, then categorise dinosaurs into different groups. This will prepare them for future lessons in which they will collect, organise and display their own data.

Introduction
● Recap the last lesson with the children, discussing what they now know about dinosaurs. Ask questions to elicit responses around how dinosaurs are similar and how they are different, For example, *Do all dinosaurs have horns? Which dinosaurs are very small? Which are very large?*
● Show the interactive activity 'Dinosaur differences' on the CD-ROM on the interactive whiteboard to stimulate further discussion.

Group/paired work
● Display the interactive activity 'Names of dinosaurs' on the CD-ROM on the whiteboard. Label the dinosaurs on screen 1 and drag and drop them into the correct alphabetical order on screen 2. Use this activity to discuss how data can be sorted and organised in different ways.
● Give each group a set of cards from the photocopiable pages 19 and 20 'Dinosaur cards 1 and 2'. Ask the children to sort the dinosaurs according to size, from largest to smallest and smallest to largest.
● Next, use the photocopiable page 21 'Sort the dinosaurs' for the children to sort the dinosaurs into different groups – for example, those with horns, those with wings, meat eaters, plant eaters, and so on.

Differentiation
● Mixed-ability pairings may be useful or less confident learners could work in a small group with adult support.
● Support: Less confident learners may need further support with the alphabet and how to identify different characteristics of dinosaurs to sort them into groups.
● Challenge: More confident learners can devise their own additional categories and sort their dinosaurs in different ways.

Review
● As a class, discuss how the children sorted their dinosaurs, how many dinosaurs there were in each group and what type of sorting was most difficult or easiest. Pose questions to encourage the children to think about what their answers mean; for example: *Were most dinosaurs plant or animal eaters?*
● Review the children's progress through their discussions and outcomes of the 'Dinosaur cards' activity.

Curriculum objectives
● To use technology purposefully to create and organise digital content.

Lesson objectives
● To identify the basic data types of image, video, audio and text.
● To match images and audio data types using a simple drag and drop activity.

Expected outcomes
● Can describe and use basic types of data.
● Can combine image and audio data types in simple ways.

Resources
Photocopiable page 22 'Match the text to the image'; media resource 'Dinosaurs in action: data types' on the CD-ROM; interactive activity 'Wild sounds' on the CD-ROM

Introduction to basic types of data

In this lesson, children learn to name and describe the four basic types of data (image, text, audio and video) through identifying different data types relating to dinosaurs. This knowledge and understanding forms the basis for working with digital content in a variety of ways in future lessons.

Introduction
● Show the media resource 'Dinosaurs in action: data types' on the CD-ROM featuring video, text, audio and image. Discuss how we can see the picture of the dinosaur, can read its name, hear its roar and see how it lived. Discuss how this all helps us to find out more about the dinosaur and together it 'brings the dinosaur to life'.

Whole-class work
● Work through the media resource 'Dinosaurs in action: data types' on the CD-ROM together, identifying the different data types and discussing the vocabulary of these data types with the children. For example, *We can see a picture of the dinosaur. This is called an 'image'. Images let us see what the dinosaur looked like.*

Group/paired work
● The children should work through the interactive activity 'Wild sounds' on the CD-ROM, matching the correct sound (audio) to the correct image.

Differentiation
● Mixed-ability pairings may be useful or less confident learners could work in a small group with adult support.
● Support: Less confident learners may need further support in remembering the data type vocabulary. The 'Dinosaurs in action' interactive resource features a slide on which the vocabulary is displayed. Leave this up for the children as a reminder.
● Challenge: More confident learners can work through photocopiable page 22 'Match the text to the image' (you can also use this as a replacement for the interactive activity 'Wild sounds' should you not have access to computers).

Review
● As a class, work through the media resource 'Dinosaurs in action: data types'. Check the children's progress as you go through this. For example, can they identify the correct data types? Do they understand the key terms? Can they make their own sound to match the correct images?
● Also, assess the children's progress through the outcomes of the matching activities. Prompt for any misunderstandings about the data types.

■SCHOLASTIC

Curriculum objectives
● To use technology purposefully to create and organise digital content.

Lesson objectives
● To draw their favourite dinosaur, add a text name and simple text description.

Expected outcomes
● Can combine text and image data for a particular purpose.

Resources
A simple drawing package, such as Microsoft Paint

Combining different data types

In this lesson, the children combine text and images using a simple drawing package. This enables them to practically apply their knowledge and understanding from the previous lesson in which they learned the names of the four basic data types and began to work with simple computer software.

Introduction

Remind the children that in the last lesson they looked at different data types and ask them to name these. Explain that they are now going to create their own images and text, and that they will use a software package on the computer to draw an image of their favourite dinosaur and add text to give it a name. Ask them to choose a favourite dinosaur from Triceratops, Tyrannosaurus rex, Pterodactyl, Diplodocus, Stegosaurus and Velociraptor.

Whole-class work

● Ask the children to log onto the computer and open up the drawing package. Show them the basic tools to use and how to draw lines and shapes and change colours. Ask them to think how they will present their dinosaur using the drawing package.

Independent work

● The children should draw their dinosaur, changing colours as appropriate. More confident learners may be able to add more colours and a background to their dinosaur picture. Show the children how to add text to their image and ask them to name their dinosaur. All children should be shown how to save their work.

Differentiation

● Support: Less confident learners may need further support with using the mouse to draw (if using desktop computers) and may need adult assistance to help them add text to their drawing and save their work.
● Challenge: More confident learners can draw more sophisticated images and may be able to add a simple text description of their dinosaur to their drawing.

Review

● If possible – if the children have saved their work in a shared area – show the children's work to the class on the whiteboard. Pick out some examples and ask the individual children to explain how they added a certain part of their dinosaur or added text in a particular way. Use this as an opportunity to encourage speaking skills, asking children to explain their work to their peers.

Curriculum objectives
● To use technology purposefully to create and organise digital content.

Lesson objectives
● To collect data using a tally sheet.

Expected outcomes
● Can collect and organise data.

Resources
Photocopiable page 23 'Tally sheet'; media resource 'Collecting data: tally marks' on the CD-ROM

Collecting and organising data

In this lesson, the children collect data using a basic tally sheet, which also allows them to organise the data and draw simple conclusions.

Introduction
● Remind the children that in the last lesson they drew their favourite dinosaur and explain that in this lesson they will be finding out which dinosaurs are the most popular within the class.

Whole-class work
● Show the children the media resource 'Collecting data: tally marks' on the CD-ROM and ask them to think how they could find out which is the most popular dinosaur in the class. Show them photocopiable page 23 'Tally sheet' and explain that this can help them to find out the most popular dinosaur easily and quickly. Ask questions about the example data, for example, *How many children said dogs were their favourite animal?*
● Give each child or pair of children a copy of photocopiable page 23 'Tally sheet'. Explain how they should record answers and how they can ensure they have asked everyone. You may need the children to access their drawing from the last lesson to remind themselves which is their favourite dinosaur.

Independent/paired work
● The children should work round the classroom asking their peers what their favourite dinosaur is. They should record answers on their tally sheet. They should then count up how many marks they have in each column and write these numbers down. Finally, ask them to check how many children are in the class to make sure this corresponds with the total number of responses they have on their tally sheets.
● You might wish to add some structure to the tally sheet activity depending on your class. For example, you could give the children the letter A and B. They pair up and swap favourite dinosaurs, then As only move round the room sequentially.

Differentiation
● Support: Less confident learners may benefit from mixed-ability pairings or further adult support in putting their tallies in the right place, counting up and writing down the numbers.
● Challenge: More confident learners can write a list of the dinosaurs in a list of most to least popular.

Review
● Bring the children together and ask them to share which dinosaurs they found were most and least popular. Organise the dinosaurs in order of preference on the board.
● There may be some discrepancies between the children's answers, but this is not really an issue. Use it as an opportunity to discuss why this could have happened (children giving different answers, making marks in the wrong column, adding up incorrectly and so on). Monitor the children's progress during the tally collection activity and their ability to draw simple conclusions from the data during the class review discussion.

Curriculum objectives
● To use technology purposefully to create and organise digital content.

Lesson objectives
● To display data using simple pictograms.

Expected outcomes
● Can manipulate data in graphical formats.

Resources
Photocopiable page 23 'Tally sheet' (now showing results); photocopiable page 'Analysing your pictogram' from the CD-ROM; photocopiable page 'Table template' from the CD-ROM; interactive activity 'Creating a pictogram' on the CD-ROM; media resource 'Pictogram example' on the CD-ROM

Displaying data

Following on from the last lesson, the children now display the data they have collected in simple pictograms, allowing them to see that representing data graphically can make it easier to understand. They learn what a pictogram is and how to create their own. Labelling the pictogram enables them to combine text and image data types, which reinforces their learning from Lessons 3 and 4.

Introduction
● Prior to the lesson, create a simple table (you can insert your data into the photocopiable page 'Table template' from the CD-ROM to show the results of the children's data collection). Explain to the children that they are going to be using the data they collected in their tally sheets and displaying it using a pictogram containing images and text.

Whole-class work
● Display the media resource 'Pictogram example' on the CD-ROM. Ask the children questions about this prepared data. For example:
  ● *How many children had a dog as a pet?*
  ● *Which pet is the least popular?*
● Explain that these pictograms are showing data that has been collected. Discuss why displaying the data in this way can make it easier to understand.

Independent/paired work
● Get the children to access the interactive activity 'Creating a pictogram' on the CD-ROM. Explain that they will use their results to create a pictogram. They may find it easier if you provide the completed photocopiable page 'Table template' for them to look at as they create the pictogram.
● Show children how to get started by working through the first dinosaur as a class. They need to drag and drop the correct number of dinosaurs into the correct box.

Differentiation
● Support: Less confident learners may benefit from mixed-ability pairings or further adult support in creating their pictogram.
● Challenge: More confident learners can answer questions on the photocopiable page 'Analysing your pictogram' on the CD-ROM, which asks them to analyse their pictogram in simple ways.

Review
● Discuss with the children why it is important to label the pictogram with text (so the viewer knows what each row/column means) and why it is important to check to ensure the numbers are correct (so the pictogram shows the correct data).
● Assess the children's progress by their pictogram and their responses to the photocopiable page 'Analysing your pictogram', if used, together with the review discussion.
● You could display the pictograms in your classroom.

Curriculum objectives
● To use technology purposefully to create and organise digital content.

Lesson objectives
● To identify simple data types.
● To know that data can be organised in different ways.
● To understand that different types of data can be combined.
● To identify the basic data types of image, video, audio and text.

Expected outcomes
● Can describe and use basic types of data .
● Can collect data using a tally sheet.
● Can organise and analyse data in simple ways.
● Can manipulate and display data in graphical ways.

Resources
Photocopiable page 19 'Dinosaur cards 1'; photocopiable page 20 'Dinosaur cards 2'; photocopiable page 23 'Tally sheet'

Dinosaurs: Assess and review

The assess and review lesson is an opportunity for the children to revisit the learning from the chapter. They will be familiar with the dinosaur theme and will carry out activities linked to the 'Data and Information' objectives.

Introduction
● Display a dinosaur from photocopiable page 19 'Dinosaur Cards (1)'. Explain that you are going to play the 'Yes/No' game. As the teacher, you are only able to answer 'Yes' or 'No' to questions. Tell the children that the dinosaur you are thinking about is the one displayed. What question could they ask to help them identify it? For example, *Does it have horns? Does it stand on two legs?* Share copies of the photocopiable page with the children, and repeat the game, but without telling them which dinosaur you have chosen.
● Ask*: What type of data are we looking at? (image and text data)*

Group work
● The children play the 'Yes/No' game in small groups or pairs. More confident learners may use photocopiable page 20 'Dinosaur Cards (2)' as well. Ask: *Can you sort your dinosaurs into an order?*
● Allow the children to sort the dinosaurs. If they remember the previous lessons, they may use alphabetical order or size to do this. Observe how they cooperate together to sort the cards and ask each group to explain their thoughts.

Whole-class work
● Before bringing the class back together, ask the children to choose their **least** favourite dinosaur (from one or both of the photocopiable pages).
● Ask: *How did you sort your dinosaurs?*
● The children have chosen their **least** favourite dinosaur. Read out the names of the dinosaurs from the photocopiable pages and ask the children to raise their hands as their least favourite one is announced. Ask them to judge which dinosaur was least popular. This could be difficult, so repeat the process moving the children to different parts of the classroom, depending on their answers. Is it easier to see the size of the groups now?
● Ask*: How could we organise the data to see more clearly which dinosaur is the least popular?* (by creating a tally chart and pictogram)

Independent work
● Remind the children about using a tally sheet and explain that they are going to use one to collect some data. Each child could use drywipe boards to record their tally or use photocopiable page 23 'Tally sheet'. Read out the names of dinosaurs and the children raise their hands for their least favourite.

Differentiation
● Support: Less confident learners will need support to explain how to sort the data.
● Challenge: More confident learners can use both photocopiable pages 19 and 20. Ask them to organise the data in more than one way.

Review
● Tell the children that they could create a pictogram with their results.
● Ask the children move to the left-hand side of the classroom if they know what a pictogram is and move to the right-hand side if they do not know. Choose individuals to give their definitions.
● Finally, return to the lesson objectives to review the learning from the lesson.

Name: _____   Date: _____

Naming dinosaurs (1)

■ Tick the boxes that are correct for the dinosaur in the picture.

Name of dinosaur:

_____

Over 10 metres ⬜

5 metres – 10 metres ⬜

Under 1 metre ⬜   ■ Add other features of your
                                       dinosaur below:

Meat eater ⬜ Armoured ⬜   _____

Plant eater ⬜ Horned ⬜   _____

_____

Name of dinosaur:

_____

Over 10 metres ⬜

5 metres – 10 metres ⬜

Under 1 metre ⬜   ■ Add other features of your
                                       dinosaur below:

Meat eater ⬜ Armoured ⬜   _____

Plant eater ⬜ Horned ⬜   _____

_____

I can record information about dinosaurs.

How did you do?

Naming dinosaurs (2)

■ Tick the boxes that are correct for the dinosaur in the picture.

Name of dinosaur:

_____

Over 10 metres ☐

5 metres – 10 metres ☐

■ Add other features of your dinosaur below:

Under 1 metre ☐

Meat eater ☐ Armoured ☐

_____

Plant eater ☐ Horned ☐

_____

_____

Name of dinosaur:

_____

Over 10 metres ☐

5 metres – 10 metres ☐

■ Add other features of your dinosaur below:

Under 1 metre ☐

Meat eater ☐ Armoured ☐

_____

Plant eater ☐ Horned ☐

_____

_____

I can record information about dinosaurs.

How did you do?

Dinosaur cards (1)

Name: Tyrannosaurus Rex
Lived: Cretaceous period
Size: 12m long x 6m tall
Diet: Meat eater (carnivore)
Features: Very short arms, ferocious hunter

Name: Allosaurus
Lived: Late Jurassic period
Size: 12m long x 3m tall
Diet: Meat eater (carnivore)
Features: Three-fingered hands and serrated teeth

Name: Velociraptor
Lived: Late Cretaceous period
Size: 2m long x 1m tall
Diet: Meat eater (carnivore)
Features: 9cm deadly retractable claw on each foot

Name: Diplodocus
Lived: Late Jurassic period
Size: 27m long x 5m tall
Diet: Plant eater (herbivore)
Features: 8m long neck and 14m long whip-like tail

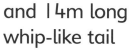

Name: Ankylosaurus
Lived: Late Cretaceous period
Size: 10m long x 1m tall
Diet: Plant eater (herbivore)
Features: thick oval armoured plates on its back, two rows of spikes on its back, club-like tail

Dinosaur cards (2)

Name: Triceratops
Lived: Late Cretaceous period
Size: 9m long x 2m tall
Diet: Plant eater (herbivore)
Features: Three horns on its face

Name: Brachiosaurus
Lived: Late Jurassic period
Size: 26m long x 16m tall
Diet: Plant eater (herbivore)
Features: tallest and largest dinosaur, walked on four legs

Name: Stegosaurus
Lived: Late Jurassic period
Size: 9m long x 2.75m tall
Diet: Plant eater (herbivore)
Features: 17 bony plates like armour on its back, spikes at the end of its tail

Name: Iguanodon
Lived: Cretaceous period
Size: 10m long x 2.7m tall
Diet: Plant eater (herbivore)
Features: Hard spike on each thumb, legs much larger than arms

Name: Megaraptor
Lived: Late Cretaceous period
Size: 8m long x 2m tall
Diet: Meat eater (carnivore)
Features: Walked on two legs, two toe claws, very fast moving

PHOTOCOPIABLE

Sort the dinosaurs!

■ Using the dinosaur cards, sort your dinosaurs into different groups and then answer the questions below.

How many dinosaurs have horns? _____

List the dinosaurs that are over 10m long. _____

_____

_____

How many dinosaurs are plant eaters (herbivores)? _____

List the dinosaurs that are meat eaters (carnivores). _____

_____

_____

How many dinosaurs lived in the late Jurassic period?

_____

■ Make up your own groupings to sort the dinosaurs in different ways. Write your questions and answers below.

_____

_____

_____

I can sort dinosaurs.

How did you do?

Match the text to the image

■ Match the correct text to the correct image using a line.

Club tail

Armour

Spikes

Claws

Serrated teeth

■ When you have finished, add your own labels to the dinosaurs.

■ Write whether the following are text or images.

Megaraptor

Allosaurus

I can sort dinosaurs.

How did you do?

Tally sheet

■ Use this sheet to record the class's favourite dinosaurs.

Name of dinosaur	Tally	Total
Tyrannosaurus rex		
Allosaurus		
Velociraptor		
Diplodocus		
Ankylosaurus		
Triceratops		
Brachiosaurus		
Stegosaurus		
Iguanodon		
Megaraptor		

I can use a tally sheet.

How did you do?

Traditional stories

This chapter uses familiar traditional stories to introduce the concepts of instructions and algorithms. The term 'algorithm' describes a sequence of instructions that are followed by humans and by computers. Therefore, it is very important that the instructions are accurate. This prepares children for when they are introduced to computer programs. The children play games to introduce the concepts. They follow pictorial instructions and then sequence them, in the correct order, using the traditional stories as themes. The story examples are 'Jack and the Beanstalk' and 'Goldilocks and the Three Bears'. They then create their own pictorial instructions for others to follow. At this stage, the algorithms use simple steps to introduce the concept of sequencing instructions to the children. This will be developed in later chapters so they understand that algorithms should be highly detailed and involve the exact steps, and sub-steps needed to perform a particular task.

Expected prior learning

- The children will have experience of playing instructional games, such as 'Simon says'. They may also be familiar with the traditional stories, but may need refreshing on the main parts, and there may be a difference between the versions that they know and the versions used in the lessons.
- Following instructions on how to wash their hands or how to get dressed should be well known and understood, as those routines are reinforced during the school day, for example, washing hands before having lunch or getting changed for a PE lesson.

Chapter at a glance

Subject area
• Algorithms and programming

National Curriculum objective
• To understand what algorithms are.

Week	Lesson objectives	Summary of activities	Expected outcomes
1	• To be able to follow a series of simple instructions through games. • To participate in giving instructions for others to follow. • To know that instructions can be given in a number of different ways (for example, verbally and using images and text).	• The children are introduced to the topic of sequencing instructions. • They follow instructions by playing the 'Simon says' game. • They act out different actions for each other, following instructions on command cards.	• Can follow a sequence of instructions. • Can verbally give instructions for someone else to follow.
2	• To identify incorrectly sequenced instructions. • To predict what will happen if incorrectly sequenced instructions are followed. • To sequence instructions into the correct order.	• The children recognise the sequence of steps involved in washing their hands and the importance of doing it in the correct order. • Reinforcing the learning, they sequence the instructions for getting dressed.	• Can understand that instructions need to be accurate. • Can rearrange a sequence of instructions.
3	• To identify the beginning, middle and end of traditional stories. • To identify errors in the sequencing of traditional stories. • To sequence traditional stories into the correct order.	• Using traditional stories, the children identify the beginning, middle and end of stories and place scenes into the correct order. • They focus on the need to be accurate with the order of the story, so that it makes sense.	• Can discuss why stories need to be in the correct order. • Can reorganise stories and number sequences into the correct order.

Week	Lesson objectives	Summary of activities	Expected outcomes
4	• To begin to know strategies to solve simple logic problems. • To be able to solve simple logic problems successfully (independently or in pairs). • To explain in simple terms the steps taken to solve simple logic problems.	• The children develop their logic and problem-solving skills, with 'Goldilocks and the Three Bears' and 'Jack and the Beanstalk' themes. • They follow clues to solve logic puzzles and describe their solutions.	• Can solve simple logic problems. • Can verbally describe solutions to problems.
5	• To be able to create a simple image plan of a sequence of instructions. • To compare the plan created by the children with a prepared plan and make adjustments, as necessary. • To follow pictorial plans to complete simple tasks.	• In this lesson, the children use their logical thinking skills to follow and create a plan of instructions, using images. • The children create a series of pictures to use as instructions for building a model tower and getting dressed to go outside in winter.	• Can plan a series of instructions. • Can check the accuracy of a series of instructions.
6	• To learn that an 'algorithm' is a term used to describe a sequence of instructions for a computer to follow. • To create algorithms for human robots. • To understand why algorithms should be accurate. • To predict what might happen if given algorithms are inaccurate.	• This lesson introduces the term 'algorithm', which is a sequence of instructions. • Algorithms are used in everyday life and it is very important that the children understand that computers follow algorithms too. • Using 'human' robots, the children follow instructions and identify why these need to be accurate.	• Can explain that an algorithm is a precise way of solving a problem. • Can explain that algorithms need to be accurate, so a computer can execute them.
Assess and review	• To assess the half-term's work.	• The children work together to draw the instructions for a game.	• Assess and review

Overview of progression

● The lessons progress from the known game of 'Simon says', to sequencing stories. They know that everyday tasks like getting dressed follow a sequence, though they may not realise that they are following instructions.
● Using traditional stories, the children begin by thinking about the beginning, middle and end of the story. They start by ordering a jumbled-up story into the correct order, then lead on to ordering pictorial instructions. They progress to creating their own pictorial instructions for others to follow.

Creative context

● The lessons have strong links to the English curriculum for instructional writing. The children must listen carefully and be accurate in their ordering of the instructions. This lays the foundations for their instructional writing, which will be developed over the following years.
● Sequences are very important in the mathematics curriculum too. To solve problems, the children often need to follow steps to achieve a solution. The emphasis on being accurate helps them to understand that the wrong answer may occur, if they are not careful.
● Instructions are used across the curriculum, from following a recipe, to games in PE, for example.

Background knowledge

● The children will know how to follow instructions, though they may not recognise how often during a day these are given and how often they follow them. The lessons should highlight as many examples as possible where they are using instructions. The children may know the traditional stories, but may know different versions of them. Therefore, it is important to re-read the stories and ask the children to follow the version used in the lessons.
● When teaching other subjects, reinforce where children are following instructions. This can help the children understand that computing is part of other subjects and everyday life.

Curriculum objectives
● To understand what algorithms are.

Lesson objectives
● To be able to follow a series of simple instructions through games.
● To participate in giving instructions for others to follow.
● To know that instructions can be given in a number of different ways (for example, verbally and using images and text

Expected outcomes
● Can follow a sequence of instructions.
● Can verbally give instructions for someone else to follow.

Resources
Photocopiable page 33 'Command cards (1)'; photocopiable page 34 'Command cards (2)' (print and cut these prior to the lesson); media resource 'Instructions review' on the CD-ROM

An introduction to sequence and instructions

This lesson introduces children to the key concepts of sequencing, giving and following instructions. Through a number of simple games and activities, the children build up understanding around what instructions are and that they can be given in different ways. As algorithms are simply a sequence of instructions to solve a problem, this is a great introduction for the children.

Whole-class work
● Play the game 'Simon says' giving different instructions to the children who should only follow the instructions if you say 'Simon says' before the instruction.
● Example instructions include:
    ● *Put your hands on your head; Put your left hand in the air; Close your eyes, stick out your tongue.*
Or if you have the room:
    ● *Jump up and down; Hop on your right foot; Turn around, touch your toes.*
● If appropriate, let the children take turns being 'Simon', This is fun, helps the children learn from their peers and can help you to assess their level of understanding at this stage in the lesson.

Group work
● Explain to the children that they have been following **verbal** instructions and now they will be using **text** and **image** instructions.
● Give out the cards made from photocopiable pages 33 and 34 'Command cards 1 and 2' to small groups of children. Children should take it in turns to take a command card from the pile and show it to the group. They should all then act out the action together. Be sure to read the cards aloud and show them to the children to reinforce recollection and memory skills.
● Alternatively, children can act out the card they pick and the rest of the group have to guess what is on their card.

Differentiation
● Mixed-ability groupings may be useful to help children to work together and share understanding.
● Support: Less confident learners will benefit from peer or adult support.
● Challenge: More confident learners could introduce 'Simon says' to their group.

Review
● Bring the whole class back together and use the media resource 'Instructions review' on the CD-ROM to assess the children's understanding of verbal, visual and textual instructions. Ask: *Which are the three ways in which instructions can be given?*
● You could also ask the children to define the key word 'instructions' if they were unable to come up with a clear definition in the introduction, or remind them of their initial definition and ask if they would change it.

■SCHOLASTIC

Curriculum objectives
● To understand what algorithms are.

● Lesson objectives
● To identify incorrectly sequenced instructions.
● To predict what will happen if incorrectly sequenced instructions are followed.
● To sequence instructions into the correct order.

Expected outcomes
● Can understand that instructions need to be accurate.
● Can rearrange a sequence of instructions.

Resources
Interactive activity 'Dressing teddy' on the CD-ROM; photocopiable page 35 'Correct the instructions' (prepare these for each pair before the lesson)

Sequencing instructions accurately

In this lesson, the children are learning about sequencing instructions. They arrange instructions into the correct order, consider what happens if instructions are in the wrong order and learn the importance of sequencing instructions to achieve the correct outcome.

Introduction
● Recap the last lesson with the children, reminding them what instructions are and that they can be verbal, visual or textual. Tell them that in this lesson they will be looking at putting instructions in the correct order. Discuss as a class why this is important, using the example of washing their hands.
● Ask: *What would happen if you dried your hands first, then rinsed them, then put soap on them?* If you have a sink in your class, or can bring in a bowl of water, a towel and some soap, you could demonstrate this.
● Your aim here is for the children to begin to understand that it's important that instructions are in the correct sequence, otherwise things can go wrong!

Whole-class work
● As a class, look at the interactive activity 'Dressing teddy' on the CD-ROM. Ask the children to identify whether the instructions are in the correct or incorrect order.
● Work as a class to put the instructions into the correct order.
● Ask one of the children to act out the instructions in the initial order to help understand that they are incorrectly arranged. Then get another child to act out the instructions once they have been rearranged correctly.

Paired work
● Give children the photocopiable page 35 'Correct the instructions', in which they are given instructions for doing The hokey cokey.
● First, they need to identify whether the instructions are in the correct order, so ask them to act the instructions out and predict what will happen if they follow the instructions as they are.
● They should then put the instructions into the right order and act them out.
● If they finish, they can write the remainder of the instructions on a piece of paper.

Differentiation
● Mixed-ability pairings may be useful or less confident learners could work in a small group with adult support.
● Support: Less confident learners may need support with understanding the instructions, although concentrating on the images rather than the text may help if reading is an issue.
● Challenge: More confident learners could add in additional detail to the existing instructions, or come up with their own sets of instructions (for example, how to put on socks and shoes, or how to paint a picture).

Review
● As a class, discuss the 'Correct the instructions' activity. Ask the children how they knew the instructions were incorrect and what would happen if they had followed the instructions. Ask one or two pairs to rearrange the instructions correctly. Assess the children's progress through the outcomes of the activities and the understanding demonstrated in the class review.

Lesson objectives
- To identify the beginning, middle and end of traditional stories.
- To identify errors in the sequencing of traditional stories.
- To sequence traditional stories into the correct order.

Expected outcomes
- Can discuss why stories need to be in the correct order.
- Can reorganise stories and number sequences into the correct order.

Resources
Interactive activity 'Jumbled stories' on the CD-ROM; photocopiable page 36 'Jumbled Goldilocks'; photocopiable page 37 'Jumbled Jack and the Beanstalk'

Sequencing stories

Having worked with instructions for the past two lessons, in this lesson children will be developing their knowledge and understanding of sequencing further by putting traditional stories and number sequences into the correct order.

Introduction

- Explain to the children that in today's lesson you will be looking at traditional stories that have been jumbled up and that it is their job to put them into the correct order. Remind them how they did this with sequences of instructions in the previous two lessons and tell them they are going to apply the same techniques to stories.
- Ask the children what they know of the story 'Jack and the Beanstalk' and ask a few children to tell the class what happens in the story, emphasising the beginning, middle and end of the story.

Whole-class work

- Show the children the interactive activity 'Jumbled stories' on the CD-ROM. As a class, rearrange the story on screen 1 so it is in the correct order. Check the children's understanding of beginning, middle and end of the story by asking questions such as: *When does Jack buy the beans – at the beginning, middle or end of the story?* You can also use photocopiable page 37 'Jumbled Jack and the Beanstalk'.

Group/paired work

- In small groups or pairs, ask the children to access screen 2 of the interactive activity 'Jumbled stories'. They need to identify errors in the sequencing of 'Goldilocks and the Three Bears' and drag and drop the story segments into the correct order. To do this activity, children need to know the story reasonably well and you may need to spend some time reading or recapping the story of Goldilocks first.
- You can also use photocopiable page 36 'Jumbled Goldilocks' for this activity should you prefer.

> **Differentiation**
> - Mixed-ability groupings may be helpful for the group/pair work and less confident learners could work in a small group with adult support.
> - Support: Less confident learners may need additional support with the story and could work with the actual storybook if this is needed and/or helpful.
> - Challenge: More confident learners may be able to retell their own favourite story in pictures using a simple beginning, middle and end approach.

Review

- Bring the children back together and discuss the correct order of the Goldilocks story, asking children to rearrange the story into the correct order on the whiteboard. Ask: *What happens at the end of the story? Which characters enter the story in the middle?*
- Assess the children's progress by their contributions to the review discussion and the outcomes of their story work.

Curriculum objectives
● To understand what algorithms are.

Lesson objectives
● To begin to know strategies to solve simple logic problems.
● To be able to solve simple logic problems successfully (independently or in pairs).
● To explain in simple terms the steps taken to solve simple logic problems.

Expected outcomes
● Can solve simple logic problems.
● Can verbally describe solutions to problems.

Resources
Selection of soft toys or different objects; interactive activity 'Logic puzzles' on the CD-ROM; photocopiable page 38 'Goldilocks logic puzzle'

Logical problem solving

In this lesson, children develop their logic and problem-solving skills, both of which are key skills in computing. Through solving a series of logic puzzles based around the traditional tales of 'Jack and the Beanstalk' and 'Goldilocks', children will learn the approaches that lead to successful resolution of logical puzzles and develop their logical thinking.

Introduction
● Line the soft toys or objects up so they are visible to the children. Ask the children questions regarding the position of the toys or objects. For example, *Which toy is in the middle? Which object is in front of ...?*
● The aim here is to get children familiar with the language of positioning: middle, between, in front of, behind, and so on. This will help them with the logical tasks they do in the lesson.

Whole-class work
● Show the children the interactive activity 'Logic puzzles' on the CD-ROM and start with the 'Jack and the Beanstalk' puzzle. Explain that they will be given instructions and need to place the characters in the correct position. Reveal the first clue and get the children to place the character. Carry on doing this until all the characters are positioned.
● Show the children how to check the characters are in the right place by checking the clues again once they have finished. Ask them questions such as, *Which characters were easiest to position? Why was that one easiest? How did you know to place that character there?*

Independent/paired work
● In pairs, children should access screen 2 of the 'Logic puzzles' interactive activity or photocopiable page 38 'Goldilocks logic puzzle'. They should work through the clues in the same way as modelled in the whole-class work, positioning the characters in the correct boxes.

> **Differentiation**
> ● Support: Less confident learners may need further support with the positioning language and in working out the more difficult character positions. Mixed-ability pairings may help with this, or adult support may be required if working in a small group.
> ● Challenge: More confident learners will be able to explain in detail to others how they approached the logic puzzle.

Review
● Ask the children for their final solutions and demonstrate this to the whole class. Ask children to explain how they knew where to place the characters, particularly how they knew that Daddy Bear was next to Mummy Bear. Ask: *Which character did you place first and why? What would happen if you didn't know where Baby Bear was? Would you still be able to solve the puzzle? What advice would you give to someone who was given one of these puzzles to solve?*
● Assess the children's progress by their response to the interactive activity 'Logic puzzles' and class discussion.

Curriculum objectives
● To understand what algorithms are.

Lesson objectives
● To be able to create a simple image plan of a sequence of instructions.
● To compare the plan created by the children with a prepared plan and make adjustments, as necessary.
● To follow pictorial plans to complete simple tasks.

Expected outcomes
● Can plan a series of instructions.
● Can check the accuracy of a series of instructions.

Resources
Media resource 'Image instructions' on the CD-ROM; photocopiable page 39 'Getting dressed to go outside in winter'; bricks for building a tower, if required

Planning sequences of instructions

In this lesson, the children use their logical thinking skills to follow and create instructions, using images.

Introduction
● Explain to the children that they will be using their logical thinking skills and understanding of instructions to follow and create image plans of instructions. Recap that instructions can be given verbally, by images and/or text.
● Show them screen 1 from the media resource 'Image instructions' on the CD-ROM, showing how to write your name. Ask questions such as: *What can you see in the picture?*, *What instruction do you think this is giving you? Why do you think it is telling you to do that?* Get the children to follow the instructions on the pictorial plan to write their name.

Whole-class work
● Show the children screen 2 in the media resource 'Image instructions', the 'Building a tower' plan, and work through this as a class to model what children will be doing. You may also wish to build a tower with bricks if you think this would help children's understanding.
● Start by showing children the first instruction and ask one child to draw an appropriate picture to illustrate the instruction in the given space. Repeat this with the other instructions with different children doing the drawing.

Group/paired work
● In small groups or pairs, give children photocopiable page 39 'Getting dressed to go outside in winter'. They should put the instructions given in the right order, drawing a picture and writing the instruction underneath. Explain that they are giving image instructions for someone else to follow. Please note there is no definitive correct order for the instructions.

Differentiation
● Mixed-ability pairings or groups may be helpful for children.
● Support: Less confident learners may need further support in understanding how to transfer the action from the instruction into an image.
● Challenge: More confident learners will be able to compare their image plan with another group and see what differences there are.

Review
● Show the children screen 3 of the media resource 'Image instructions', showing the completed plan, and ask them to compare it to their image plan. Ask questions such as: *What differences can you spot between your image plan and this one? Which do you think is clearer? Why do you think that plan is clearer? How would you change your plan?* Try to get children not to focus on whether the drawing is better/worse, but rather how the instructions are shown.
● If you have time, the children could make adjustments to their plan, or draw a neater version, and you could use the plans as display work.

Curriculum objectives
● To understand what algorithms are.

Lesson objectives
● To learn that an 'algorithm' is a term used to describe a sequence of instructions for a computer to follow.
● To create algorithms for human robots.
● To understand why algorithms should be accurate.
● To predict what might happen if given algorithms are inaccurate

Expected outcomes
● Can explain that an algorithm is a precise way of solving a problem.
● Can explain that algorithms need to be accurate, so a computer can execute them.

Resources
Photocopiable page 'Robot instructions' from the CD-ROM; space to move (this may be the classroom, a hall or outside space)

Understanding algorithms

This lesson introduces the term for an 'algorithm', which is a sequence of instructions. We use algorithms every day and it is very important that the children understand that computers follow algorithms too. Using 'human' robots, the children follow instructions and identify why they need to be accurate.

Introduction
● Write the word 'algorithm' on the board and ask the children to clap out the word as al-go-ri-thm. This is to help them get to know the vocabulary and remember the 'rithm' (or rhythm) part of the word.
● Explain to them that an 'algorithm' is simply a sequence of instructions, so they have been creating algorithms for the past five lessons. Ask the children to recap some of the sequences of instructions that they have been creating.

Whole-class work
● Explain that algorithms are a sequence of instructions to complete any task. This definition is also shown on the media resource.
● Ask for a volunteer and explain that they are going to be acting as a robot who cannot think for themselves (you may prefer to choose a child you know will respond well to this task).
● Explain that the class needs to give the 'robot' instructions to walk to the door of the classroom (or any other suitable place depending on space). Ask the children to give one instruction each to the robot to get him or her to the chosen spot.
● As the children give instructions, ask them if the robot would know how to do that; for example, they may say, *Go to the door*. That is a valid instruction, but only if the robot already knows how to walk!
● You are aiming to get children to understand that algorithms need to be precise, accurate and specific.

Group/paired work
● In pairs, or small groups if necessary, ask the children to name themselves either 'A' or 'B'. Explain that they are going to take turns being human robots. A is the robot and B will give the instructions, and then they will swap.
● Give the children photocopiable page 'Robot instructions' from the CD-ROM. Explain that they should give their robot instructions and use the photocopiable page to help them. Remind them that the robot does not know how to do anything, so they must give it specific instructions that expand on the ideas given. For example, they must tell the robot how to walk to the door! It will help if you demonstrate at least the first instruction and correct any clear misunderstandings prior to the children starting the activity.

Differentiation
● All children should be encouraged to focus on giving clear, accurate instructions.
● Support: Less confident learners may benefit from mixed-ability pairings or further adult support in giving instructions.
● Challenge: More confident learners can give more detailed instructions to their robot and be encouraged to think about how instructions could be *repeated*, or how they could tell their robot to keep going *until* they get to a certain place.

Review
● Ask suitable pairs to demonstrate their instructions, perhaps those you have noticed whose instructions are particularly clear and accurate. Ask questions of the other children such as: *How is A making it really easy for robot B to understand what she wants him to do? How could you make the instruction even easier for robot B to understand?*
● Assess children's progress by their robot activity and their understanding of how and why to give accurate instructions.

Curriculum objectives
● To understand what algorithms are.

Lesson objectives
● To be able to create a simple image plan of a sequence of instructions.
● To compare the plan created by the children with a prepared plan and make adjustments, as necessary.
● To follow pictorial plans to complete simple tasks.

Expected outcomes
● Can plan a series of instructions.
● Can check the accuracy of a series of instructions.

Resources
Photocopiable page 'Chopping down the beanstalk' from the CD-ROM

Traditional stories: Assess and review

The assess and review lesson enables the children to consolidate their learning about algorithms and instructions. They recall the stories they have been studying and then play a game and create the pictorial instructions.

Introduction
● Remind the children that one of the characters in 'Jack and the Beanstalk'. was the Golden Goose. Continue the theme by playing the 'Duck, duck, goose' game. The children sit on the floor, in a circle. One child is 'on' and they walk around the outside of the circle, touching each child on the head and saying 'Duck' until they choose someone and say 'Goose'. They then run clockwise around the circle chased by the 'Goose'. The aim is to run around the circle and then sit in the space where the Goose used to be before the Goose catches them. Play the game several times, so children are sure of the rules.
● Ask: *Can you explain the rules of 'Duck, duck, goose'?*

Paired work
● The children work in pairs to think about the rules of the game. Allow discussion time before asking them to draw a picture to describe the game. The children can then explain the rules, using their picture as a prompt.

Group work
● Place the children into groups of four. Explain that they are going to draw the instructions for 'Duck, duck, goose'. Give each group three pieces of paper. Divide the children into four roles – the 'bossy instructor', the 'beginner', the 'middler' and the 'ender'. The bossy instructor has to describe the game. The beginner draws a picture to describe the start of the game, Then the middler must decide what happens next and draw that picture. Finally, the ender draws the end of the game. Each child must listen to the bossy instructor to remind them of the steps. Once finished, they check to see whether their instructions make sense.

Whole-class work
● Bring the class together and explain that they are going to compare their instructions. Choose one group to share their pictures and the bossy instructor can describe the game. Choose another group and repeat. Ask: *Were the pictures the same? Were the instructions different? Were the instructions clear?*

> **Differentiation**
> ● Support: Less confident learners will need support to describe the instructions. They could be the bossy instructor, telling the others how to play.
> ● Challenge: More confident learners could identify and draw further steps in the game. They could fold their paper into four panels and draw the instructions.

Review
● Ask the children to think about their instructions. If they could draw one more picture, what would it be? Would it make the instructions clearer?
● Conclude the lesson by playing the 'Chopping down the beanstalk' game. Prior to the lesson, prepare multiple versions of the cards from the photocopiable page 'Chopping down the beanstalk' from the CD-ROM. In groups, the children take turns to collect a scene card, then act out that picture. The first team to collect the 'Climbing down the beanstalk', 'Fetching the axe' and 'Chopping the beanstalk wins the game and acts out the 3 scenes in order. If they get the 'Giant's coming' card, they start again, placing all of the cards back on the table.

Command cards (1)

Giggle

Sit

Stand

Jump

Hop

Point

PHOTOCOPIABLE

Command cards (2)

Grin

Sit and grin

Sit and clap

Jump and clap

Jump and point

Hop and giggle

Correct the instructions

■ Look at the instructions for 'The hokey cokey'. Are they in the correct order?

> The hokey cokey
> Put your left arm in
> In,
> In,
> Out,
> Out
> Shake it all about
> Your left arm out

■ Write out the correct order of the instructions below.

1. _____

2. _____

3. _____

4. _____

5. _____

6. _____

7. _____

8. _____

I can rearrange instructions to the right order.

How did you do?

Jumbled 'Goldilocks'

■ Look at the images below and number them in the order they appear in the story.

I can put a story into the correct order.

How did you do?

PHOTOCOPIABLE

Jumbled 'Jack and the Beanstalk'

■ Look at the images below and number them in the order they appear in the story.

I can put a story into the correct order.

How did you do?

'Goldilocks' logic puzzle

■ Read the clues and then draw a line from the character to the box they should go in.

1	2	3	4	5

 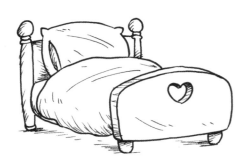

Clues:

Baby Bear is next to Mummy Bear.

Mummy Bear is in the first box.

The porridge bowl is in the middle box.

Daddy Bear is next to the porridge bowl.

I can solve a logic puzzle.

How did you do?

Getting dressed to go outside in winter

■ Write the instructions in order under the boxes and draw the image for each one.

```
┌─────────────────────┐        ┌─────────────────────┐
│                     │        │                     │
│                     │        │                     │
│                     │        │                     │
│                     │        │                     │
│                     │        │                     │
└─────────────────────┘        └─────────────────────┘
```

_____   _____

_____   _____

_____   _____

```
┌─────────────────────┐        ┌─────────────────────┐
│                     │        │                     │
│                     │        │                     │
│                     │        │                     │
│                     │        │                     │
│                     │        │                     │
└─────────────────────┘        └─────────────────────┘
```

_____   _____

_____   _____

_____   _____

Instructions:
Put on your coat.
Put on your gloves.
Put on your hat.
Put on your wellington boots.

I can draw instructions for someone else to follow.

How did you do?

Computers in everyday life

This chapter considers computers in everyday life. Children are surrounded by computers, but may not always realise it. In their home, the library, the classroom or the school office, they will have seen desktop-style computers. Starting with this desktop computer model, the children identify the main features, for example the monitor, mouse and keyboard. They are also introduced to the central processing unit (or CPU) as the 'brain' of the computer.

Expected prior learning

● The children will have seen computers around the home and in school and this is all the knowledge that is required for this chapter.

Chapter at a glance

Subject area
● How computers work

National Curriculum objective
● To recognise common uses of information technology beyond school.

Week	Lesson objectives	Summary of activities	Expected outcomes
1	● To learn the names of basic parts of the computer. ● To be able to name mouse, screen, keyboard and CPU. ● To explain, in simple terms, the functions of main parts of a computer.	● The children name the parts of the computer and begin to use the correct terminology. ● They then discuss the functions of each of the main parts of the computer.	● Can name parts of the classroom computer. ● Can describe how the children use the keyboard, mouse and screen.
2	● To learn that a mouse is an input device that controls a pointer on the screen. ● To learn that a mouse allows a user to control elements on the screen. ● To become more confident using a mouse when completing simple tasks.	● The focus of the lesson is on the mouse. The children think about the name 'mouse' and where they have heard it before (as an animal). They consider what a mouse does on the computer, clicking on icons. ● The children practise with a mouse to explore what the mouse can do within a simple word processing document.	● Can explain that a mouse is an input device. ● Can use a mouse to complete simple tasks.
3	● To learn that a keyboard is an input device that allows a user to input letters, numbers and symbols. ● To become more confident using a keyboard by typing simple words and sentences combining numbers, letters and symbols.	● This lesson focuses on the keyboard as an input device. Children type different letters and numbers and see these appear on the screen. ● For practice, they type different words, exploring how to use the keyboard for letters, numbers and symbols.	● Can explain that a keyboard is an input device. ● Can accurately use a keyboard to type simple sentences.
4	● To learn that a screen is an output device that displays information for the user. ● To be able to explain what they can usually expect to see on a screen.	● Building on the previous mouse and keyboard lessons, the children look at screens as output devices. ● They consider different types of screens and where they might see them, in everyday life.	● Can explain that a screen is an output device. ● Can recognise the common features of different types of computer screens.
5	● To learn that a CPU contains the computer 'brain'. ● To be able to explain that a CPU processes instructions given by input devices. ● To be able to explain that a CPU gives instructions to output devices.	● Children learn about the main functions of a CPU. They will be able to explain what the acronym stands for (central processing unit) and explain how it works. ● They pass and process instructions, acting like a CPU.	● Can understand in simple terms how a CPU works. ● Can explain simply that a CPU follows instructions.

Week	Lesson objectives	Summary of activities	Expected outcomes
6	• To know the main parts of a computer. • To verbally explain the main parts of a computer. • To identify input and output devices on a simple computer model. • To identify the CPU and explain how it works in simple terms.	• Children pull together their learning from this chapter and build a simple model of a computer using a template. • They label their computer and explain verbally their understanding of how the different elements of the computer work.	• Can build a simple computer model. • Can explain in simple terms the main parts of a computer and how a computer works.
Assess and review	• To assess the half-term's work.	• Children remember what they have studied, by creating a box model of the computer.	• Assess and review.

Overview of progression

● The children may have many different starting points, depending on their previous experience of computers. If their home has different computers and they have had access to them, they will be familiar with the mouse or a touchscreen.

● Other children may have experienced computers previously, so will know the name of a mouse and have some typing skills. Most children will not have considered that the computer has a 'thinking part' and will not have used the term CPU. Therefore, all children will progress in their skills and knowledge of the mouse, keyboard, screen and CPU over the lessons.

Creative context

● The lessons link to English through the use of nouns for the components and the instructional language used to explain how to use the features. The children will develop their use of the alphabet and lower-case and upper-case letters.

● For maths, they will encounter numbers and symbols and reinforce the place value of numbers. Using the mouse requires muscle control in the arms and shoulders, so benefiting coordination for PE and also their handwriting. The subject of computers in the environment could link to geography and the local area.

Background knowledge

● The children may know the name of the mouse and keyboard from previous use of the computer. The name of the screen may vary, such as TV or monitor. However, they may not know where the 'thinking' happens, in the CPU. They may call it the 'box' or 'where the CD or DVD goes', so they need to become familiar with finding and naming that part.

● With advances in technology, the CPU can be integrated into the screen, as an all-in-one computer. A tablet computer can also contain the CPU and touchscreen in one device.

Curriculum objectives
● To recognise common uses of information technology beyond school.

Lesson objectives
● To learn the names of basic parts of the computer.
● To be able to name the mouse, screen, keyboard and CPU.
● To explain, in simple terms, the functions of main parts of a computer.

Expected outcomes
● Can name parts of the classroom computer.
● Can describe how the children use the keyboard, mouse and screen.

Resources
Photocopiable page 49 'Name the parts of the computer'; interactive activity 'What do I do?' on the CD-ROM; headphones for independent/paired work as necessary

An introduction to the parts of a computer

This lesson introduces the children to the main parts of the computer – the keyboard, mouse, screen and CPU. By the end of the lesson, the children will be able to name and explain in simple terms the main parts of a computer and understand their basic functions. This will be extended in subsequent lessons when children will examine each element in more detail.

Introduction
● Explain to the children that you will be learning about computers for the next few lessons; how they work and what all the different parts are called.
● Ask them what they already know and use this to prompt discussion. For example:
    ● *Can you point to the computer in the room?*
    ● *What is this called?* (Holding up mouse/keyboard)
    ● *What is this part called?* (Pointing to screen)

Whole-class work
● Give the children photocopiable page 49 'Name the parts of the computer' and explain that they should match the words to the images.
● Use this to introduce the children to the correct terminology (getting them to repeat the words back to you).
● If you have the space and the computers, develop this by next asking the children to point to each of the different elements on their computers as you call out the word.

Independent/paired work
● Ask the children to open the interactive activity 'What do I do?' on the CD-ROM in which they will match the part of the computer to what it does.

Differentiation
● Mixed-ability pairings may be useful to help children to work together and share understanding.
● Support: Less confident learners may benefit from peer or adult support, particularly in working out which part of the computer carries out which function.
● Challenge: More confident learners could draw a computer and label it with the correct terminology. They could also explain verbally what each part of the computer does.

Review
● As a class, review the interactive activity 'What do I do?' and use this as an opportunity to correct any misunderstandings.
● Re-emphasise the names of each of the different parts of the computer and explain that they will be learning about each part in more detail in the following lessons.
● Review children's progress through their understanding of the names and simple functions of the main parts of the computer.

Curriculum objectives
● To recognise common uses of information technology beyond school.

Lesson objectives
● To learn that a mouse is an input device that controls a pointer on the screen.
● To learn that a mouse allows a user to control elements on the screen.
● To become more confident using a mouse when completing simple tasks.

Expected outcomes
● Can explain that a mouse is an input device.
● Can use a mouse to complete simple tasks.

Resources
Interactive activity 'What can your mouse do?' on the CD-ROM; photocopiable page 50 'Spot the mice!'; word processing package such as Microsoft Word

Understanding about a computer mouse

In this lesson children will be learning about computer mice in more detail. They will be introduced to the term 'input device' and will learn how to control a mouse and use it to tell the computer what they want it to do.

Introduction
● Give the children photocopiable page 50 'Spot the mice!' and ask them to spot the 'mice' on the page. This should be a fun and simple activity for them.
● Use this to explain that they will be learning about mice in a lot more detail today. Show the children a mouse in the classroom (a few different ones if possible) and show them where it plugs into the computer.
● Ask the children what they think a mouse is used for. You can help them by asking children to come to the front and click on icons, clicking on the screen, clicking play on a video or on a document to open it up.
● Explain to the children that a mouse is an *input device* because it allows us to input data into the computer, so we can tell it where we want to open and where we want to click. We can use it to insert a picture or to click on a video to play. We can give the computer instructions with the mouse. Show the children how to click the left and right buttons on the mouse.

Independent/paired work
● Explain to the children that they will be working through an activity to explore what they can do with their mouse.
● Show the children the interactive activity 'What can your mouse do?' on the CD-ROM, in which they are prompted to undertake a variety of operations with their mouse.
● You may need to work through the instructions with some or all of the class prior to their attempting the interactive activity independently so that they know what is expected of them.

Differentiation
● Support: Less dextrous learners may need more support in using their mouse.
● Challenge: More confident learners could find out two more things they can do with their mouse that have not been covered by the lesson (for example, changing the fonts on a word processing document).

Review
● As a class, recap with the children what a mouse can do.
● Ask questions such as:
  ● *What can a mouse be used for?*
  ● *What does a mouse allow a user to do?*
  ● *What type of device is a mouse?* You may need to prompt them here by asking, *Is it an input device?*
  ● *How does a user control the mouse?*

Curriculum objectives
● To recognise common uses of information technology beyond school.

Lesson objectives
● To learn that a keyboard is an input device that allows a user to input letters, numbers and symbols.
● To become more confident using a keyboard by typing simple words and sentences combining numbers, letters and symbols.

Expected outcomes
● Can explain that a keyboard is an input device.
● Can accurately use a keyboard to type simple sentences.

Resources
● Photocopiable page 51 'What can your keyboard do?'

Understanding about keyboards

In this lesson, the children will be increasing their understanding about keyboards. They will be able to identify what a keyboard can be used for and become more confident in using a keyboard to type using numbers, letters and symbols.

Introduction
● Explain to the children that in today's lesson you will be looking at keyboards. Remind them that they already know about what a mouse does and where it plugs into the computer.
● Show them a keyboard (several different keyboards if possible) and explain that a keyboard is also an input device that allows them to tell the computer what they want it to do.

Whole class work
● Open up a simple word processing document and ask for volunteers to come to the front and find different keys on the keyboard. For example:
  ● *Who can find the 'F' for Freddie?*
  ● *Where is the number 5?*
● Type a short word, such as 'blackdog'. Ask: *Who can put a space in the middle to make it correct?*

Independent/paired work
● Ask the children to look at photocopiable page 51 'What can your keyboard do?'. They should work through the exercises, which involve typing simple words and sentences using letters, numbers and symbols.
● Depending on children's confidence and your computer resources, you may wish to put the children into pairs for this exercise.
● The children should be encouraged to work independently, 'investigating' the keyboard to find the right key.

> **Differentiation**
> ● Support: Less confident learners may require adult help, or mixed-ability pairing, for the 'What can a keyboard do?' activity.
> ● Challenge: You could use an online typing tutorial, such as those available at www.bbc.co.uk/schools/typing/levels/level1.shtml for children who are more confident typists.

Review
● Bring the children back together and ask them to demonstrate what they can do on the class board.
● Encourage them to write simple words and very short sentences that use letters, numbers and symbols. For example, 'The dog ate 2 bones.'
● Ask questions such as:
  ● *What do we use a keyboard for?*
  ● *What kind of device is a keyboard?* (Again, you may need to prompt by asking: *Is a keyboard an input or an output device?*)
● Assess the children's progress by their contribution to the review discussion and the outcomes of the 'What can your keyboard do?' activity.

Curriculum objectives
● To recognise common uses of information technology beyond school.

Lesson objectives
● To learn that a screen is an output device that displays information for the user.
● To be able to explain what they can usually expect to see on a screen.

Expected outcomes
● Can explain that a screen is an output device.
● Can recognise the common features of different types of computer screens.

Resources
● Media resource 'Different displays' on the CD-ROM; photocopiable page 52 'What can you see on the screen?'

Learning about computer screens

In this lesson, the children will be developing their understanding around what a computer screen is and what it does. Building on their understanding of input devices in the previous two lessons, they now learn that a screen is an output device and recognise the common features of different types of screen.

Introduction
● Show the children the media resource 'Different displays' on the CD-ROM and ask them what these displays all have in common (they are all different types of computer screen).
● Explain to the children that in today's lesson they are going to be learning about computer screens in the same way as they have already learned about mice and keyboards.
● Recap what they remember about mice and keyboards (prompting them with, *What kind of device are mice and keyboards, input or output devices?* as necessary).

Whole-class work
● Ask the children to look at their computer screens (or you could do this on the whiteboard projecting the start screen) and ask them to tell you what they can see. They can see images, text and icons ('icons' may be a new word for them). They can also see the on/off button on the monitor – explain that this doesn't turn the computer on/off, it just turns the screen on/off.
● Explain that icons are the picture labels that tell us which programs we can use by clicking on them. The children can explore clicking on different icons at this point if you wish.
● Explain that a screen is an output device as the instructions that are given by the mouse and keyboard come 'out' on the screen.

Independent work
● Children work through photocopiable page 52 'What can you see on the screen?' in which they match up the names of the different parts of the screen to images showing these parts.

Differentiation
● Support: Less confident learners may need further support in the individual activity and mixed-ability pairings may help with this, or adult support may be required if working in a small group.
● Challenge: More confident learners will be able to explain to others what they have learned about screens and be able to discuss the functions of a screen. Ask them to make a list of all the screens they have in their house or that they see everyday.

Review
● Think-pair-share: Ask the children to think of one thing they now know about screens and share this with a partner. Then ask pairs to share back to the class.
● You will hopefully get a good variety of facts about screens from this. However, you may need to prompt children with questions such as;
  ● *Where would you find a screen in your home?*
  ● *Why is a screen an output rather than input device?*
  ● *How do you turn on and off the screen on your computer?*
● Assess the children's progress by their response to the individual activity and their responses to the think-pair-share review at the end of the lesson.

Curriculum objectives
● To recognise common uses of information technology beyond school.

Lesson objectives
● To learn that a CPU contains the computer 'brain'.
● To be able to explain that a CPU processes instructions given by input devices.
● To be able to explain that a CPU gives instructions to output devices.

Expected outcomes
● Can understand in simple terms how a CPU works.
● Can explain that the CPU follows instructions.

Resources
Media resource 'CPU'; interactive activity 'What does CPU stand for?'; photocopiable page 53 'Computer instruction cards (1)'; photocopiable page 54 'Computer instruction cards (2)'

Learning about the CPU

In this lesson, the children will learn about the main functions of a CPU and be able to explain what the acronym stands for and, in simple terms, how it works. This lesson will bring together their understanding about computers from previous lessons as they learn that the CPU contains the computer 'brain'.

Introduction
● Display the first screen of the media resource 'CPU' on the CD-ROM on the whiteboard.
● Explain to the children that they will be learning about the 'brains' of the computer today.
● Explain that this is the part that gets the information from the input devices (mouse and keyboard) and tells the output device (screen) what to show.
● Use the interactive activity 'What does CPU stand for?' on the CD-ROM to help the children find out what the letters stand for. In simple terms, try to explain what each word in 'central processing unit' means.

Whole-class work
● Show the children screen 2 in the media resource 'CPU' and explain that the instructions they give the computer are processed by the CPU.
● Ask three volunteers to stand in a row at the front of the class and have ready the cards prepared from photocopiable page 53 'Computer instruction cards (1)'.
● Explain that child 1 is the 'input', child 2 in the middle is the 'CPU' and child 3 is the 'output'. You could recap here what input and output devices they know.
● Give the first card to child 1 who is 'inputting' the instruction into the CPU. The child should pass the instructions to the middle child. The middle child should then whisper the instruction to the third 'output' child, who should then action the instruction.
● Ask the rest of the class to guess what the instruction was.
● Repeat this with the remaining two instructions, emphasising that the input device is telling the CPU what it wants to happen and the CPU must tell the output device what this is (so the CPU is following the instructions given to it).

Group work
● Ideally in groups of three, ask the children to decide who will be 'input', 'CPU' and 'output' and distribute the photocopiable page 54 'Computer instruction cards (2)'.
● Ask the 'input' child to pass the instruction card to the 'CPU', who should then whisper the instructions to the 'output' device, who should carry out the instruction (as modelled in the whole-class activity).
● They should then check whether the instruction has been processed correctly.
● They can swap roles around if you/they wish.

Differentiation
● Support: Less confident learners may benefit from mixed-ability groupings or further adult support when undertaking the small group task.
● Challenge: More confident learners could make up their own instructions in addition to the computer instruction cards.

Review
● Ask groups to demonstrate the processing of a card for the rest of the class to guess. This is helpful for groups who made up their own instructions.
● Review the children's understanding of a CPU by asking questions such as:
  ● What does a CPU do?
  ● Where does a CPU get the instructions from?
  ● How does a CPU know what to do?
  ● Where would you find a CPU in this computer? (Point to a class computer.)

Curriculum objectives
● To recognise common uses of information technology beyond school.

Lesson objectives
● To know the main parts of a computer.
● To verbally explain the main parts of a computer.
● To identify input and output devices on a simple computer model.
● To identify the CPU and explain how it works in simple terms.

Expected outcomes
● Can build a simple computer model.
● Can explain in simple terms the main parts of a computer and how a computer works.

Resources
Photocopiable page 55 'Computer template' prepared and cut out prior to the lesson; glue or sticky tape

Building a simple computer model

Following the work the children have been doing in the previous lessons, they reinforce their understanding of the main parts of a computer by building a simple model, which they label and use to verbally demonstrate their understanding.

Introduction
● Prior to the lesson, make up one of the computer models from photocopiable page 55 'Computer template'.
● Show the children the model and explain that they will be building their own model computer, which they will label with all the different parts they already know.

Whole-class work
● Go over the model with the children, showing them the different parts and asking them to name these as a class if you think they will benefit from this. As well as naming the keyboard, mouse and screen, they should say whether these are input or output devices.
● Give the children a ready cut-out template from photocopiable page 55 'Computer template' and, as a class, work through the first few folds so they understand what they need to do.

Group work
● The children construct their computer model.
● They should then stick the labels from photocopiable page 55 'Computer template' in the correct place on their model.

Differentiation
● Support: Mixed-ability pairings or groups may be helpful for less confident children and the time taken to complete the computer may depend on the children's dexterity in sticking their template.
● Challenge: More confident learners may be able to add and explain further detailed elements, such as icons and spacebar.

Review
● Invite each group to demonstrate their computer model to you, explaining how each element fits together and how it works. This is a good opportunity for assessment as you can ask questions or give prompts such as:
   ● Which parts of your computer are input devices?
   ● How does the CPU know what to do?
   ● Explain how each part of your computer works.
● If time allows, bring the class together and ask groups to share their understanding with the rest of the class.
● You could use the completed computers in a display.

Curriculum objectives
● To recognise common uses of information technology beyond school.

Lesson objectives
● To learn the names of the basic parts of the computer.
● To be able to name mouse, screen, keyboard and CPU.
● To explain, in simple terms, the functions of the main parts of a computer.

Expected outcomes
● The children name the parts of the computer and begin to use the correct terminology.
● They then discuss the functions of the parts of the computer.

Resources
Cardboard boxes and craft materials to create a model of a computer

Computers in everyday life: Assess and review

The assess and review lesson is an opportunity for the children to revisit the learning from the chapter. They have learned about the parts of the computer, the names and the basic functions. In this lesson, they remember what they have studied, by creating a box model of the computer.

Introduction
● Remind the children about their lessons about computers. For example, they have looked at different types of computer, where they might find these and what the main parts are. Explain that they are now going to make a model of a computer and label it.
● Ask: *What are the main parts of the computer?*

Group work
● The children work in small groups, or pairs, to use cardboard boxes and craft materials to create the main CPU, the screen, the mouse and the keyboard of a desktop-style computer. Allow them the freedom to create it as they want to. For example, if they decide to make a tablet computer, see how they model the touch screen or keyboard. If they make a desktop-style computer, see how they connect the parts together.
● Ask: *Can you label the parts of the model computer?*
● Allow the children to add labels, using paper and pens. Ask them individually to name the parts of the computer.
● Ask: *Can you tell me what each part of the computer does?*
● Ask the children to explain the function of the keyboard, mouse, screen and CPU. Finally, ask them to say whether it is an 'input' or 'output' device.

Whole-class work
● Arrange the model computers as a gallery, so that the children can view each others' work. Ask them to take turns to be the guide to identify the parts of the computer for another child's model. Can they also explain the functions?

> **Differentiation**
> ● Support: Less confident learners may need adhesive labels to add to their computers, with writing prompts, for example, 'This is the... We use it to...'
> ● Challenge: More confident learners could write description cards, to display next to their models, to show their understanding of the names and functions of the parts.

Review
● Tell the children that there are many different types of computers around them in their everyday life. Ask them to give examples, such as the school photocopier.
● Ask: *Where else might they see computers outside of school?*
● This question lays the foundations for their future work in Year 2 about computers in the local environment.

Name the parts of the computer

■ Draw a line to match the word to the image.

Mouse

CPU

Screen

Keyboard

I can name the main parts of a computer.

How did you do?

Spot the mice!

■ Find and circle the computer mice in the image below.

I can spot a computer mouse.

How did you do?

SCHOLASTIC
www.scholastic.co.uk

What can your keyboard do?

■ Type the following with your keyboard:

Your name

Your friend's name

Your teacher's name

Your favourite food

Your favourite book

■ Can you type and finish these sentences?

I like to _____

My pet is called _____

I am _____ years old.

I have _____ brothers and _____ sisters.

I can type using a keyboard.

How did you do?

What can you see on the screen?

■ Match up the words to the parts of the screen.

image   mouse pointer   on/off button   text   icon

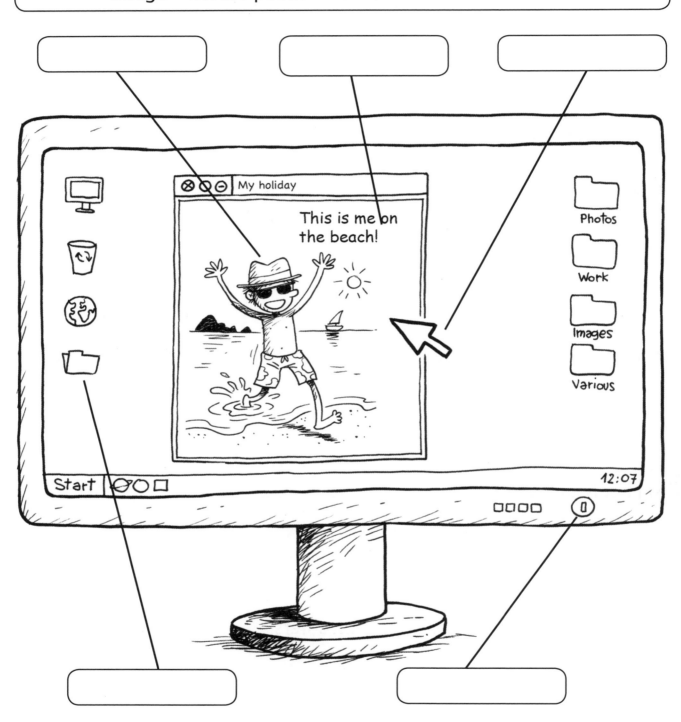

I can name the things you see on a computer screen.

How did you do?

PHOTOCOPIABLE

Computer instruction cards (1)

Bend down

Wave your arms

Point to the door

Turn around

Computer instruction cards (2)

Smile

Jump

Dance

Hop

Name: _____   Date: _____

Computer template

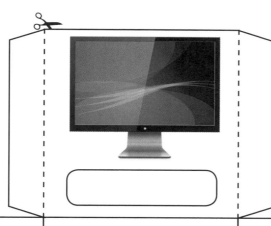

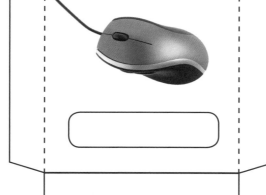

Plants and animals

This chapter uses a plants and animals theme to build on the children's knowledge and understanding of sequencing instructions and algorithms. They are also introduced to programming for the first time and a number of key concepts including flowcharts, repetition, debugging and controlling objects. The main aim is to get the children thinking about how they can sequence instructions accurately, create algorithms and give precise instructions to control objects. At this stage, the algorithms use simple steps to introduce the concept of sequencing instructions. This will be developed in later chapters so children understand that algorithms should be highly detailed and involve the exact steps, and sub-steps, needed to perform a particular task.

Expected prior learning

● The children have already learned about giving and sequencing instructions accurately and have been introduced to the term 'algorithm' in Autumn 2. They may also know about controlling objects, such as remote-control toys. For this topic, the children will need some understanding of plants and animals, including the life cycles of frogs and butterflies, simple food chains and growing a plant from seed.

Chapter at a glance

Subject area
• Algorithms and programming

National Curriculum objective
• To understand what algorithms are, how they are implemented as programs on digital devices, and that programs execute by following precise and unambiguous instructions.

Week	Lesson objectives	Summary of activities	Expected outcomes
1	• To rearrange images into the correct sequence. • To explain verbally the reasons behind their choice of sequencing. • To identify and correct errors in sequencing. • To be introduced to the term 'debugging'.	• Children rearrange images of life cycles into the correct order. • They learn how to identify and correct errors in their sequences.	• Can rearrange a sequence of images into the correct order. • Can identify and correct errors within a sequence of images.
2	• To create a sequence of images. • To identify and correct errors in sequences of images. • To know and understand the term 'debugging'. • To understand the importance of accurate sequences.	• Children create food chain sequences using images and arrows. • They debug their own and others' food chain sequences.	• Can create sequences of images in the correct order. • Can explain why accuracy is important and how they debug their work.
3	• To know what a flowchart is and understand how it can be followed. • To rearrange a simple flowchart into the correct order. • To debug their own and others' flowcharts. • To identify and represent repetition in a flowchart.	• Children are introduced to flowcharts. • They create a flowchart to represent the growth of a plant from seed. • They identify where repetition occurs in the sequence of instructions and represent this in the flowchart.	• Can use simple flowcharts to represent instructions. • Can identify and represent repetition in flowcharts.

Week	Lesson objectives	Summary of activities	Expected outcomes
4	• To be able to explain that an algorithm is a term used to describe a sequence of instructions for a computer to follow. • To create simple, accurate algorithms to move an object. • To explain how they have created their algorithms to ensure accuracy. • To be able to debug algorithms to ensure accuracy.	• Children are reminded of the term 'algorithm' – a sequence of instructions. • Creating algorithms to control a cut-out butterfly on a simple grid. • Creating algorithms to move the butterfly to different squares around the grid.	• Can explain that algorithms need to be accurate so they can be followed. • Can create simple algorithms to control an object.
5	• To control an onscreen device. • To predict what will happen when controlling an onscreen device. • To give instructions accurately to an onscreen device. • To begin to understand that a computer program executes an algorithm.	• Building on the work they have already completed in this unit, the children will now control onscreen ladybirds using simple algorithms. • This first step into onscreen programming encourages them to experiment with different instructions and see what happens.	• Can control an onscreen device. • Can give instructions and predict the outcome.
6	• To control an onscreen device accurately. • To predict what will happen when controlling an onscreen device. • To give instructions to an onscreen device to achieve specific goals. • To be able to spot errors and debug instructions to achieve specific goals. • To begin to understand that a computer program executes an algorithm.	• Working with controlling an onscreen object again; this time a slug. • Working through a number of challenges in which they have to get their slug to specific places on the grid. • They will be encouraged to think about how they debug their programs in order to get to the right position.	• Can control an onscreen device using precise instructions to achieve a specific goal. • Can debug instructions to ensure a specific goal is achieved.
Assess and review	• To assess the half-term's work.	• Playing a game and considering the importance of precise rules. • Creating flowcharts to represent stages of games.	• Assess and review

Overview of progression
● Throughout the lessons, the children build upon their knowledge of sequencing and putting instructions into the correct order. They begin by sequencing simple images and using arrows to represent direction. Through this, they are then introduced to flowcharts. Debugging is introduced and children develop their understanding over several lessons as they identify and correct errors.
● Revisiting and developing their knowledge and understanding of algorithms, first looked at in Autumn 2, helps children to establish this important concept. They are introduced to the idea that a computer program executes an algorithm and this will help them in future years when they develop their programming skills.

Creative context
● The lessons have strong links to the mathematics curriculum with children using grids and moving objects. There are also links with English, especially books, such as *The Very Hungry Caterpillar* and *Monkey Puzzle*.
● Linking to science, there is reference to the life cycle of a butterfly along with other plants, insects and animals.

Background knowledge
● Children will be familiar with many of the insects and animals referred to. They will know, from their work completed in Autumn 2, about sequencing instructions and this knowledge and understanding is developed here.
● You will need to assess the children's capability in sequencing in the correct order and provide additional support as necessary. Children may also need support with their first steps in programming and controlling an object, although no prior knowledge is assumed.

Curriculum objectives
• To understand what algorithms are, how they are implemented as programs on digital devices, and that programs execute by following precise and unambiguous instructions.

Lesson objectives
• To rearrange images into the correct sequence.
• To explain verbally the reasons behind their choice of sequencing.
• To identify and correct errors in sequencing.
• To be introduced to the term 'debugging'.

Expected outcomes
• Can rearrange a sequence of images into the correct order.
• Can identify and correct errors within a sequence of images.

Resources
Interactive activity 'Life cycles' on the CD-ROM; interactive activity 'Jumbled stories' on the CD-ROM (optional); *The Very Hungry Caterpillar* by Eric Carle.

Sequencing images

In this lesson, the children develop their understanding of sequencing further in order to reinforce the importance of giving instructions clearly, accurately and precisely. They sequence images of frog and butterfly life cycles into the correct order, identifying and correcting mistakes as these occur.

Introduction
• Remind the children of the work they completed earlier in the year where they sequenced the stories 'Jack and the Beanstalk' and 'Goldilocks' into the correct order. You may wish to show them the interactive activity 'Jumbled stories' on the CD-ROM (Autumn 2) as a reminder. Ask questions such as:
  • *How did you know which image came first in the sequence?*
  • *How did you work out the rest of the sequence?*
  • *What happens if an image is in the wrong place?*
• Explain that the children are going to be working with sequencing images again in this lesson, this time to sequence life cycles.

Whole-class work
• Show the children the first screen from the interactive activity 'Life cycles' on the CD-ROM. As a class, arrange the sequence of images of the frog life cycle.
• Emphasise to the children as you work that arrows and images are being used to show the correct order of the frog life cycle.
• Ask questions such as:
  • *How did you work out which image went first?*
  • *Why do you think that image came next?*
• If children make mistakes, use this as an opportunity to highlight that spotting and correcting errors is a very important part of computing and that this is called 'debugging'.
• If you wish, read *The Very Hungry Caterpillar* to the children as a class to recap the stages of the butterfly life cycle.

Independent/paired work
• Ask the children to access screen 2 of the interactive activity 'Life cycles', which shows the butterfly life cycle.
• Explain that they should identify the correct sequence of images, dragging and dropping them into the correct place to show the butterfly life cycle.
• If they make a mistake, they should try to work out what error they have made and correct it if possible (debug their work). They can help each other to do this.

> ### Differentiation
> • Support: Less confident learners may need further support with the sequencing of the butterfly life cycle and/or dragging and dropping the images. Mixed-ability pairings or adult support may help with this.
> • Challenge: More confident learners will be able to help others to 'debug' their work and explain verbally how they sequenced their images correctly.

Review
• Display screen 2 of the interactive activity 'Life cycles' showing the butterfly life cycle and ask for volunteers to drag and drop one element into the correct place. Children can self-assess their own work as this is done. Again, discuss mistakes as 'debugging' errors in the sequence.
• At this stage, you are trying to get children to think about the process of sequencing their work if possible. Ask questions to prompt this, such as:
  • *Why do you think it's important to check for errors (debug)?*
  • *Who had to debug their work and how did you do it?*
  • *How did you know what the correct sequence was?*
  • *What is the first thing you need to do when you have to create a sequence?*
• Assess the children's progress through the 'butterfly life cycle' activity and class discussion.

■SCHOLASTIC

Curriculum objectives
● To understand what algorithms are, how they are implemented as programs on digital devices and that programs execute by following precise and unambiguous instructions.

Lesson objectives
● To create a sequence of images.
● To identify and correct errors in sequences of images.
● To know and understand the term 'debugging'.
● To understand the importance of accurate sequences.

Expected outcomes
● Can create sequences of images in the correct order.
● Can explain why accuracy is important and how they debug their work.

Resources
Media resource 'Food chains' on the CD-ROM; photocopiable page 65 'Food chain cards (1)'; photocopiable page 66 'Food chain cards (2)'; photocopiable page 67 'Food chain arrows'; space for group activity

Understanding the importance of accuracy when creating sequences

In this lesson, the children develop their sequencing skills further by working with food chains. They sequence images in the correct order, checking for accuracy and developing their understanding that debugging is an important part of computing.

Introduction
● Remind the children that in the last lesson they sequenced images into the correct order using images and arrows to show life cycles.
● Explain that in this lesson they will be again using images and arrows, this time to create sequences of images to explain how food chains work.

Whole-class work
● Briefly discuss what the children know about food chains and how these work. You may have covered this in science lessons; if not, you are looking for them to understand that a food chain shows where animals get their food from and who eats what.
● Show the children the media resource 'Food chains' on the CD-ROM. Tell them that some of the animals in the food chain on screen 1 are in the wrong place and ask whether they can tell you which ones. Remind them that spotting mistakes and correcting them is called 'debugging'.
● Again, point out that images and arrows are used in food chains to represent who eats what.
● Explain that in small groups they will be 'creating' food chains. Ask four volunteers to demonstrate. Give them each one card from photocopiable page 65 'Food chain cards (1)'. Ask them to hold the cards in one hand.
● Ask the class to rearrange the four children into the correct order for who eats what.
● Add the arrows (using photocopiable page 67 'Food arrows') to show who eats what (they can hold the image in one hand and an arrow in the other).

Group work
● Give a volunteer group the cards from photocopiable page 66 'Food chain cards (2)' and then give each group a set of either set of cards.
● The children should then rearrange themselves into the correct order for their food chain, using images and arrows.
● Encourage groups to debug the food chains of other groups who have the same cards as them.

> **Differentiation**
> ● Support: Less confident learners may benefit from mixed-ability groups or adult support in sequencing their food chain correctly, or understanding where to stand and how the arrows represent who eats who.
> ● Challenge: More confident learners can help to debug their own and other groups' food chains and could draw out their own food chain on paper.

Review
● Go through the correct order of both food chains.
● Ask the children questions such as:
  ● *Why is it important to get your images and arrows in the right order?* (Ask them to imagine if a caterpillar ate a lion!)
  ● *How did you spot mistakes in other groups?* (Checking against each other's work, working out which one was right, changing it accordingly.)
● Assess the children's understanding through the group activity and the review discussion.

Lesson objectives
● To know what a flowchart is and understand how it can be followed.
● To rearrange a simple flowchart into the correct order.
● To debug their own and others' flowcharts.
● To identify and represent repetition in a flowchart.

Expected outcomes
● Can use simple flowcharts to represent instructions.
● Can identify and represent repetition in flowcharts.

Resources
Media resource 'Flowchart' on the CD-ROM; photocopiable page 68 'Flowchart cards' prepared prior to the lesson, physical gardening objects (optional) such as watering can, pot, seed, compost

Understanding and using flowcharts

Following on from the last two lessons, the children apply their knowledge and understanding of sequencing using images and arrows to begin working with flowcharts. They create flowcharts of simple image and text instructions for 'how to grow a plant' and begin to understand how repetition can be used and represented in flowcharts.

Introduction
● Remind the children that they have been using images and arrows to create sequences. Explain that in computing we can use images and arrows to create *flowcharts* to give instructions for others to follow.
● Tell the children that they will be giving instructions for growing a plant from seed using a flowchart.

Whole-class work
● Ask for volunteers to draw one of the steps for how to grow a plant from seed on the board (optionally you could use a pot, seed, compost and watering can to help work out the sequence).
● Show the children screen 1 of the media resource 'Flowchart' on the CD-ROM which shows the steps of watering a plant in a simple flowchart.
● Discuss with the children how the flowchart is representing the steps.
● Ask the children to identify where actions are repeated (watering the plant every day).
● Show screen 2 of the media resource, which shows how the repeat can be represented in the flowchart.
● Discuss with the children how the repeat instruction is instructing you to keep repeating the watering instruction every day.

Group/paired work
● Give out the cards from photocopiable page 68 'Flowchart cards' (apart from the 'repeat' card) and explain to the children that they are going to arrange these in the correct order to give instructions for growing a plant from seed.
● Explain that they have to place the images in the correct order and then add arrows in the correct places.
● Once they think they have finished, they should swap with a neighbouring pair and check their work for errors, adjusting their flowcharts as necessary. Remind them that this is 'debugging'.
● Give the children the 'repeat' cards from photocopiable page 68 'Flowchart cards' and ask them to put the repeat card in where they think it should go.
● Again, they can debug each other's work.

> **Differentiation**
> ● Support: Less confident learners may benefit from mixed-ability pairings or further adult support in ordering their flowcharts and you may choose to leave out the repeat card.
> ● Challenge: More confident learners could answer questions about how they sequenced the instructions into the correct order. They could also work with other groups to help them debug their work.

Review
● As a class, work through the correct order of the cards, asking questions such as:
  ● *How did you work out the correct order?*
  ● *Why did you choose to put that card there?*
  ● *What debugging did you do and how did you correct any errors?*
  ● *How did you know where to put your repeat card?*
  ● *Is there anywhere else you could use your repeat card?* (It could also be used to keep giving the plant light.)
● Ask the children whether they can remember what a sequence of instructions is called. Explain that they have been creating algorithms for growing a plant from seed today.

Using algorithms to control an object

This lesson introduces the concept of controlling an object with an algorithm. Children learn how they can give precise instructions to control their object's movement around a grid. This reinforces learning around algorithms and emphasises important fundamental computational thinking skills.

Curriculum objectives
● To understand what algorithms are, how they are implemented as programs on digital devices and that programs execute by following precise and unambiguous instructions.

Lesson objectives
● To be able to explain that an algorithm is a term used to describe a sequence of instructions for a computer to follow.
● To create simple, accurate algorithms to move an object.
● To explain how they have created their algorithms to ensure accuracy.
● To be able to debug algorithms to ensure accuracy.

Expected outcomes
● Can explain that algorithms need to be accurate so they can be followed.
● Can create simple algorithms to control an object.

Resources
Media resource 'Caterpillar grid' on the CD-ROM; photocopiable page 69 'Caterpillar'; photocopiable page 70 'Butterfly' printed onto card and cut up; photocopiable page 71 'Butterfly grid'

Introduction
● Start by asking the children to recall the work they did previously on algorithms when they were human robots and gave each other instructions (Autumn 2, Lesson 6).
● You may need to remind them of the word 'algorithm'. Clap out the word as al-go-rith-m. Ask what an algorithm is and what is does.
● Explain to the children that in this lesson they will be creating their own algorithms to move objects in the classroom.

Whole-class work
● Show the children the media resource 'Caterpillar grid' on the CD-ROM on the board and the caterpillar cut out from photocopiable page 69 'Caterpillar'. Put sticky tack on the back of the caterpillar so it can be stuck to the board easily.
● Explain that their job is to give the caterpillar instructions to get to the different places on the grid.
● Explain how the directions should work, for example 'go forward 1' will get the caterpillar to move forward one space, 'turn left' will get the caterpillar to turn left, and so on.
● Ask the class to give instructions to the caterpillar to reach different squares. Ask the children questions such as:
  ● *The caterpillar needs food. What direction should he move in first?*
  ● *How many steps does he need to move in that direction?*
  ● *In which direction does the caterpillar need to turn now?*
  ● *Is there any other way we could get the caterpillar to his food (or whichever square you are aiming for)?*
  ● *Could you repeat an instruction in your algorithm?*
  ● *What would we do if we made a mistake?*

Group/pair work
● Explain to the children that they are now going to create algorithms for their own caterpillar to move around a grid.
● In small groups or pairs, give the children photocopiable page 71 'Butterfly grid' and a butterfly printed from photocopiable page 70 'Butterfly'.
● The children should draw four different-coloured flowers in four squares of the grid.
● The children should then put their butterfly on the starting point and create verbal algorithms for the butterfly to get to each flower.

> **Differentiation**
> ● Support: Mixed-ability groupings may be useful or less confident learners could work with adult support to help with giving accurate instructions.
> ● Challenge: More confident learners could write down one of their algorithms (for example, to get to the purple flower move forward 1, turn left, move forward 2).

Review
● Ask volunteers to demonstrate their instructions and ask questions such as:
  ● *How did you work out the best route for the butterfly to take?*
  ● *How did you know in which direction the butterfly should turn?*
  ● *What other instructions could get the butterfly there?*
  ● *How did you correct any errors you made?*
● Review the children's progress through their discussions and through the outcomes of the 'Butterfly' activity.

Curriculum objectives
● To understand what algorithms are, how they are implemented as programs on digital devices and that programs execute by following precise and unambiguous instructions

Lesson objectives
● To control an onscreen device.
● To predict what will happen when controlling an onscreen device.
● To give instructions accurately to an onscreen device.
● To begin to understand that a computer program executes an algorithm.

Expected outcomes
● Can control an onscreen device.
● Can give instructions and predict the outcome.

Resources
Interactive activity 'Ladybird controller' on the CD-ROM

Controlling an onscreen device

In this lesson, the children discover that they can use a computer to control an onscreen device. They extend the skills they have developed making predictions and selecting the correct instructions to use. This may be their first foray into programming and this terminology will be introduced during the lesson.

Introduction
● Recap the last lesson with the children, discussing with them what they know about controlling objects and giving instructions. For example: *How did you get your butterfly to go to a flower? Give me an example of one of the instructions you gave to your butterfly to move it to a flower.*
● Explain that in this lesson the children will be controlling an object like the butterfly, but this time doing it on a computer. Explain that they will be creating algorithms for computer 'programs' to complete and that this is called programming.

Whole-class work
● Display the interactive activity 'Ladybird controller' on the CD-ROM.
● Ask the children what they think might happen if you press each of the arrows on the 'ladybird' (they are predicting what will happen – a key computational thinking skill).
● Ask for a volunteer to make the 'ladybird' move forward and turn and see whether this matches up with their prediction.
● Show the children how they can change the size of the step.
● Ask them to predict what will happen when a number 3 step size is chosen and get a volunteer to show the results, discussing whether their predictions were correct.
● Ask them to predict what will happen when a number 1 step size is chosen and get a volunteer to show the results, discussing whether they were correct.
● Ask the children to predict what the 'trail colour' controls will do and get a volunteer to change colours and move the ladybird around to show the effect.

Independent/paired work
● Show the children how to access the interactive activity 'Ladybird controller' and ask them to experiment with the controls, moving their ladybird around the screen.
● At this stage, there is no need for specific goals, just experimentation. However, if you wish you could add further structure, giving the children instructions, such as, *The ladybird wants to move to the leaf, can you get her there?*

> **Differentiation**
> ● Support: Less confident learners may need support with the computer controls, left and right, or moving their ladybird to the correct position. You may wish to use mixed-ability pairings to help with this.
> ● Challenge: You can set more confident learners the task of making shapes such as squares and rectangles using the ladybird.

Review
● As a class, discuss how the children found ways to get their ladybird to different places and ask volunteers to demonstrate what they have discovered. You could set simple tasks to facilitate this. For example: *Who can show me how to get to the bottom right of the screen? How would I make a square with green and red sides?*
● Reiterate that they have been using a computer 'program' to carry out the algorithms that they have created.
● Review children's progress through their discussions and the outcomes of their independent work.

■SCHOLASTIC

Curriculum objectives
● To understand what algorithms are, how they are implemented as programs on digital devices and that programs execute by following precise and unambiguous instructions

Lesson objectives
● To control an onscreen device accurately.
● To predict what will happen when controlling an onscreen device.
● To give instructions to an onscreen device to achieve specific goals.
● To be able to spot errors and debug instructions to achieve specific goals.
● To begin to understand that a computer program executes an algorithm.

Expected outcomes
● Can control an onscreen device using precise instructions to achieve a specific goal.
● Can debug instructions to ensure a specific goal is achieved.

Resources
Interactive activity 'Ladybird controller' on the CD-ROM; interactive activity 'Slug controller' on the CD-ROM; photocopiable page 'Slug challenge' from the CD-ROM

Controlling an onscreen device to achieve specific goals

In this lesson, children build on the last lesson and develop further their understanding of controlling onscreen devices and giving instructions to achieve specific goals. They build on the work completed in the last lesson, reinforcing the importance of giving an exact sequence of instructions.

Introduction
● Remind the children of their last lesson in which they controlled a ladybird device. Display the interactive activity 'Ladybird controller' on the CD-ROM and ask them questions such as:
  ● How did you get the ladybird to move/turn?
  ● How did you make sure that you were taking the right-sized steps?
  ● What did you do if you made a mistake?
● Reiterate that they have been using a computer 'program'. They create the algorithm (instructions) and then input it into the program to make it work. This is called programming.

Whole-class work
● Display the interactive activity 'Slug controller' on the CD-ROM.
● Explain to the children that this works in a similar way to the ladybird and that this time they will be controlling the slug to get to the different fruits.
● Show them the photocopiable page 'Slug challenge' from the CD-ROM and work through the first challenge with them.
● First, ask them what instructions they think they need to give the slug. Write these down on the board.
● Second, ask a volunteer to follow these instructions using the slug. Do they work? What do they need to change?
● Note down the changes they needed to make on the board. Explain that this is called 'debugging' and is used a great deal in computing. Getting it 'wrong' is a very important part of the process.

Independent/paired work
● Ask the children to access the interactive activity 'Slug controller' and give them the photocopiable page 'Slug challenge'.
● Explain that they should complete the tasks, writing down the instructions they think they need first and then trying out their instructions with the slug. They should then write down the instruction they actually used, if this was different (this is debugging their program).

Differentiation
● Support: Mixed-ability pairings may be useful or less confident learners could work in a small group with adult support to help in writing down their instructions and following them. They may also need help with how to debug their instructions.
● Challenge: More confident learners could explain how they used debugging in their instructions and how this helped them to improve on the next set of instructions. Ask, How did you correct your mistakes? How did you make sure you did not make the same mistakes again?

Review
● Work through one or two of the 'slug challenges' asking volunteers to show you their instructions.
● Discuss how they approached the slug challenges, asking questions such as:
  ● Were your first instructions always right or did you have to debug your instructions every time?
  ● What happened when your instructions were wrong?
  ● How did you work out how to make your instructions correct?
● Assess the children's progress through the outcomes of the slug challenges

Curriculum objectives
● To understand what algorithms are, how they are implemented as programs on digital devices and that programs execute by following precise and unambiguous instructions

Lesson objectives
● To know what a flowchart is and understand how it can be followed.
● To order a simple flowchart into the correct order.
● To follow the instructions on a simple flowchart.

Expected outcomes
● Can use simple flowcharts to represent instructions.
● Can follow a sequence of instructions.
● Can identify repetition.

Resources
Photocopiable page 'Beetle game' from the CD-ROM; six-sided dice

Plants and animals: Assess and review

This assess and review lesson focuses on programming by controlling objects. The children have thought about giving instructions to objects and that those instructions need to be accurate and precise. By looking at plant and animal life cycles, the children have reinforced their knowledge of sequencing. They have been introduced to the term 'debugging', meaning identifying and correcting errors in an algorithm.

Introduction
● Display the photocopiable page 'Beetle game' from the CD-ROM to the class. Explain the rules – the children take turns in rolling the dice. The game has precise rules, they have to throw a 6 to begin – then they can draw the body. Once they have a beetle body, if they get a 'I' that means they can add an eye and so on. Once the game has been demonstrated, place the children into small groups of four to play the game.
● Ask: *What happens if someone cheats and doesn't follow the rules?*

Group work
● After the children have played the game, explain that now they can choose any rules they would like to use. By letting them invent their own rules, the games will probably not work and disagreements may follow.
● Ask: *What happens if the rules are not clear or precise?*

Whole-class work
● Bring the class together and ask the children to explain how the game needed to start, that is, they needed to throw a 6 to start, because they needed a beetle's body.
● Remind them of the flowcharts that they saw in earlier lessons. *What does a flowchart start with? What could come next?*
● Ask: *How could you draw the start of the game as a flowchart?*

Paired work
● In pairs, ask the children to draw a flowchart to represent the start of the game. Begin with the 'Start' oval shape. Which shape will come next?

> ### Differentiation
> ● Support: Less confident learners will need support to choose the correct shapes and to write the instructions. Asking them to explain verbally will help them to summarise the instructions.
> ● Challenge: More confident learners could draw a flowchart for the next stage of the game – for example, throwing a I for an eye and so on.

Review
● Tell the children that they could write flowcharts for many activities they do in their lives. Choose three children to share their flowchart for the game. Ask another child to follow the flowchart – does it work?
● Model the next stage of the game, asking the children to identify whether there are repeated instructions

Food chain cards (1)

Sunflower seed (in a flower)

Insect

Frog

Snake

Food chain cards (2)

Leaf

Caterpillar

Bird

Cat

Food chain arrows

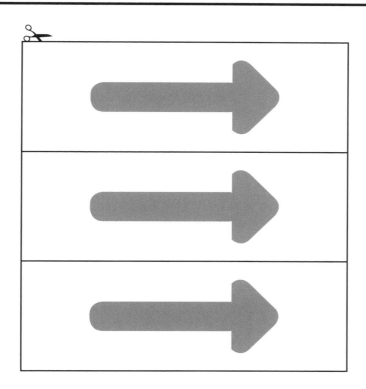

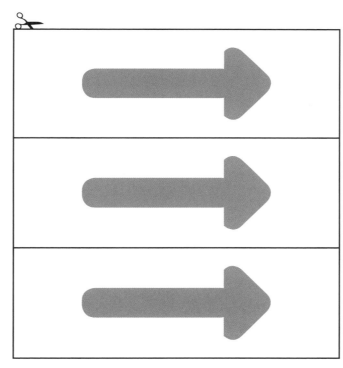

Flowchart cards

 Fill a pot with soil	 Place the seed in the soil
 Cover the seed with soil	 Water the seed
 Put pot in sunlight	 Water every day
	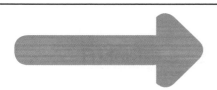

Caterpillar

■ Use the caterpillar size that fits best on the grid on your whiteboard.

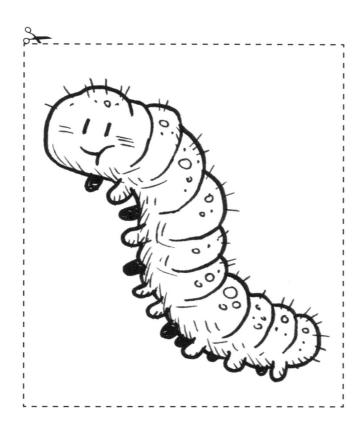

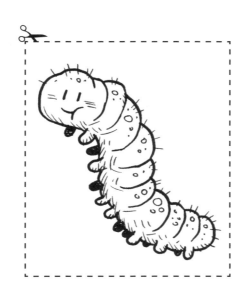

Butterfly

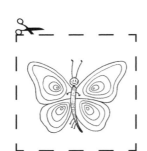

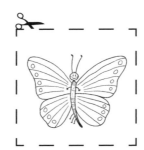

Butterfly grid

- Draw four flowers in four different squares.
- Can you give your butterfly instructions to reach the flowers?

✂ ̶

I can give instructions to an object to move it round a grid.

How did you do?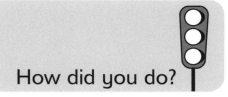

Handa's Surprise

The children are introduced to the story *Handa's Surprise*. They use it as an example to recognise the main events and to sequence them in the correct order. In each lesson, the children will re-read the story and role play part of it, so the introductory lesson is important for them to grasp the main features of the story: the beginning, where Handa's starts her journey; the middle, where she loses the fruit to different animals; and the end, where she is surprised to find tangerines in her basket. Sequencing events links to algorithms and sorting – important aspects in computing. Children use digital cameras for capturing images and video and audio devices to capture sound effects and narration. Finally, they combine images and audio to create their version of the story. Throughout the process, the children focus on sequencing *Handa's surprise* into the correct order.

Expected prior learning

● The children will be familiar with telling stories and should be able to recognise the beginning, the middle and the end. They may have used digital cameras previously. Also, they may have listened to 'read-a-long' books.

Chapter at a glance

Subject area
• Data and information

National Curriculum objective
• To use technology purposefully to create, organise and manipulate digital content.

Week	Lesson objectives	Summary of activities	Expected outcomes
I	• To identify the correct order of a story. • To be able to explain and describe the beginning, middle and end of a story. • To be able to sequence a story into the correct order. • To create a simple, pictorial storyboard, retelling a story in the correct order.	• The children are introduced to the story of *Handa's surprise* and read it together as a class. • They discuss the order of the beginning, middle and end of a story and place the corresponding three images from the story into the correct order. They then add the other key events in sequence. • To reinforce the learning, they retell the story as a storyboard.	• Can sequence a series of events into the correct order.
2	• To role play a sequence in a story. • To capture role play, using a simple digital camera. • To work effectively in small groups.	• Re-reading the story, the children focus on its beginning (Handa preparing, setting off and meeting the monkey). • They roleplay the scenes by following instructions and capture them using a digital camera.	• Can follow a sequence of instructions. • Can use digital cameras to capture content.
3	• To role play a sequence in a story. • To capture role play, using a simple digital audio device (microphone). • To work effectively in small groups.	• Re-reading the story, the children focus on the next three scenes (meeting the ostrich, the zebra and the elephant). • Using audio devices such as microphones, they record themselves making animal sounds and playing instruments.	• Can use audio devices to record accompanying music.

Week	Lesson objectives	Summary of activities	Expected outcomes
4	• To role play a sequence of a story. • To capture role play, using a simple digital audio device (microphone). • To work effectively in small groups.	• Re-reading the story, the children focus on the narration during the next three scenes (meeting the giraffe, the antelope and the parrot). • They capture their narrations using audio devices and replay them to listen to their own voices reading.	• Can use audio devices to record narration.
5	• To role play a sequence of a story. • To capture role play, using a simple digital camera. • To work effectively in small groups.	• Re-reading the story, the children focus on the twist in the story (the goat becoming loose and colliding with the tree). • Using video cameras (handheld video cameras or digital cameras), the children role play the goat scenes and the tangerines falling into Handa's basket.	• Can use digital cameras to capture video content.
6	• To learn that images, audio and video can be combined using software. • To evaluate images, audio and video and give simple feedback.	• Finally, the children combine their learning from the lessons to create a digital story. They role play the story and capture images and narration, to add to the editing software. • The children watch the final stories and evaluate their learning.	• Can combine digital content purposefully. • Can understand that images, audio and video can be combined effectively.
Assess and review	• To assess the half-term's work.	• To consolidate the learning, the children are given a new activity to sequence a story and capture images, video or audio.	• Assess and review.

Overview of progression
● The children will be familiar with listening to stories and most should know the terms 'beginning', 'middle' and 'end'. The lessons reinforce the concept of sequencing the events in a story into the correct order. This prepares them for programming in the following years, where sequencing instructions is very important.
● They encounter a range of digital devices, including a digital camera and digital audio recorder. They should progress their skills in using the equipment for a specific purpose. They will especially develop their collaborative group-working skills.

Creative context
● The content of this chapter has strong links with the English curriculum, with children engaging in a number of speech and drama activities. They will be reading, re-reading and retelling stories, recognising the beginning, middle and end.
● The African context of the story links to geography with opportunities to investigate where the story is set, where the animals live and to estimate how far Handa travels.

Background knowledge
● During the lessons, the children build up their knowledge of Africa and its animals. They may already know the names 'monkey', 'ostrich', 'zebra', 'elephant', 'giraffe', 'antelope', 'parrot' and 'goat'. However, they may not know the sounds that these animals make.
● Using digital cameras may be new to the children. They might have used a mobile phone to take a photograph. Combining image, video and audio will be new to most children.

Curriculum objectives
● To use technology purposefully to create, organise and manipulate digital content.

Lesson objectives
● To identify the correct order of a story.
● To be able to explain and describe the beginning, middle and end of a story.
● To be able to sequence a story into the correct order.
● To create a simple, pictorial storyboard, retelling a story in the correct order.

Expected outcomes
● Can sequence a series of events into the correct order.

Resources
Handa's Surprise book; photocopiable page 81 'Cover memory game'; photocopiable pages 'Handa's Surprise cards (1) and (2)' from the CD-ROM; photocopiable page 82 'My scenes (1)'; photocopiable page 83 'My scenes (2)'; photocopiable page 84 'Adding scenes'; glue

Introduction to *Handa's Surprise* and sequencing

In this lesson, the children are introduced to the story. They make the link between parts of a story and sequencing the beginning, middle and end. They retell the story through a simple storyboard, which emphasises the sequencing of the scenes in the correct order.

Introduction
● Explain to the children that they are going to read *Handa's Surprise*. Show them the front cover and say they are going to play a memory game. Using photocopiable page 81 'Cover memory game', ask the children to work in small groups to draw the cover. Hold the book up, and then one person from each group looks for 10 seconds, goes to their group and draws part of the picture. The next person in the group then looks at the cover, returns and draws the next part. Repeat until all of the children have had a turn.
● Show them the cover again and ask them to predict what the surprise might be. In addition, you could ask:
  ● *Where do you think the story is set?*
  ● *How old is Handa?*
  ● *Which fruits can you see?*
  ● *What is a surprise?*
  ● *Can you tell a story of when you had a surprise?*

Whole-class work
● Read the story from the beginning to the end. How much can they remember? Ask a child whether they can remember the first animal who took the fruit and which fruit it was? Use photocopiable pages 82 and 83 'My scenes (1) and (2)' to note down how many scenes the class remembers.

Paired or Group work
● Give the children three scene cards (cut out from photocopiable pages 'Handa's Surprise cards (1) and (2)' from the CD-ROM), which are the beginning (scene 1), middle (scene 7: giraffe and the pineapple) and the end (scene 14). Ask the children to put the cards in order. Can they remember what happened in between?
● Using photocopiable page 84 'Adding scenes', ask children to stick the three scene cards into the boxes on the left and draw a scene that occurs in between the three scene cards, for example scene 3 with the monkey and scene 9 with the parrot. Ask children why they remembered those scenes.

Differentiation
● Mixed-ability groupings may be useful to help children to work together and share understanding.
● Support: Less confident learners will benefit from peer or adult support to reinforce the vocabulary of 'beginning', 'middle' and 'end'. They may also need help to choose which scenes to draw.
● Challenge: More confident learners could order the cards and draw four scenes.

Review
● Bring the whole class back together and display the beginning scene. Ask the question, *What happened next?* See whether any of the children have drawn the next scene. If so, ask them to show it to the class and describe what happened. Continue through the story, pausing at each scene to see whether one or more of the children have drawn it. Conclude with the final scene.
● Link the learning to computing by stating that stories are like a series of instructions. Each part of the story follows in order. Remove the final scenes (where Handa gets the tangerines). Ask the more confident learners to give an example of another ending. Replace the scenes, and ask the less confident learners to think of another animal and fruit that could appear in the middle.

Curriculum objectives
● To use technology purposefully to create, organise and manipulate digital content.

Lesson objectives
● To role play a sequence in a story.
● To capture role play, using a simple digital camera.
● To work effectively in small groups.

Expected outcomes
● Can follow a sequence of instructions.
● Can use digital cameras to capture content.

Resources
Handa's Surprise by Eileen Browne; photocopiable page '*Handa's Surprise* cards (1)' from the CD-ROM; digital camera or tablet device with a camera

Developing sequencing using digital images

The children re-read the story and then focus on the opening scenes. They retell the beginning by role playing the scenes and capture them using a digital camera.

Introduction
● Show the *Handa's Surprise* book to the children. Can they remember the story? Ask one child to say what happened at the beginning. Ask one child what happened at the end. Now ask for examples from the middle of the story. Re-read the story to the children.
● Display the cards from photocopiable page '*Handa's Surprise* cards (1)' from the CD-ROM. Ask: *Does it matter in which order they are placed?* Show the children the cards placed out of order, for example scene 2 then scene 1. Does the story still make sense? Can Handa begin her journey before she has filled her basket with fruit? Explain that in the original story the basket was filled with fruit and then Handa set off. The next stage was to meet the monkey. Ask the children if that could come before the first two scenes. The aim is to show that in the *Handa's Surprise* story, the first three scenes need to be in order (if the children were composing a new story, then they could invent new sentences to correspond to the pictures).

Whole-class work
● Explain to the children that they are going to role play the first three scenes. Ask three children to play the parts of Handa, the monkey and the photographer. The child playing Handa can act out putting fruit in a basket and setting off on her journey. The child playing the monkey can pretend to snatch a banana. Meanwhile, the photographer can pretend to take photographs of the action (ask them to say 'snap' whenever they think it is appropriate to take a picture, encouraging them to wait for an important scene).
● Show the children the digital camera and explain how to take a photograph. They need to collect images at appropriate parts in the story.

Group work
● Place the children into groups of three and ask them to repeat what the first group did, pretending to take images. Depending on the number of digital cameras available, distribute the cameras to the photographers, as they perform their role plays (if there is only one camera, let the groups use it in turn). To allow every child the opportunity to use the camera, they should change roles and play each part.

Differentiation
● Mixed-ability groupings may be useful to help children to work together and share understanding.
● Support: Less confident learners may need support with remembering the scenes.
● Challenge: More confident learners may be able to understand and use the cameras more easily than less confident learners, though this may depend on prior experience of cameras outside of school. They might write the narration down, for others to read.

Review
● Bring the whole class back together. If possible, share some of the images the children have just captured on a large display. Do the images match the story scenes 1, 2 and 3? Which photo most clearly shows the action from the story?
● Conclude the lesson by repeating the aim of sequencing the scenes in order to retell the story. Explain that computers also need instructions in the correct order.

Curriculum objectives
● To use technology purposefully to create, organise and manipulate digital content.

Lesson objectives
● To role play a sequence in a story.
● To capture role play, using a simple digital audio device (microphone).
● To work effectively in small groups.

Expected outcomes
● Can use audio devices to record accompanying music.

Resources
Handa's Surprise by Eileen Browne; photocopiable page 'Handa's Surprise cards (1)' from the CD-ROM; digital audio recorder or laptop/tablet device with audio recording capability; percussion instruments

Developing sequencing using audio (sound effects)

Following on from the lesson on digital images, the children record animal sounds and then accompanying music for the *Handa's Surprise* story.

Introduction
● Remind the children of the *Handa's Surprise* story. Ask one of the more confident children to read the first two pages. Now ask another child to make a monkey sound for scene 3. Continue to read the story yourself, asking different children to make the animal sounds. Some sounds may be more familiar, for example the elephant. For other sounds, they will need to be creative, for example, the antelope.
● Explain to the children that they are going to capture their sounds using an audio recorder (a microphone or suitable recording software on a computer or mobile device).

Whole-class work
● Show the children the audio recorder and demonstrate how to capture a recording. Ask a child to be a monkey and record their sound, then play it back. The children role play the sounds for scenes 4 (ostrich), 5 (zebra) and 6 (elephant) and record them on the audio recorders.

Group work
● In small groups of three, the children can role play the three scenes and take turns to record the animal sounds. If only one recorder is available, it could be shared around from group to group, as they role play.

Whole-class work
● Bring the class back together and explain that they are going to record percussion sounds to add to the story. For each animal, can they imagine which sounds would match with their character?

Group work
● Back in their small groups of three, the children can role play the three scenes and take turns to play their instruments. Each child uses one instrument to represent the animal, while another child records the sound.

> **Differentiation**
> ● Mixed-ability groupings may be useful to help children to work together and share understanding.
> ● Support: Less confident learners will benefit from peer or adult support to think about how the audio would match the characteristics of the animal.
> ● Challenge: More confident learners could organise their group to record for a set time period or while they are reading the story.

Review
● Bring the whole class back together. Show scene 4 and ask a child to play their instrument, while you read the story. Emphasise how the sound should stop when the reader is ready to move onto the next scene. Now choose an audio recording to play for the next scene–does it continue for the duration of the reading?
● Finally, conclude the lesson by stating that you are sequencing the story in order to retell it. The audio recordings add to the experience, by adding animal sounds and accompanying music.

Curriculum objectives
● To use technology purposefully to create, organise and manipulate digital content.

Lesson objectives
● To role play a sequence in a story.
● To capture role play, using a simple digital audio device (microphone).
● To work effectively in small groups.

Expected outcomes
● Can use audio devices to record narration.

Resources
Handa's Surprise by Eileen Browne; photocopiable pages 'Handa's Surprise cards (1)' and (2) from the CD-ROM; photocopiable page 85 'Scenes 7–9 with narration text'; digital audio recorder or laptop/tablet device with audio recording capability

Developing sequencing using audio (narration)

In this lesson, children narrate the *Handa's Surprise* story and capture the audio, improving their audio-recording skills.

Introduction
● Explain to the children that they are continuing on from their previous lessons, focusing on sequencing the story *Handa's Surprise* and recording audio. Ask more confident readers to read pages from the book – you may need to support them with their reading. Remind the children how to use the audio recorder and give an example of one of the children reading from the pages that precede scenes 7 (giraffe), 8 (antelope) and 9 (parrot).

Whole-class work
● Display the three scene cards 7, 8 and 9 from photocopiable pages 'Handa's Surprise cards (1) and (2)' from the CD-ROM. Mix them up and ask whether it matters which order the cards appear. Here the children may disagree – to retell the story as in the book, they should put them in the same order but, in the middle of the story, it may not matter if the scenes are in a different order, as long as all of the fruit is missing by the end of the story. This can highlight that computers will follow instructions and not try to reorder them, whereas humans may consider doing things in a different order.

Group work
● Place the children into groups of three and ask them to tell the story of scenes 7–9 in their own words. Use photocopiable page 85 'Scenes 7–9 with narration text'. The children can sketch out scenes 7–9 in the boxes and add their narration text underneath. While they are narrating, one of the other children should record the audio. Ask them to experiment recording the story in different orders.

Differentiation
● Mixed-ability groupings may be useful to help children to work together and share understanding.
● Support: Less confident readers will benefit from adult support or they could retell the story in their own words.
● Challenge: More confident readers could read the words and support their group.

Review
● Bring the whole class back together and ask them again about the order of the scenes 7, 8 and 9, perhaps playing some recordings that were not in order. Do they think it matters which order the scenes are in for the story to make sense? Now ask a less confident learner, *Could the end come before the beginning?* They should say that it can't. Emphasise how stories have a beginning, middle and end.
● Conclude that, to retell the story exactly as the original, the scenes must follow the same order. Explain that computers follow the instructions in order without question.

Curriculum objectives
● To use technology purposefully to create, organise and manipulate digital content.

Lesson objectives
● To role play a sequence in a story.
● To capture role play, using a simple digital camera.
● To work effectively in small groups.

Expected outcomes
● Can use digital cameras to capture video content.

Resources
● *Handa's Surprise* by Eileen Browne; photocopiable pages 'Handa's Surprise cards (1)' and (2)' from the CD-ROM; digital camera (that can record video) or tablet device with a camera

Developing sequencing using video

In this lesson, the children experiment with video to capture role play of *Handa's Surprise*. They re-emphasise the importance of sequencing the story in order.

Introduction
● Re-read *Handa's Surprise* to the children, however, miss words out on each page. Ask the children if it changes the story for them. Are they missing out on the description of the story or on the events, because words are missing? Then think about taking photographs and watching a video. Is video better than a still image, because you get to see more?

Whole-class work
● Show the children the video camera (or digital camera with video function or mobile device). Explain that they are going to role play scenes 10 (goat becoming loose), 11 (goat hitting tree) and 12 (tangerines falling) and capture them on video.
● Ask three children to model the activity, one being the goat, one being Handa and one filming the scenes. As they film, they will often move the camera around, which means the final film is not easy to follow. Encourage them to hold the camera still and keep the scene short (the children could count to 10 quietly for each scene). Also, encourage them to say 'cut' after each one.

Group work
● In groups of three, the children take turns to be the different characters and the camera person (if there are not enough cameras for each group, share the camera with each one, while the others rehearse). If they cannot hold the camera steady, they could rest it on a table and press record.
● Another way of improving the videos is to introduce 'slow motion'. Describe how the children can move really slowly. Examples on the television include athletics (100-metre sprints) and action replays of football and cricket. This may help them recreate the scene where the goat hits the tree, ensuring that the camera can catch the video.

Differentiation
● Mixed-ability groupings may be useful to help children to work together and share understanding.
● Support: Less confident learners may need reminding of the key scenes from the story or the instructions for using the video cameras.
● Challenge: More confident learners could describe how they decided to film the action and why they chose to say particular words.

Review
● Before bringing the class together, choose one group to share their videos. (The videos may need to be transferred to the computer to display them or you may be able to connect the camera to the projector directly.) Check that their videos play back correctly.
● Bring the class together to watch the three videos created by your chosen group. Ask the children whether the videos show the action from the book. Do they think videos are better than still images?
● Remind the children that they are sequencing the story, using different ways of capturing the scenes.

Curriculum objectives
● To use technology purposefully to create, organise and manipulate digital content.

Lesson objectives
● To learn that images, audio and video can be combined using software.
● To evaluate images, audio and video and give simple feedback.

Expected outcomes
● Can combine digital content purposefully.
● Can understand that images, audio and video can be combined effectively.

Resources
Handa's Surprise by Eileen Browne; photocopiable pages '*Handa's Surprise* cards (1) and (2)' from the CD-ROM; digital camera (that can record video) or tablet device with a camera; digital audio recorder or laptop/tablet device with audio recording capability; software (for example, Microsoft PhotoStory or a movie editor); percussion instruments

Developing sequencing using images, audio and video

In this lesson, the children consolidate their learning from the previous lessons to combine images, audio and video. They remember that they are sequencing a story.

Introduction
● Give the children the percussion instruments and place them into eight groups called 'Monkey', 'Ostrich', 'Zebra', 'Elephant', 'Giraffe', 'Antelope', 'Parrot' and 'Goat'. Choose two children to be 'Handa' and 'Akeyo'. Begin by showing the pictures of the scenes from *Handa's Surprise* on photocopiable pages '*Handa's Surprise* cards (1) and (2)'. As each scene is displayed, the relevant group should make music to match the scene (Handa can make a sound for each scene, for example, the sound of Handa walking steadily.)
● Now, repeat the story with narration and with the children's groups making the appropriate animal sound and playing their instruments.
● Finally, tell the story without the book with the children making the sounds of the animals and using the percussion instruments, along with your narration.
● Ask individual children: *Which version did you like the best? Is it better to have just images, just narration, just animal sounds or just music?* Explain that they are going to retell the story *Handa's Surprise* using images and audio.

Group work
● In their animal groups, the children role play the scene in which their animal appears. When they have practised this, bring the class together to perform the story in the correct sequence.

Whole-class work
● Choose a camera person to record the scenes so one camera contains all the images. Firstly, Handa acts out the first two scenes, to begin the story. Each group in turn performs their role play and the camera person takes photographs. At the end of the story, Handa and Akeyo act out the final scene. Load the scenes in order, into Microsoft PhotoStory or video editing software. Then you can record the narration into the software directly (the children could retell the story for their part).

Differentiation
● Mixed-ability groupings could be used in the lesson, as the children act out their scenes.
● Support: Less confident learners may need support to focus on the role play or when ordering their scene cards.
● Challenge: More confident learners may try using the software to create their own stories.

● **Note**: using the software to combine images and audio can take a long time. Therefore, the lesson could conclude here. You can then add the elements together after the lesson. It is possible to add a background music track, chosen from a list of digital music or imported as an mp3 from a CD.

Review
● Bring the class back together for the final performance of *Handa's Surprise*. Using software, the images and narration have been combined. Ask the children to watch the final film carefully and compare it to the original story.
● Ask the children whether their story is in the same order as the original story. Ask: *What happens at the beginning? What happens at the end? Why do you think Handa was surprised?*
● Conclude the lesson by reinforcing the concept of sequencing the story and by combining images and audio. Explain that videos could be combined with audio narration and sound effects too, using video-editing software.

Curriculum objectives
● To use technology purposefully to create, organise and manipulate digital content.

Lesson objectives
● To role play a sequence of a story.
● To capture role play, using a simple digital camera.
● To work effectively in small groups.

Expected outcomes
● Can use digital cameras to capture video content.
● Can work effectively in small groups.

Resources
Photocopiable page 86 'Speech bubbles'; photocopiable page 87 'Handa's happy ending'

Handa's Surprise: Assess and review

The children will be very familiar with the story of Handa by now and should be able to retell the series of events. They have also experienced using digital cameras, voice recorders and video cameras to capture their role plays. In this assess and review lesson, they will revisit the skills they have developed and create a new scene in the story.

Introduction
● Re-read the story of *Handa's Surprise*. Ask the children to predict what will happen next. Also, ask them to add detail to the story, for example: *What is the name of the village? How far does she walk? Which other animals might she meet? What could happen next in the story?*

Group work
● The children work in small groups to role play the story. Ask them to add extra words to the action using photocopiable page 86 'Speech bubbles'. For example, Handa might say to herself, *It is a long way to the village* or *I am really hot.*
● Using a video camera, the children capture their acting and voices.
● Bring the class together and ask the children to plan the next two scenes in the story. Display the final scene, so that they can see Handa and her friend together. Using photocopiable page 87 'Handa's happy ending', the children sketch the scenes and imagine the words that are being used.
● Ask: *Can you work together as a group to plan what happens next?*
● Allow the children time to discuss the next scenes in groups. They can then sketch them on to the photocopiable sheet. Can they add dialogue for the characters?
● Once they are ready, they capture the scenes, using the video camera. Observe how they are working together – are some children dominating? Are all being listened to?

Whole-class work
● Bring the class together and share their videos, so that they can all see the performances. Ask the children to think about how they worked together.
● Ask: *Was it easy working together? Did everyone get to share their ideas?*
● Explain to the class that everyone should be listened to and have an opportunity to share their ideas. Also, sometimes, it can be good that one person takes a lead to organise a group. The key learning is that they reflect upon how they worked together and whether it made the task easier or the results better?

> ### Differentiation
> ● Support: Less confident learners will need support to explain their ideas and to organise them into actions for the role play.
> ● Challenge: More confident learners could write the script for the characters, using the boxes on photocopiable page 87 'Handa's happy ending'.

Review
● Remind the children of the story and how they have used technology to capture it in a different way. Choose three children to explain how to use the digital camera to capture stills and to capture video. Ask them how to capture audio using a voice recorder. If they have used a tablet computer, ask them whether they find it easier to have all of the tools in one device.
● Finally, ask the children to think about working in groups. What are the advantages of working in groups? When do they prefer to work alone?

Cover memory game

■ Draw the front cover of the book *Handa's Surprise.*
Each person in your group can draw part of the picture.
■ What do you think will happen in the story?

(blank drawing box)

I can look at the front cover of a book and predict
what will happen.

How did you do?

My scenes (1)

■ How many scenes from Handa's Surprise can you remember?
Describe or draw the scenes.

1	2	3
4	5	6

7

PHOTOCOPIABLE   ■SCHOLASTIC
www.scholastic.co.uk

My scenes (2)

■ How many scenes from Handa's Surprise can you remember?
Describe or draw the scenes.

✂--

8	9	10

11	12	13

14

Adding scenes

■ Paste the scenes described into the boxes on the left. Draw pictures in the boxes on the right to show something that happened in between these scenes.

Paste the picture of Handa putting fruit in the basket in this box.	
Paste the picture of the giraffe taking the pineapple in this box.	
Paste the picture of Handa and Akeyo eating tangerines in this box.	

I can remember events in a story and order them.

How did you do?

PHOTOCOPIABLE

Scenes 7–9 with narration text

7	8

9

Speech bubbles

■ Draw Handa and write what she might say when she is walking to the village.

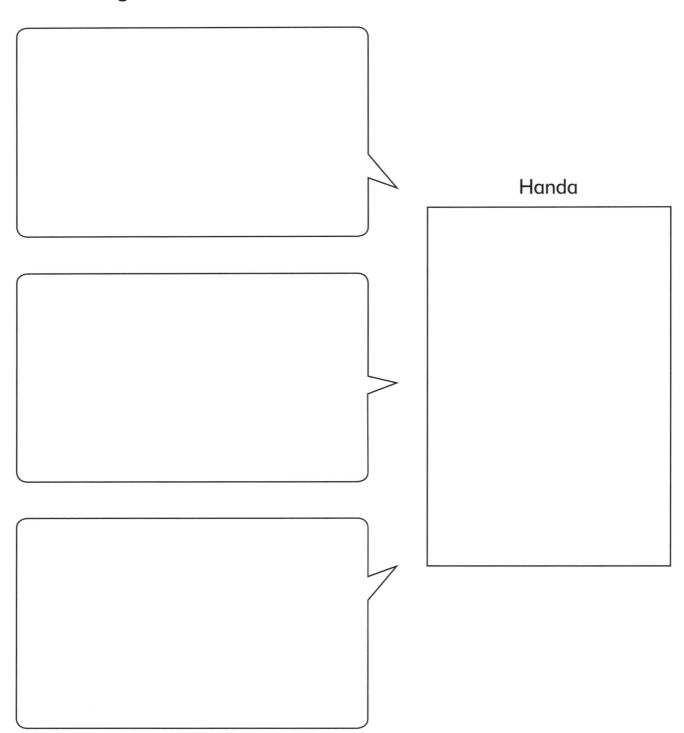

Handa

I can write speech.

How did you do?

Name: _____ Date: _____

Handa's happy ending

■ What could happen after the end of *Handa's Surprise*? Draw two extra scenes in the boxes and add words to go with them.

I can draw new scenes to add to the end of the story *Handa's Surprise*.

How did you do?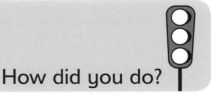

Sea and coast

The theme of this chapter is 'Sea and coast' and the focus is the story of *The Lighthouse Keeper's Lunch*. The children think about communication between friends. They learn that friends are kind to each other, whether they are face-to-face or communicating using a computer. They consider their personal information, such as name, address and password and create avatars to use when online. Looking at websites, the children sort a selection into an order of popularity and discuss the need to type addresses accurately. The children learn that if they feel upset by something they see on the web or by communication with people online, they should tell their teacher or a parent.

Expected prior learning

● Before the lesson, the children will have experienced visiting websites and some may have typed a web address into a browser. They will need to be able to type simple words and use a mouse to navigate a website (pressing onscreen buttons to select tools).

Chapter at a glance

Subject area
• Communication and safety

National Curriculum objective
• To keep personal information private.
• To know where to go for help and support when they have concerns about material on the internet.

Week	Lesson objectives	Summary of activities	Expected outcomes
1	• To list what makes a 'good' friend. • To identify how 'good' friends communicate through role play. • To discuss methods of face-to-face communication. • To discuss methods of communication that are not face-to-face (for example, letters, postcards, email, Facebook).	• Children are introduced to the story *The Lighthouse Keeper's Lunch*. • The story describes how the lighthouse keeper looks after the lighthouse. The children identify how they can look after each other as friends. • They act out a scene to show clear, kind communication. • They discuss ways of communicating when not face to-face.	• Can identify what makes a good friend both offline and online. • Can identify features of appropriate behaviour online.
2	• To create a list (for example, objects you would see at the seaside). • To identify and discuss how to stay safe at different physical locations. • To begin to understand how to stay safe when online.	• The children begin by thinking about safety in real life. • Analogies are made between staying safe at the seaside and online.	• Can create a list using text. • Can order a list alphabetically and numerically.
3	• To understand how to behave positively with others when face-to-face and online. • To learn how to protect private information when online (for example, considering when to share address details).	• The children read about the negative behaviour of the seagulls in *The Lighthouse Keeper's Lunch* when they steal the keeper's food. • Analogies are drawn with protecting private information online.	• Can protect their identity online by not using their full name. • Can protect their identity online by choosing an avatar.
4	• To create a memorable password that is not easily identified by others. • To understand why passwords need to be kept private.	• The children try different ways of creating passwords that are secure. • Through discussion, the children describe why they need to keep passwords private.	• Can create a secure password and understand the need to protect it.

■SCHOLASTIC

Week	Lesson objectives	Summary of activities	Expected outcomes
5	• To create a list of websites. • To sort a list based on one criteria. • To stay safe by accurately entering the website address. • To understand what to do if they visit a website they don't recognise.	• The children look at different seaside websites. • They sort the websites into order of popularity. • In the story, the sea gulls taste sandwiches filled with mustard, so they fly away. Following the analogy, children discuss what to do if they find something unpleasant online.	• Can create a list of websites that the children visit and sort, in order of popularity. • Can understand the need for accuracy when entering website addresses.
6	• To begin to understand how to stay safe when online. • To discuss friends they meet in-person and online. • To identify what to do when a friend upsets them – tell someone. • To discuss people who are not friends, who they might meet online. • To know that online friends should behave kindly and if they upset you, tell someone.	• Children review the learning about friends they meet in person and online. • They discuss what to do if they meet someone who is unkind and who they can tell about this. • The children write a poem based on being safe online.	• Can write a poem based on staying safe online.
Assess and review	• To assess the half-term's work.	• The children complete their own website profile. • They consider protecting their identity when online.	• Assess and review.

Overview of progression

● The children progress in their understanding of being kind when communicating with people. They begin with communication when face-to-face, then to communicating online. They consider the information they use, such as user names and addresses and think about whether they need to share it. They also progress their knowledge of passwords and how to create a more secure password.

● The children may have a basic understanding of visiting websites, though they may not have typed the address into the browser before. Therefore, they learn about the need for accuracy when typing, so that they arrive at the correct address.

● Finally, they consider if they find unpleasant material on the web or if someone makes them feel uncomfortable, then they need to tell someone they trust, such as their teacher or a parent.

Creative context

● Many links can be formed with English in this chapter. Encourage them to identify the new vocabulary and practise using it. They could practise spelling days of the week and ordering the story and the food. They construct an acrostic poem, with musical accompaniment. During role plays, they can narrate their actions.

● Linking to maths, they could think about the recipes for the food and the numbers of items in the basket. They could use times of the day to describe day and night. For science, they could conduct some simple water experiments with light and observe how water moves, including mentioning the tides.

Background knowledge

● When discussing communication when not face-to-face, they should have experienced sending a birthday card and so the idea of sending messages using a computer can be described, for example, an email or typing a text message. Some children may have used a video communication tool, such as Skype or FaceTime, with family members who live in other places of the world.

● The children will have encountered websites before, but may not know about the address bar or where they would type to enter an address. They will need to be able to use a mouse to navigate a web page.

Curriculum objectives
• To keep personal information private.
• To know where to go for help and support when they have concerns about material on the internet.

Lesson objectives
• To list what makes a 'good' friend.
• To identify how 'good' friends communicate through role play.
• To discuss methods of face-to-face communication.
• To discuss methods of communication that are not face-to-face (for example, letters, postcards, email, Facebook)

Expected outcomes
• Can identify what makes a good friend both off and online.
• Can identify features of appropriate behaviour online.

Resources
The Lighthouse Keeper's Lunch by Ronda Armitage; photocopiable page 97 'Best friends'; photocopiable page 98 'Different communication'

Introduction to The Lighthouse Keeper's Lunch

Introduction

• Ask the children, *What are friends?* Choose two children who you know are friends and ask them to stand at the front of the class. Ask the others, *How do you know they are friends?* Responses could be because they spend time together, they like similar things, their families are friends, they sit next to each other or they live near each other. With all responses, try to draw out that they are kind to each other. For example, they may live near each other, but if one was unkind to the other, then that may not be friendly. They spend time together, but if one teased the other or stole their toys, they would not be friends. So, it is the way they act that keeps them friends.

• Using photocopiable page 97 'Best friends', ask the children to draw a picture of two best friends. This could be themselves or imaginary best friends.

• Introduce the story *The Lighthouse Keeper's Lunch*. Ask the children to predict what it is about. Who are the characters? What might they be like? Then read the story.

Whole-class work

• Re-read the start of the story, which describes the lighthouse keeper (being an *industrious* person and *come rain or shine, he tended his light* – the children may need help to think what this means). Can the children tell what the lighthouse keeper was like by his actions?

• Read the next part of the book to describe the lighthouse keeper's wife. She cooked *delicious* lunches. *What does that tell us about her?*

Group work

• The children think of something that they do together as friends. Each pair or small group must think of an idea and then act out how they do it. For example, they may play a game at play time, such as 'Tig' or 'Stuck in the mud', so they would act out how to play that game.

Whole-class work

• Bring the class together and ask the children to act out their role play. The other children guess what they are doing. Once they have the correct answer, they identify how they are being good friends (for example, including others, not being too rough, taking turns). On the computer or a large piece of paper, list the ways the children are being good friends.

> **Differentiation**
> • Mixed-ability groupings will enable the children to work together and share understanding. More confident learners could write a list of 'What makes a good friend' for their group and less confident learners will benefit from peer or adult support.

Review

• Returning to the story, the lighthouse keeper is in his cottage at night-time and he can talk face-to-face with his wife. When he is on the lighthouse, ask, *How does she send the food to him?* She sends it over the wire and she is not face-to-face. Also, at night the ships sound their horns to 'toot' him and the lighthouse sends out its light to communicate (not face-to-face).

• Using photocopiable page 98 'Different communication', the children review their understanding of the different methods of communication.

• Ask more confident learners to describe how email works. Ask less confident learners to describe how a letter is sent. Both methods are ways of communicating at a distance.

• Finally, describe how we can send messages using mobile phones and through social media sites like Facebook, Twitter or Google+? Explain that these are not face-to-face but we still need to think about our behaviour.

Staying safe at the seaside

To focus on safety, the children begin by thinking about safety in real life. They begin by listing objects they would see at the seaside. The children discuss how to stay safe at the seaside. Analogies are then made between staying safe at the seaside and online.

Curriculum objectives
● To keep personal information private.
● To know where to go for help and support when they have concerns about material on the internet.

Lesson objectives
● To create a list (for example, objects you would see at the seaside).
● To identify and discuss how to stay safe at different physical locations.
● To begin to understand how to stay safe when online.

Expected outcomes
● Can create a list using text.
● Can order a list alphabetically and numerically.

Resources
individual whiteboards and pens; photocopiable page 99 'Trip to the seaside'

Introduction
● Begin the lesson by using the story *The Lighthouse Keeper's Lunch* and play 'I-spy' using the pictures from the first few pages to recap on the previous lesson. Let the children take turns to choose an item and then identify the first letter. Make a list of the items and display it on a large piece of paper or in a word processing document.
● Once the children have played the game and ten items have been identified, ask the children to look at the list. Can they sort it into alphabetical order? Help the children to sort the words into alphabetical order.

Whole-class work
● Ask the class, *Who has been to the seaside?* Choose three children to describe where they went, what they saw and what they did. Use the format, 'I went to...', 'I saw...' and 'I did...', for example, 'I went to Skegness, I saw the sea and I made a sand castle.'

Group work
● Place the children into small groups or pairs. Those who have been to the seaside tell others when they went, what they saw and what they did. Now, pause everyone and ask them to discuss a new question, *What did you have to be careful about, when at the seaside?*
● Using the photocopiable page 99 'Trip to the seaside', the children record their answers about their visits to the seaside and also, what they needed to be careful about.

Differentiation
● Mixed-ability groupings would be beneficial to help children work together and share understanding.
● Support: Less confident learners may need images of the seaside as prompts. Alternatively, they could use scenes in *The Lighthouse Keeper's Lunch* to identify dangers.
● Challenge: More confident learners could write their own notes to describe how they needed to take care at the seaside.

Review
● Bring the whole class back together and ask the children to share the 'dangers' or what they need to be careful about at the beach, for example the tide coming in, broken glass, jellyfish or strangers. Write a list of ten dangers on a large piece of paper or, preferably, in a word processor. Explain that they are going to decide which is the biggest danger and put that at number one on the list. Continue to order the list until they have reached number ten. The word processor or equivalent digital text tool will allow the text to be re-ordered, by dragging and dropping it.
● Conclude the lesson by making the analogy with being safe online. Describe that a website might have lots of great content. You can say *I went to...* and name a website, then *I saw...* and describe what you saw on the website and *I did...* describe an activity you did on that website. For example, *I went to Cbeebies website, I saw 'Grandpa in my pocket' and I played a game.* Then explain that some websites are better than others and also that sometimes the things on that website might not be nice or kind. Explain that the children need to be careful in real life and also when they are online.

Curriculum objectives
● To keep personal information private.
● To know where to go for help and support when they have concerns about material on the internet.

Lesson objectives
● To understand how to behave positively with others when face-to-face and online.
● To learn how to protect private information when online (for example, considering when to share address details).

Expected outcomes
● Can protect their identity online by not using their full name.
● Can protect their identity online by choosing an avatar.

Resources
Photocopiable page 100 'Food in the basket'; photocopiable page 101 'My avatar'; an online avatar creator, such as the Voki website (www.voki.com/create.php)

Keeping private

Following *The Lighthouse Keeper's Lunch* story, the focus is on the seagulls and how they behave negatively. Reversing this, the children form opinions about how to behave in a positive manner. In the story, the seagulls steal food from the basket and the lighthouse keeper has to protect it. The children consider protecting private information online, such as their name and by using an avatar.

Introduction
● Begin the lesson by playing a game of 'Opposites'. The children have to do the opposite action to the instruction, for example, you say *Stand up*, so the children sit down. Other instructions could be: *Be very noisy; Arms up; Close your eyes.*
● Explain to the children that the seagulls are being naughty in the story. Ask what the seagulls are doing and why it is naughty. For example, they are stealing Mr Grinling's food. Now ask the children to think of the opposite behaviour – being kind and not stealing the food.

Whole-class work
● Read the next part of the story. Ask: *How does the lighthouse keeper try to protect the basket on each day?* On Tuesday, he tied the napkin over the basket. On Wednesday, he placed the cat in the basket. On Thursday and Friday, he put mustard in the sandwiches. Using photocopiable page 100 'Food in the basket', the children draw which foods were in the basket each day.
● Explain to the children that when going online, we can protect ourselves by not using our full name and we can also use an avatar, instead of our real photograph. An example would be that they might use their real first names and their initial for the second name. For example, Anna Ross could say that her online name was Anna R. Alternatively, the children might use the name of an animal starting with that letter, for example, Anna Rhino.

Group work
● Tell the children to design an avatar for themselves, using photocopiable page 101 'My avatar'. They could simply draw a picture of themselves, using colouring pens and paper or they could use a paint package on the computer. There are online avatar creators, such as 'Voki' which allows the user to create an avatar and, if required, add a recorded voice (www.voki.com/create.php). Demonstrate using Voki to help the children.

Differentiation
● Mixed-ability groupings can help the children to share ideas about their avatars.
● Support: Less confident learners could work with a partner to support their creation of the avatars and check that they have understood how to create an online name.
● Challenge: More confident learners could create avatars for Mr and Mrs Grinling, in addition to their own avatars.

Review
● Bring the whole class back together to share examples of their avatars. Ask three children to tell the class their online name and show their avatar. Ask them to explain why they chose the features (hair style, eye colour and so on).
● Ask the children whether they should share their address when online. They may infer that they should never share their address, so that someone online could not find their house. Explain that sometimes the address is needed, for example, when joining the LEGO club, a magazine is sent to their address. They need to think carefully – do they really need to add their address on the computer?
● Finally, conclude the lesson by reiterating how important is it to protect themselves online by not using their full names, using an avatar and thinking about other information, such as whether to give their address.

■SCHOLASTIC

Curriculum objectives
● To keep personal information private.
● To know where to go for help and support when they have concerns about material on the internet.

Lesson objectives
● To create a memorable password that is not easily identified by others.
● To understand why passwords need to be kept private.

Expected outcomes
● Can create a secure password and understand the need to protect it.

Resources
Photocopiable page 102 'Passwords'; photocopiable page 103 'Strong passwords'

Protecting passwords

In the story, the lighthouse keeper tries different ways to protect the basket, so the children try different ways of creating secure passwords. Through discussion, the children describe why they need to keep passwords private.

Introduction
● Begin by playing the 'Password' game. One child stands outside the classroom door and knocks. A second child opens the door and says 'What's the password?' The first child has to guess. This could be impossible for them, so the second child gives a hint, for example, *It's my favourite fruit.* The first child has three tries to guess correctly. They then swap places. The other children can play this in pairs (they can sit at their desks, pretending to knock on a door and then guess the password). Ask whether a password of their name would be a good password? *Would it be too easy to guess?*
● Re-read T*he Lighthouse Keeper's Lunch* and remind the children of the previous lesson, where the lighthouse keeper tried different approaches to protecting the basket. Can they remember the different ways?
● Explain that passwords are a way of protecting the children online. However, if the passwords are too easy to guess, they will not be protected, like the basket with the napkin and the cat.

Whole-class work
● Ask the children to think of a hobby, for example, a favourite TV programme or a favourite celebrity. Choose one child to share their idea. An example could be, *I like watching Strictly Come Dancing.* Write the words, so the children can read the sentence. Now, take the first letter of each of the words 'ilwscd'. Ask the children whether this would be easy to guess. Change the letters to include some capital letters, for example, 'ilwSCD'. Ask: *Does this make it easier or harder to guess?* Finally, replace the 'i' with a digit, '1lwSCD'. Ask again: *Does this make it easier or harder to guess?*

Group work
● In small groups or pairs, the children think of their own example of a password and write it down. Then, they underline the initial letters of each word and write that down. The next steps are to replace some letters with capital letters and numbers. Using photocopiable page 102 'Passwords', will help to structure the process.

Differentiation
● Mixed-ability groupings may be useful to help children to work together.
● Support: Less confident learners will need support with their writing and identification of the initial letters. They could simply stop at that step or if you think they can use capital letters, they could swap all of their letters to capitals.
● Challenge: More confident learners will be able to do all of the steps from writing the sentence, identifying the initial letters, changing to capital letters and using digits.

Review
● Bring the whole class back together and ask three children to share their sentences and then the passwords that they have created. Do they think that they are 'strong' passwords? Do they think that they can remember the passwords? Explain that many people forget their passwords and that a sentence about something they like can make it easier to remember.
● To check that the children have understood what makes a secure password, use photocopiable page 103 'Strong passwords' to check their understanding.
● To conclude the lesson, highlight that the three children who shared their examples have actually given away their secret. The whole class now know their passwords! What should they do? Establish that they should change their password and, from now on, keep it secret!

Curriculum objectives
● To keep personal information private.
● To know where to go for help and support when they have concerns about material on the internet.

Lesson objectives
● To create a list of websites.
● To sort a list based on one criteria.
● To stay safe by accurately entering the website address.
● To understand what to do if they visit a website they don't recognise.

Expected outcomes
● Can create a list of websites that the children visit and sort, in order of popularity.
● Can understand the need for accuracy when entering website addresses.

Resources
Photocopiable page 'Favourite foods' from the CD-ROM; photocopiable page 'Seaside websites' from the CD-ROM; a washing line across the classroom; clothes pegs to attach paper to the washing line

Favourite places to visit

In this lesson, the children look at different seaside websites and vote on their favourites. They sort the websites into order of popularity. In the story *The Lighthouse Keeper's Lunch*, the sea gulls taste sandwiches that are filled with mustard, so they fly away. Following this analogy, the children discuss what to do if they find something unpleasant online.

Introduction
● Re-read the story and ask the children, *How does the basket get across from the cottage to the lighthouse?* Describe the wire that connects the two places. Before the lesson, put a washing line or string across the room.
● Remind children that in the story, there is food in the basket. Ask the children to name their favourite foods. Using photocopiable page 'Favourite foods' from the CD-ROM, the children draw their favourite food. When complete, choose five examples and attach them to the washing line. Ask the children to vote on their favourite foods (for example, fish and chips = 10 votes, burger = 7 votes, curry = 1, beans on toast = 3). Order the foods from the most to least votes, going from left to right, so if the children were on the lighthouse, then fish and chips would be sent over, as it is most popular.

Whole-class work
● Explain that the children will be looking at different websites linked to the seaside topic. Display the websites listed on photocopiable page 'Seaside websites' from the CD-ROM.

Group work
● In small groups, discuss which website they like the best. Why do they like it? Ask children to cut out the websites from the photocopiable page 'Seaside websites' and organise them into an order they all agree on.

> **Differentiation**
> ● Support: Less confident learners will benefit from peer or adult support to organise their websites into an order.
> ● Challenge: More confident learners could try to identify why the children have chosen their particular order.

Whole-class work
● Bring the class together and draw their attention to the web addresses. They are all very long and a mistake could be made when typing it into the browser. Ask, *What happens if you type in the wrong words?* Explain that if you address a letter to the wrong house, it will not get there, the same is true of websites.
● Tell the children that if, when they are typing a web address, they accidentally find a website that upsets them, they should turn off the screen or close the browser. Demonstrate this action, then tell the children that afterwards they should tell a parent or teacher.

Review
● Remind the children that, in groups, they have looked at websites and put them in order of popularity. Attach the pieces of paper with the websites' names along the washing line. Ask one person from each group to describe their order. As each list is read out, move the pieces of paper along the washing line to reflect the order.
● Did they notice that the order changed for each group? This is because they decided on personal preference. If they had been told to sort them in alphabetical order or by number of words on a page, it may have been easier. This is ordering with one criteria. Explain to the children that when sorting they used the criteria of 'which is the most popular'.

Curriculum objectives
● To keep personal information private.
● To know where to go for help and support when they have concerns about material on the internet.

Lesson objectives
● To begin to understand how to stay safe when online.
● To discuss friends they meet in person and online.
● To identify what to do when a friend upsets them – tell someone.
● To discuss people who are not friends, who they might meet online.
● To know that online friends should behave kindly and, if they upset you, tell someone.

Expected outcomes
● Can write a poem based on staying safe online.

Resources
Photocopiable page 'Kind or unkind?' from the CD-ROM; photocopiable page 'Safe online poem' from the CD-ROM; book or magazine; individual whiteboards and pens

Being kind online

The Lighthouse Keeper's Lunch story is reviewed looking at the relationship between the characters. The children think about friends they meet in person and online. They discuss what to do if they meet someone who is unkind and who they can tell. Finally, the children write a poem based on being safe online.

Introduction
● Ask the children to listen to T*he Lighthouse Keeper's Lunch* story, thinking about who is being kind. They may say that the wife is kind, as she makes the food for the lighthouse keeper. However, she is not really kind to the cat, making it go in the basket. The seagulls are not kind, as they steal the food and make unkind comments. Finally, the lighthouse keeper is possibly unkind at the end of the story, as he sees the gulls eating another person's lunch and says, *Ah well, such is life.* Use photocopiable page 'Kind or unkind?' from the CD-ROM to discuss how people's actions can be kind or unkind.

Whole-class work
● Explain that the children are going to act out a play, where they are unkind and then kind. Choose three children to act and ask two of them to hold a book or comic. Then the third child will try to join in, but the two will not talk with them and turn their backs to not allow them to see the book. The third child is upset and tells the teacher. Finally, the two children apologise and let the other child join in looking at the book.

Group work
● Organise the children into groups of three and ask them to act out the play. If it helps the children to remember, read out the main points:
  ● Two children are reading together.
  ● Another child tries to join them, but they do not let them see the book.
  ● The child tells the teacher.
  ● The children let the other child join them and they all read together.
● The children could adapt the play, by having a different activity, instead of a book, for example, playing football or a game of 'Tig'.

Whole-class work
● Bring the whole class back together and ask one group to act out their play. Describe being kind when face-to-face and when using the computer. Ask whether they have communicated with people using a video communication tool, such as Skype or FaceTime. They may have used a tool like this with their own families to contact other family members. Explain that in the future they may meet people who they do not know on the internet.
● Explain that the same rules apply – if the person online is being unkind, they should tell a parent or teacher. Hopefully, at this age, it is unlikely that they would be communicating either by text or video unsupervised. However, this is building understanding for future years.

> **Differentiation**
> ● Mixed-ability groupings would allow the children to share ideas.
> ● Support: Less confident learners will benefit from peer or adult support to direct them through the stages of the play.
> ● Challenge: More confident learners could narrate the play for the group to act out and write it on an individual whiteboard.

Review
● To conclude the lesson, ask the class to create a 'staying safe online' acrostic poem. Using photocopiable page 'Safe online poem' from the CD-ROM, it shows the letters, K-I-N-D. Ask the children to think of a tip that starts with these letters. For example, K*now who to tell, I can play with friends, No one is left out, Do be kind.*

Sea and coast: Assess and review

The assess and review lesson is an opportunity for the children to revisit the learning from the chapter.

Introduction
● Ask the children, to think about the story of *The Lighthouse Keeper's Lunch*. Explain that the lighthouse keeper has set up a website for children to send messages to him. Firstly, they need to join the Lighthouse keeper club before they can send a message.
● *Ask: How do we find a website?* (Search or 'Google', or typing in an address)
● *Ask: If we type in an address, why do we need to be careful?* (To make sure the correct website is reached)

Paired/independent work
● The children complete their website profile on the photocopiable page 'Lighthouse keeper club membership' from the CD-ROM. They add a user name in the box 'Name' then it asks for their 'Address'. Let the children complete the boxes, without prompting.
● In the picture box, ask the children to draw the picture they would like to use as their avatar. Allow them to choose how they would like to represent themselves. Then the children add their age to the profile.
● Finally, they need to create a password for their login. Allow them to write any text, without prompting.

Whole-class work
● Ask the children to look at their completed membership sheets.
● *Ask: Did you put your first name and surname into the 'Lighthouse keeper club name' box?*
● *Ask: Did you need to put in your surname or could you use your first name and then an animal or another object for your surname?*
● *Ask: Did you need to add your address?*
● Next, look at the profile picture on their sheets. Highlight that, instead of using a real photograph, they could use an avatar. Key learning: *Use an avatar instead of a picture of yourself. Be careful sharing your images.*
● The date of birth or age is often requested when joining online clubs.
● *Ask: Why does the Lighthouse keeper club want to know how old you are?* (Potentially so they can send information about offers)
● Finally, look at the passwords the children created.
● *Ask: Is your password easy to guess? How will you remember it?*

> ### Differentiation
> ● Support: Less confident learners will need help with spelling addresses and with the date of birth.
> ● Challenge: More confident learners could add an 'About me' piece of writing, to share about their interests, but without giving away information about addresses, dates and times.

Review
● Tell the children that they have successfully joined the 'Lighthouse keeper club' and that they could send a message to each other.
● *Ask: If someone says something unkind at playtime, what can you do?* (Tell the teacher)
● *Ask: If someone says something unkind when online on the computer, what can you do?* (Tell the teacher, parent or carer)

Best friends

■ Draw two best friends. Show what they like to do together.

I can talk about best friends and say why they are friends.

How did you do?

Different communication

We can communicate face-to-face or not face-to-face.
- Look at the pictures below. Draw the missing picture.

Face to face	NOT face to face
Communicating in the classroom	Communicating by writing a birthday card
Communicating on the school playground	Communicating using a computer

I can draw a picture that shows communicating using a computer.

How did you do?

PHOTOCOPIABLE   **SCHOLASTIC**
www.scholastic.co.uk

Name: _____   Date: _____

Trip to the seaside

I went to...

I saw...

I did...

I was careful about...

I can record details of a trip to the seaside.

How did you do?

Food in the basket

■ Draw the food in the basket for each day.

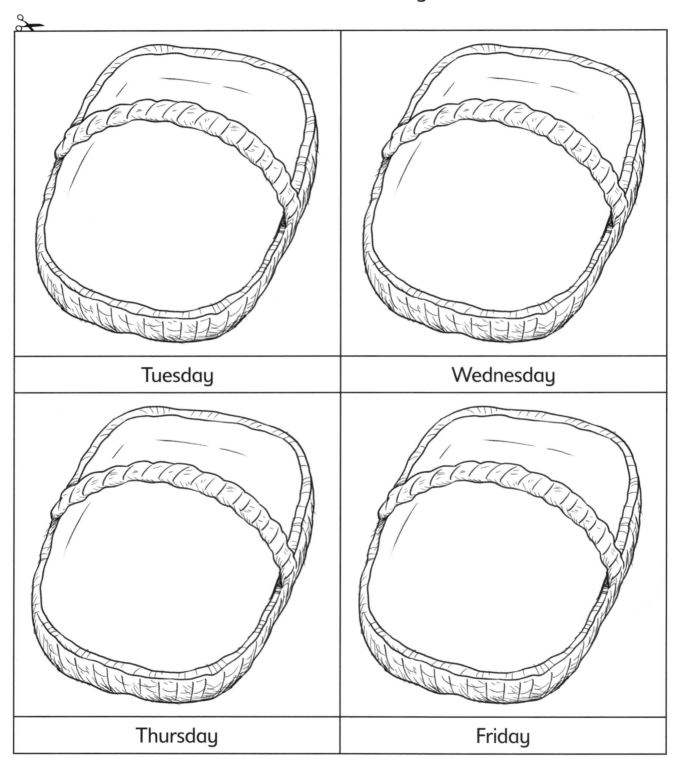

Tuesday	Wednesday
Thursday	Friday

I can recall the sequence from the story.

How did you do?

PHOTOCOPIABLE

My avatar

■ Draw your avatar picture. It could be a cartoon picture of you or a superhero. You decide!

My name is _____

I can create an avatar to use on the computer.

How did you do?

Passwords

1. Think of a hobby, a favourite TV programme or a favourite celebrity.
2. Think of a sentence about your hobby.
3. Take the first letter of each word.
4. Add some capital letters.
5. Change some letters for numbers.

Example:

1. Bike riding
2. I like riding on my bike
3. ilromb
4. ilromB
5. I lromB

Now, it's your turn!

1. _____

2. _____

3. _____

4. _____

5. _____

I can create a strong password.

How did you do?

Strong passwords

Passwords that are easy to guess are weak.
Passwords that are difficult to guess are strong.

■ The class have chosen new passwords. Are they strong or weak?

Name	Password	Strong or weak?
Peter	Peter	
Jane	liwarm	
Ravi	RIght	
Anna	12345	
William	Lwif8	

■ Which password do you think is the strongest? Why?

_____

_____

_____

■ Which password do you think is the weakest? Why?

_____

_____

_____

I can tell how strong passwords are.

How did you do?

Oliver's Vegetables

This chapter uses the book *Oliver's Vegetables* as a theme and builds on the knowledge and understanding of algorithms that the children have developed in Year 1. Key aspects such as flowcharts, algorithms, debugging and programming are developed further and prior learning is consolidated.

Expected prior learning

● The children have already been introduced to algorithms and made their first attempts at simple programming in Year 1. For this topic, they will need to know the story of *Oliver's Vegetables* and have some basic understanding of how vegetables are grown.

Chapter at a glance

Subject area
• Algorithms and programming

National Curriculum objective
• To understand what algorithms are, how they are implemented as programs on digital devices and that programs execute by following precise and unambiguous instructions. • To create and debug simple programs. • To use logical reasoning to predict the behaviour of simple programs.

Week	Lesson objectives	Summary of activities	Expected outcomes
1	• To know what a flowchart is and understand how it can be followed. • To arrange a simple flowchart into the correct order. • To use 'repeat', 'repeat until' and 'wait until' instructions within a flowchart. • To debug their own and others' flowcharts.	• Children create flowcharts to give instructions for planting vegetables. • They debug their own and others' flowcharts.	• Can use simple flowcharts to represent instructions. • Can identify and represent repetition in flowcharts.
2	• To be able to identify algorithms represented in flowcharts that will create 2D shapes. • To identify and correct errors in flowchart algorithms. • To understand how repetition can be used in flowcharts and algorithms to achieve a specific goal.	• Children create flowcharts to plant vegetables in common 2D shapes. • They identify and correct errors in flowcharts.	• Can identify flowchart algorithms to create common shapes. • Can debug flowchart algorithms.
3	• To follow simple algorithms to plant vegetables in specific patterns. • To begin to understand that computers need more accurate instructions than humans. • To begin to understand that computers use programs to implement algorithms.	• Children create simple algorithms to create specific patterns. • They follow algorithms to plant vegetables in specific patterns on a grid. • They use simple programming-type abbreviations in algorithms.	• Can follow simple algorithms with accuracy. • Can explain that algorithms need to be accurate and precise so they can be implemented.
4	• To control an onscreen device. • To predict what will happen when controlling an onscreen device. • To give instructions accurately to an onscreen device. • To begin to understand that a computer program executes an algorithm.	• Children use a simple program to implement algorithms to create patterns of vegetables. • They check and debug their work to improve accuracy.	• Can control an onscreen device using a simple program. • Can create programs to achieve specific goals.

■ SCHOLASTIC

Week	Lesson objectives	Summary of activities	Expected outcomes
5	• To write simple algorithms to create specified patterns. • To control an onscreen device accurately in order to test their algorithms. • To be able to spot errors and debug algorithms and programs. • To begin to understand that a computer program executes an algorithm.	• Children create their own algorithms to create specific patterns. • They test and debug their algorithms using a simple computer program.	• Can create simple algorithms to achieve specific goals. • Can debug algorithms.
6	• To create simple accurate algorithms using images and/or text. • To test and debug others' algorithms. • To understand that a computer program executes an algorithm.	• Children write their own algorithm for making chips from potatoes. • They work collaboratively to debug their own and others' algorithms. • They make their algorithm suitable for implementation by a computer program.	• Can create simple, accurate and precise algorithms. • Can test and debug algorithms.
Assess and review	• To assess the half-term's work.	• A choice of tasks is given to assess knowledge and understanding.	• Assess and review

Overview of progression

• Throughout the lessons, the children build upon their knowledge and understanding of algorithms. They begin with a reminder of flowcharts, using image and text instructions to create a simple algorithm showing how to sow carrots. Through this, they are first introduced to the important commands of 'repeat', 'repeat until' and 'wait until'. Debugging is covered across all lessons as children are encouraged to review and test their algorithms in order to identify and correct errors.

• First introduced in Year 1, children are reintroduced to the important concept that a computer program executes an algorithm and for the first time they both follow and create their own algorithms using a simple computer program.

Creative context

• The lessons have strong links to the mathematics curriculum with children using grids, moving objects using numbers (for example *Plant 3 carrots*) and using algorithms to draw patterns and 2D shapes. The computing lessons should also draw upon the children's learning in English, especially because they utilise *Oliver's Vegetables* in every lesson.

• Linking to the science curriculum, this chapter includes reference to plants and growing and eating vegetables.

Background knowledge

• The children may not have specific knowledge of some of the vegetables, but they should be aware of the more common vegetables, particularly if they are already familiar with *Oliver's Vegetables*. From the work they have already completed in Year 1, they will know about sequencing, algorithms and programming, and this knowledge and understanding is developed further in this chapter.

• From assessing children's understanding in the Year 1 units, you will need to assess their capability in following and creating algorithms and provide additional support as necessary.

● To understand what algorithms are, how they are implemented as programs on digital devices, and that programs execute by following precise and unambiguous instructions.

Lesson objectives
● To know what a flowchart is and understand how it can be followed.
● To arrange a simple flowchart into the correct order.
● To use 'repeat', 'repeat until' and 'wait until' instructions within a flowchart.
● To debug their own and others' flowcharts.

Expected outcomes
● Can use simple flowcharts to represent instructions.
● Can identify and represent repetition in flowcharts.

Resources
Media resource 'Oliver's Vegetables flowchart' on the CD-ROM; photocopiable page 113 'Carrot cards'; photocopiable page 114, 'Help Oliver'; plastic rake (optional); Oliver's Vegetables by Vivian French

Understanding and using flowcharts

The children create simple flowcharts consisting of image and text instructions to show Oliver how to sow a row of carrots, developing their understanding of how repeat instructions can be used both in algorithms and flowcharts.

Introduction
● Explain that today the children will be creating flowcharts to give instructions to Oliver who wants to help his Grandpa sow a row of carrots.
● You may wish to recap/read the story of Oliver's Vegetables or go over how a vegetable (carrot) seed is planted and grows as the children need to understand how to grow a seed to be able to give the correct instructions.

Whole-class work
● Using photocopiable page 113 'Carrot cards' and the plastic rake, ask for volunteers to demonstrate how to sow a row of carrots.
● Give out the carrot seed cards from the photocopiable page and ask the rest of the class to give instructions to the volunteer to role play sowing the carrot seeds in a straight line. (See photocopiable page 114 'Help Oliver' or media resource 'Oliver's Vegetables flowchart' for the correct sequence.) This is simply raking the soil, planting the seed, raking over the soil, then moving forward one step and repeating until the end of the row. You can prompt the children with questions such as: What do you think you have to do first to plant a seed? What should you do once the soil has been raked?
● Show the children screen 1 of the media resource that shows these steps in a simple flowchart and discuss with the children how the flowchart is representing the steps.
● Ask the children to identify where actions are repeated (plant and cover seed, then move 1 step forward).
● Ask the children to highlight how Oliver knows when to stop (repeat until you reach the end of the row).
● If the children complete this confidently, you could swap the seed card for the carrot card and ask the children to go through the sequence for how to pick the carrots (wait until the carrots have grown, then pick one carrot, move forward one step and repeat until the end of the row). The flowchart with this extension is shown on the final screen of the media resource.

Group/paired work
● Give out photocopiable page 114 'Help Oliver' and explain to the children that they are going to complete their own flowcharts to show Oliver how to plant his row of carrots.
● Explain that they have to place the images in the correct order and add arrows in the correct places.
● Highlight cards 5–6, which show the repeat and wait instructions.
● When they think they have finished, they should swap with a neighbouring pair and check their work for errors, adjusting their flowcharts as necessary. Remind them that this is 'debugging'.

Review
● As a class work through the correct order of the cards, asking questions such as:
  ● How did you work out the correct order?
  ● Why did you choose to put that card there?
  ● How did you choose the correct position for the 'keep going until'/'wait until' cards?
  ● How do these cards help Oliver?
  ● What debugging did you do and how did you correct any errors?
● Discuss with the children that they have been creating algorithms using repeat commands and wait until commands. Explain that these are used a great deal in computing and programming.

Curriculum objectives
● To understand what algorithms are, how they are implemented as programs on digital devices and that programs execute by following precise and unambiguous instructions.

Lesson objectives
● To be able to identify algorithms represented in flowcharts that will create 2D shapes.
● To identify and correct errors in flowchart algorithms.
● To understand how repetition can be used in flowcharts and algorithms to achieve a specific goal.

Expected outcomes
● Can identify flowchart algorithms to create common shapes.
● Can debug flowchart algorithms.

Resources
Interactive activity 'Algorithms and shapes' on the CD-ROM; media resource 'Plant in a square' on the CD-ROM

Using flowcharts to create squares

This lesson develops the children's understanding of algorithms and flowcharts as they help Oliver to sow his vegetables in different-sized squares. They build on the algorithms and flowcharts they created in the last lesson to provide instructions to Oliver to help him to sow seeds in a square pattern. The children are introduced to the 'turn' command, which they will use in later lessons in this chapter.

Introduction
● Remind the children of the work they completed in the last lesson, in which they created algorithms to help Oliver sow a row of carrots. Display the media resource 'Plant in a square' on the CD-ROM and talk through screen 1, which shows the steps used last week to sow the seeds in a straight line. Particularly highlight the use of *repeat*, *repeat until* and *wait until* instructions, using questions such as:
  ● *What instruction did we use to get Oliver to sow more than one seed?*
  ● *How did Oliver know when to stop?*
  ● *Which instruction tells Oliver when to pick the carrots?*

Whole-class work
● Explain that in this lesson you will be helping Oliver to sow his vegetables into a square pattern.
● Show screen 2 of the media resource and explain that this is the planting area and that you are going to create an algorithm and a flowchart to help Oliver to plant his vegetables in a square.
● As a class, work out the instructions that need to be added to the existing flowchart you have talked through on screen 1, displaying this again. You could add the instructions on the board as the children give them and use photocopiable page 113 'Carrot cards' if you wish from Lesson 1 to help 'walk through' the planting of the square. This will involve sowing in a straight line, turning right and repeating this four times.
● Show screen 3 and talk children through the correctly sequenced instructions, highlighting the *turn* commands and any differences in the commands the class came up with.

Independent/paired work
● Ask the children to access interactive activity 'Algorithms and shapes' on the CD-ROM and explain that they have to work out what shape would be made if Oliver planted using these flowcharts. You may wish to do the first one with the children to check their understanding.

Differentiation
● Support: Less confident learners may benefit from mixed-ability pairings or further adult support in the independent/paired task and could focus on creating one square only.
● Challenge: More confident learners could also create their own flowchart (on paper) for a shape of their own choosing (a rectangle, for example).

Review
● Ask a few children to demonstrate the correct answers to the 'Algorithms and shapes' task on the board, highlighting and correcting any common areas of misunderstanding.
● Ask questions to probe their understanding, such as:
  ● *How did you work out when Oliver should turn?*
  ● *Did it matter which way Oliver turned? Why not?*
  ● *How would Oliver plant the seeds in a rectangular pattern?*
  ● *What shape would be the trickiest for Oliver to plant and why?*
● Assess the children's progress through class discussion and the children's responses to the independent/paired task.

Curriculum objectives
● To understand what algorithms are, how they are implemented as programs on digital devices and that programs execute by following precise and unambiguous instructions.

Lesson objectives
● To follow simple algorithms to plant vegetables in specific patterns.
● To begin to understand that computers need more accurate instructions than humans.
● To begin to understand that computers use programs to implement algorithms.

Expected outcomes
● Can follow simple algorithms with accuracy.
● Can explain that algorithms need to be accurate and precise so they can be implemented.

Resources
Interactive activity 'Sowing grid' on the CD-ROM; photocopiable page 115 'Vegetables'; photocopiable page 116 'Vegetable patterns (1)'; photocopiable page 117 'Vegetable patterns (2)'; media resource 'Vegetable pattern solutions' on the CD-ROM; glue or sticky tack

Using algorithms to control an object

Bridging the gap between representing algorithms with flowcharts and programming an onscreen device, in this lesson the children follow given algorithms to *create* specific patterns. This helps them to begin to understand that computers use programs to implement algorithms and develop their understanding that algorithms need to be specific, precise and accurate.

Introduction
● Remind the children that they have been creating algorithms and representing these as flowcharts to help Oliver to sow his vegetables in different ways.
● Explain that in this lesson they will be following these flowcharts to plant paper vegetables for Oliver in different shapes and patterns.

Whole-class work
● Show the children the interactive activity 'Sowing grid' on the CD-ROM. This shows some vegetables which can be dragged into the grid.
● Explain that their job is to create algorithms (instructions) to help Oliver sow the correct pattern.
● Explain how the instructions should work, for example *Plant 1 carrot* will plant one carrot, *Plant 1 spinach* will plant one spinach, *repeat until end* will repeat the last instruction until the end of the row (spend some time getting familiar with this prior to the lesson).
● Ask the class to create algorithms to create specific patterns, using *repeat* commands where possible. They should write their algorithms on paper. Example patterns:
    ● One row of carrots, followed by one row of spinach.
    ● Two rows of rhubarb, followed by three rows of peas.
    ● Alternative rows of each vegetable.
    ● One alternative plant of each vegetable.

Independent/paired work
● Independently or in pairs, give the children one of each of photocopiable pages 115, 116 and 117 'Vegetable patterns (1)' and/or 'Vegetable patterns (2)' and 'Vegetables' (cut out prior to the lesson). They will also need sticky tack or glue to stick down their 'vegetables' onto the grid.
● Explain that they need to look at the first set of instructions and then follow the algorithm to create the pattern using their vegetables and one of their grids. You may need to go through one as a class.
● There are two patterns for the children to create, so you may wish to give out the grids one at a time and check their work when they have finished one before giving out the next.

Differentiation
● Support: Mixed-ability pairings may be useful for the pattern exercises or less confident learners could work with adult support to help with following the instructions and/or sticking their vegetables in the right place. You may wish to give less confident learners the first, easier pattern only.
● Challenge: More confident learners could create their algorithm for another pattern, exchanging this with a partner for them to create. You could also show them the media resource 'Vegetable pattern solutions' from the CD-ROM if they finish early to identify and correct any errors in their own work.

Review
● Show the children the media resource. As a class, talk through the correct outcomes, asking volunteers to share their work.
● Emphasise that rows can go across or up and down as the algorithm does not tell them which way it wants them to go. Ask: *How could this be improved?*
● Ask the children to review their work as you do this and identify any errors.

Curriculum objectives
● To understand what algorithms are, how they are implemented as programs on digital devices and that programs execute by following precise and unambiguous instructions.

Lesson objectives
● To control an onscreen device.
● To predict what will happen when controlling an onscreen device.
● To give instructions accurately to an onscreen device.
● To begin to understand that a computer program executes an algorithm.

Expected outcomes
● Can control an onscreen device using a simple program.
● Can create programs to achieve specific goals.

Resources
Interactive activity 'Planting Oliver's Vegetables' on the CD-ROM; photocopiable page 118 'Planting patterns'

Programming an onscreen device to create patterns

In this lesson, the children develop their understanding of how computers implement algorithms as programs. Following on from the last lesson, they take given algorithms and use these to program an onscreen device to achieve specified goals. In doing so, they develop their knowledge and understanding of programming onscreen devices and how algorithms are implemented by computers as programs.

Introduction
● Remind the children that in the last lesson they followed algorithms to create patterns of vegetables on paper.
● Explain that in this lesson they will be inputting their algorithms into a computer *program* to plant the vegetables and that this is called 'programming'.

Whole-class work
● Display the interactive activity 'Planting Oliver's Vegetables' on the CD-ROM and ask the children how they think they could plant the vegetables into the grid. (Use the controls on the *Themes* tab to add objects.)
● Ask for volunteers to move around the grid and select and plant each of the vegetables, seeing if this fits in with their predictions.
● Spend some time on the functionality so that the children are confident with how to use the controls for the next task.

Independent/paired work
● Ask the children to access the interactive activity and give out photocopiable page 118 'Planting patterns'.
● Explain that they should follow the instructions to create the patterns given.
● You may wish to go through the first pattern together.
● Encourage the children to 'debug' their work by checking the algorithm against their finished pattern (they could do this in pairs) and making any necessary changes before ticking the 'complete' box on the photocopiable page.

Differentiation
● Support: Less confident learners may need support with the computer controls and how to plant their vegetables in the right location. You may wish to use mixed-ability pairings to help with this, or give them adult support when following the 'planting patterns'.
● Challenge: More confident learners can create a variety of their own patterns and could write down on paper the algorithms they have used.

Review
● As a class, discuss how the children followed the patterns and implemented them. If you have time, you could go through the work as a class with volunteers and get some of the children to show the patterns they created.
● Reiterate that they have been using a computer 'program' to carry out the algorithms.
● Review children's progress through their discussions and outcomes of their independent work.

Curriculum objectives
● To understand what algorithms are, how they are implemented as programs on digital devices and that programs execute by following precise and unambiguous instructions.

Lesson objectives
● To write simple algorithms to create specified patterns.
● To control an onscreen device accurately in order to test their algorithms.
● To be able to spot errors and debug algorithms and programs.
● To begin to understand that a computer program executes an algorithm

Expected outcomes
● Can create simple algorithms to achieve specific goals.
● Can debug algorithms.

Resources
Interactive activity 'Planting Oliver's Vegetables' on the CD-ROM; photocopiable page 119 'Planting algorithms'

Creating algorithms to achieve a specific goal

In this lesson, children develop further their understanding of controlling onscreen devices, creating patterns and programming objects to achieve specific goals. They write their own algorithms to create different patterns, testing and debugging them using an onscreen device.

Introduction
● Display the interactive activity 'Planting Oliver's Vegetables' and remind the children of their last lesson in which they planted Oliver's Vegetables in different patterns using the program. Ask them questions such as:
    ● *How did you follow the algorithm?*
    ● *How did you check whether you had created the correct pattern?*
    ● *What did you do if you made a mistake in your programming?*
● Reiterate that they have been using a computer 'program' to implement the algorithms and that this is called 'programming'.

Whole-class work
● Display photocopiable page 119 'Planting algorithms' on the CD-ROM and explain that in this lesson they will be given a pattern/shape and will need to work out the exact and correct algorithm for that shape.
● Work through the first example with the children, coming up with the correct algorithm for planting that pattern as a class.
● Go to the interactive activity 'Planting Oliver's Vegetables' to try out the algorithm. Make sure that you explain to the children how they can do the same for their paired work. This is an important step.
● Depending on the progress of your class, you may wish to stick to 'plant one row of carrots' and so on, although the children should be used to using abbreviated forms such as *P1 carrots* now.
● Ask the children to 'debug' the algorithm as you create it, asking questions such as: *Will that do what we want? What might be a better instruction?*
● Encourage them to use *repeats* and *repeat until* where possible.

Paired work
● Give out the photocopiable page and ask the children to access the interactive activity 'Planting Oliver's Vegetables' to test their algorithms.
● The children should work through the tasks, writing down their algorithms to create the shape in the image.
● Remind them that they should test out their algorithms when they are creating them and when they have finished, to debug their algorithm.

Differentiation
● Support: Mixed-ability pairings may be useful or less confident learners could work in a small group with adult support to help in writing down their algorithms. You may wish to allow them to write one or two simple algorithms and then create their own patterns.
● Challenge: More confident learners could explain how they used debugging in their algorithms and how this helped them to improve their work. Ask: *How did you correct your mistakes and how did you make sure you did not make the same mistakes again?* They could also come up with their own algorithms and patterns.

Review
● As a class, work through one or two of the 'Planting algorithms' tasks asking volunteers to share their instructions, which another volunteer could implement on the board, using the interactive activity.
● Discuss how the children wrote their algorithms, asking questions such as:
    ● *How did you test whether your algorithm was correct?*
    ● *How did you correct it if it was wrong?*
    ● *What advice would you give someone else who was writing an algorithm?*

Curriculum objectives
● To understand what algorithms are, how they are implemented as programs on digital devices and that programs execute by following precise and unambiguous instructions.

Lesson objectives
● To create simple accurate algorithms using images and/or text.
● To test and debug others' algorithms.
● To understand that a computer program executes an algorithm.

Expected outcomes
● Can create simple, accurate and precise algorithms.
● Can test and debug algorithms.

Resources
Media resource 'How chips are made' on the CD-ROM; photocopiable page 'My algorithm for making chips' from the CD-ROM

Creating and debugging algorithms

In this lesson, the children start to consolidate the work they have completed during this chapter and create their own algorithm. They then identify, test and debug their algorithm, adding greater precision where necessary to ensure that it is ready for a computer program to implement.

Introduction
● Recap Lesson 4 with the children, reminding them that they wrote their own algorithms for planting Oliver's Vegetables in patterns, tested them out and debugged them using the computer program.
● Explain that today they will be creating another algorithm for a different task. Remind them that at the end of the book Oliver picks the potatoes and gets his chips! In this lesson, they will be creating an algorithm for making chips from potatoes.

Whole-class work
● As a class, come up with a list of instructions of how chips are made. Depending on your class's knowledge, you may only have to fill in a few gaps.
● Use the media resource 'How chips are made' on the CD-ROM to show the children the actual steps involved.
● Explain that they are going to write an algorithm for how to make chips using pictures and text that they will create themselves.

Independent/paired work
● Give the children photocopiable page 'My algorithm for making chips' from the CD-ROM and explain that they are going to create their own algorithm in the boxes given. They can use images or text, or both.
● Ask the children to use the media resource to work out the correct steps.
● You may wish to complete the first step together.
● Once children have completed their algorithm, they should swap with a partner and compare their algorithms to test and debug them. Ask: *Are there any differences? Which one is correct? What needs to be changed?*
● Using the back of the photocopiable sheet, ask them to see whether they can break down their algorithm into more exact and precise instructions (for example, cutting the chips could include exact instructions and a repeat).

Differentiation
● Support: You may wish to use mixed-ability pairings for the independent task and less confident learners could work with adult support to help them write/draw the steps. You could print out a copy of the steps to help them if necessary.
● Challenge: More confident learners can help others to debug their work and should focus on creating a precise and accurate algorithm that a computer program could follow.

Review
● As a class, review the steps in the algorithm and ask children to self- or peer- assess their work depending on the stage they are at.
● Ask the children to share how they think the algorithm can be improved in order to increase the accuracy and precision and ensure that a computer program could implement it.
● You could create a collaborative whole-class algorithm on the board.
● Assess the children's understanding by looking at their work in the independent task and the review discussion.

Curriculum objectives
● To understand what algorithms are, how they are implemented as programs on digital devices and that programs execute by following precise and unambiguous instructions.

Lesson objectives
● To create simple algorithms.
● To identify repetition in an algorithm.
● To implement algorithms using a simple computer program.
● To understand that a computer program executes an algorithm.

Expected outcomes
● Can create simple, accurate and precise algorithms.
● Can understand that a computer program implements an algorithm.
● Can follow simple algorithms with accuracy.
● Can test and debug algorithms.

Resources
Interactive activity 'Algorithms quiz' on the CD-ROM; photocopiable page 'Algorithms challenge (1)' from the CD-ROM photocopiable page 'Algorithms challenge (2)' from the CD-ROM

Oliver's Vegetables: Assess and review

This lesson provides an opportunity to review the key learning points from the chapter. The children write, test and debug a simple algorithm and then use a simple program to implement their algorithm. They will be able to demonstrate their understanding of algorithms and their emerging knowledge of programming. Through the outcomes of children's work and observation, you can undertake teacher assessment, review aspects of the chapter and adjust future learning as necessary.

Introduction
● Remind the children that throughout this chapter they have been creating algorithms around the theme of *Oliver's Vegetables* including matching algorithms to the correct patterns and shapes, using a program to implement their algorithms and writing their own algorithms.
● Explain that today they will be working through different tasks (or you may give them choice or allocate tasks to them, or indeed give all your children the same task, according to your professional judgement).
● Display photocopiable pages 'Algorithms challenge (1) and (2)' on the CD-ROM and go through the appropriate tasks with the children, explaining the requirements briefly as appropriate.

Independent work
● The children should work through their task as independently as possible.

Differentiation
● Support: You may wish to allocate tasks to all children, particularly less confident learners, and these learners may need more adult help to complete their task.
● Challenge: More confident learners can be allocated the more challenging tasks and should be able to complete the task with full independence.

Review
● Using the interactive activity 'Algorithms quiz' on the CD-ROM, review the main learning points from the chapter with the children in a fun way.
● Review children's progress through the outcomes of their independent work and adjust learning in the next chapter as appropriate.

Carrot cards

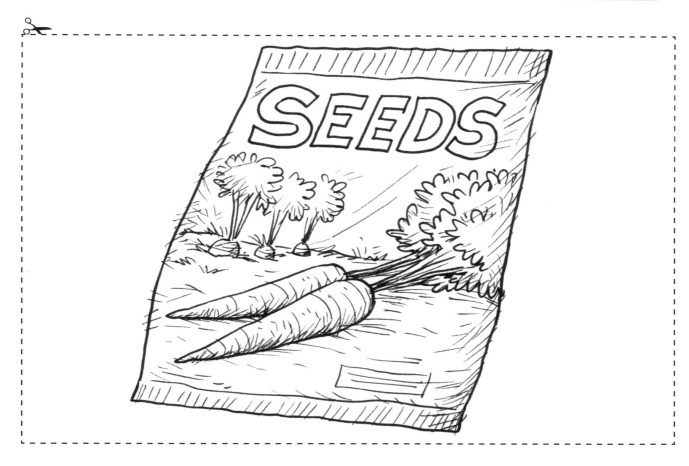

Help Oliver

■ Help Oliver sow the vegetables.

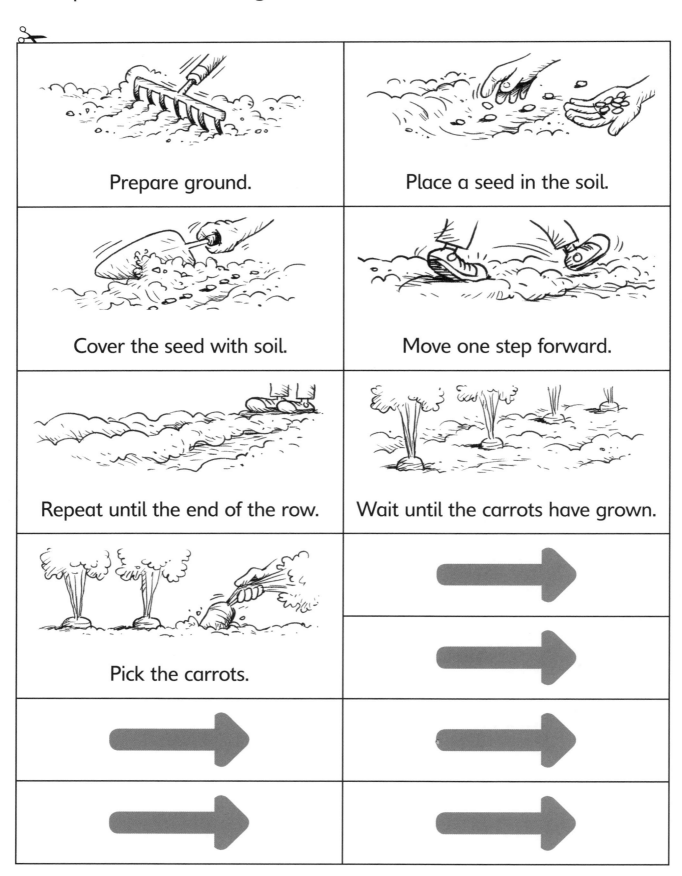

Prepare ground.	Place a seed in the soil.
Cover the seed with soil.	Move one step forward.
Repeat until the end of the row.	Wait until the carrots have grown.
Pick the carrots.	→
→	→
→	→

Name: _____   Date: _____

Vegetables

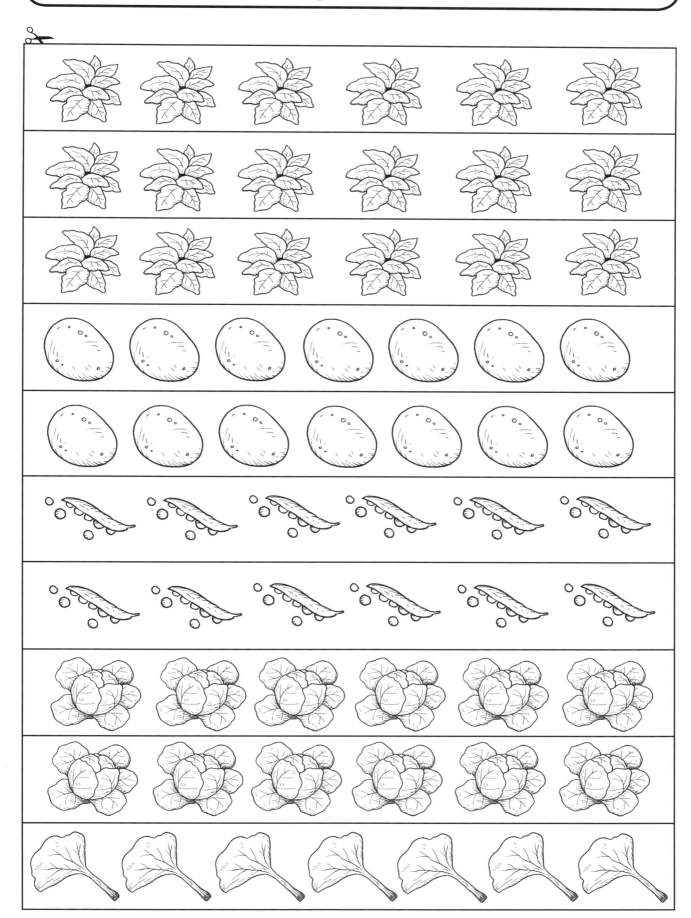

Vegetable patterns (1)

■ Create the pattern by sticking the vegetables onto the grid.

Pattern:

P1 row spinach

P1 row cabbage

Start here				

Remember P1 = plant 1

I can follow an algorithm to create a pattern.

How did you do?

PHOTOCOPIABLE

SCHOLASTIC
www.scholastic.co.uk

Vegetable patterns (2)

■ Create the pattern by sticking the vegetables onto the grid.

Pattern:

P2 peas

P1 rhubarb

P2 potatoes

Repeat

Remember:

P1 = plant 1

P2 = plant 2

Start here				

I can follow an algorithm to create a pattern.

How did you do?

Planting patterns

■ Can you program Oliver to plant his vegetables in these patterns?

Pattern 1:

P1 row of each vegetable ☐

Pattern 2:

P2 rows of carrots ☐

P1 row of peas ☐

P1 row of potatoes ☐

P1 row of any vegetable you like ☐

Pattern 3:

P1 of each vegetable ☐

Repeat until end ☐

Pattern 4:

Carrots in the corners ☐

Peas in the middle square ☐

Rhubarb plants anywhere ☐

Pattern 5:

Create a pattern of your own on the back of the sheet.

I can program an onscreen device to create a pattern.
I can use a program to carry out an algorithm.
How did you do?

Name: _____ Date: _____

Planting algorithms

■ Can you create algorithms for these patterns?

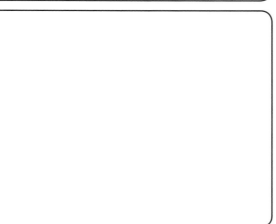

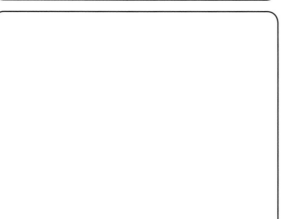

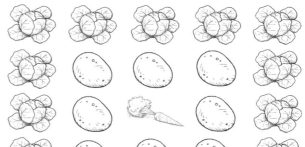

I can create algorithms to draw patterns.
I can debug my algorithms.

How did you do?

Fairy tales

This chapter builds on the Autumn 1 algorithms chapter and uses a fairy tales theme to develop children's understanding of algorithms and, in particular, programming. Using a programmable floor robot, such as a Bee-Bot, the children develop their learning in this key area of the computing curriculum, including sequencing, prediction, algorithms and repetition. Although the lessons are designed with the Bee-Bot in mind, other floor robots such as Pro-Bots and Roamer Turtles could also be used.

Expected prior learning

The children have already been introduced to programming simple onscreen devices in Year 1 and in the previous chapter and the lessons in this chapter are a natural and fun extension of this, giving them a physical object to program. For this topic, the children will need to have a basic understanding of common fairy tales.

Chapter at a glance

Subject area
• Algorithms and programming

National Curriculum objective
• To understand what algorithms are, how they are implemented as programs on digital devices and that programs execute by following precise and unambiguous instructions. • To create and debug simple programs. • To use logical reasoning to predict the behaviour of simple programs.

Week	Lesson objectives	Summary of activities	Expected outcomes
1	• To understand that a programmable robot can be controlled by pressing buttons. • To predict what will happen when programming a floor robot. • To be able to give simple instructions to a programmable robot, including moving forwards, backwards and making left and right turns. • To program a floor robot to reach specified positions.	• Children learn how to move a programmable floor robot in simple ways. • They move a floor robot to the correct place on a mat to 'catch the wolf'.	• Can move a floor robot in simple ways. • Can program a floor robot to reach a specified position.
2	• To give simple sequences of instructions to a programmable floor robot. • To program a floor robot to follow the specific sequence of a story. • To identify and correct errors in programs (debugging).	• Children program sequences of instructions into a floor robot to get it to move to the correct place and to re-enact the 'Three Little Pigs' story. • They test their program, identifying errors and correcting them (debug).	• Can program a floor robot with a sequence of instructions in order to achieve specific goals. • Can debug a simple program.
3	• To program a floor robot with devised sequences of instructions. • To test and debug a programmed algorithm to achieve an intended goal. • To be creative and experimental.	• Children create a pig disguise for their robot. • They create sequences of instructions to make their robot dance to music.	• Can program a floor robot with sequences of instructions. • Can debug a program.
4	• To plan an algorithm to allow a floor robot to reach a specific goal in the most efficient way. • To program a floor robot with sequences of instructions to follow a planned path. • To test and rewrite their algorithm as necessary to achieve a specific goal (debugging). • To understand how the floor robot executes an algorithm.	• Children plan a maze and the best route through a maze for Little Red Riding Hood to reach Grandma's house. • They program a floor robot with the algorithm they have planned. • They debug their algorithm and program to get the best route through the maze.	• Can plan, implement, test and debug an algorithm to achieve a specific goal. • Can begin to understand that a computer program within a floor robot executes an algorithm.

■SCHOLASTIC

Week	Lesson objectives	Summary of activities	Expected outcomes
5	• To use problem-solving and logical thinking skills to plan the best algorithm for a robot to take to achieve a specific goal. • To plan an algorithm to allow a floor robot to reach a specific goal in the most efficient way. • To program two floor robots with sequences of instructions to follow a planned path. • To test and rewrite algorithms as necessary to achieve their goal (debugging). • To explain verbally how they chose the best algorithm and programmed their robot.	• Children program a second 'wolf' robot to follow along a path. • They make sure that the wolf robot reaches Grandma's house before the first Little Red Riding Hood robot.	• Can use problem solving and logical thinking to program multiple floor robots, debugging them as necessary to follow a chosen path. • Can explain how they wrote an algorithm and programmed a floor robot in simple terms.
6	• To be creative, experimental and work cooperatively with their peers. • To use problem-solving and logical thinking skills to plan the best algorithm for a robot to take to follow a planned path in the most efficient way. • To explain verbally how they chose the best algorithm and programmed their robot. • To explain how they would change their approach in the future.	• Children create a classroom obstacle course. • They have a fairy tale robot race. • They consider how they would change their approach to the task in the future.	• Can confidently program a floor robot to follow a path in the most efficient way. • Can use problem solving and logical thinking to quickly and effectively debug their algorithm. • Can begin to evaluate their own work.
Assess and review	• To assess the half-term's work.	• Children plan and write an algorithm to send a floor robot along a chosen path. • They program their algorithm into a floor robot. • They debug their algorithm. • They explain this process to others.	• Assess and review.

Overview of progression

• The children build upon their knowledge and understanding of algorithms and programming through the use of programmable floor robots. They learn how to move the robot in simple ways and to program the robot with sequences of instructions. Children are introduced to programming physical objects to follow a specific path and also develop their problem-solving, logical and creative thinking skills throughout.
• This chapter develops their knowledge and understanding that a computer program executes an algorithm and they create, test and debug their algorithms across all lessons.

Creative context

• The lessons have strong links to the mathematics curriculum with children using grids, and moving and turning objects in different directions.

Background knowledge

• The children may know the fairy tales used in this chapter, although refreshing their knowledge by reading the stories may be helpful. From the work they have already completed in Year 1 and in the previous chapter, they should have a sound base from which to build their understanding of sequencing, algorithms and programming.
• From assessing children's understanding in the previous chapter, you will need to assess the children's capability in following and creating algorithms and programming and provide additional support as necessary.

Curriculum objectives
● To understand what algorithms are, how they are implemented as programs on digital devices and that programs execute by following precise and unambiguous instructions.

Lesson objectives
● To understand that a programmable robot can be controlled by pressing buttons.
● To predict what will happen when programming a floor robot.
● To be able to give simple instructions to a programmable robot, including moving forwards, backwards and making left and right turns.
● To program a floor robot to reach specified positions.

Expected outcomes
● Can move a floor robot in simple ways.
● Can program a floor robot to reach a specified position.

Resources
A 'robot mat' (this can be a commercially available mat, a printed mat downloaded from the internet or a drawn 4 × 4 grid with 15cm squares); photocopiable page 129 'Three little pigs cards (1)', photocopiable page 130 'Three little pigs cards (2)'; floor robots; ruler

Introduction to using a programmable floor robot

This lesson provides a gentle introduction to using a programmable floor robot. Children provide simple instructions to the robot to move in different directions and become familiar with the idea of programming the robot using the correct buttons in order to reach specified positions.

Introduction
● Remind the children that they have been working with algorithms and programming onscreen devices to follow their algorithms.
● Explain that they will now be programming robots to follow algorithms.
● Show the children a floor robot.

Whole-class work
● As a class, discuss how the floor robot might work. Ask questions such as: *What can you see on the robot? What do you think will happen if we press this?*
● Put the robot down on to the floor or on a large table and ask volunteers to press the buttons to get it moving forwards, backwards, left and right so the children can see how it works.
● Ask the children to make predictions about the robot, for example: *How far do you think the robot will move if we press forward once and then press go?* You could measure this with a ruler to see whether their predictions are correct.
● Highlight to the children any eye movements or sounds the robot makes after moving, asking them, *How do you know the robot has finished your instruction?*
● Explain to the class that they will be using the robot to 'catch the wolf' that often features in fairy stories.

Group work
● Depending on how many robots you have, you may need to complete this activity as a whole class or you may be able to split the class into groups.
● You will need a robot mat. Your school may have a commercially available mat for use with Bee-Bots. If not, you can download free printable mats from the internet, or you could draw out a 4 × 4 grid with squares of 15cm.
● Give each group a robot mat and the wolf card from the set of cards on photocopiable pages 129 and 130 'Three little pigs cards' (1) and (2).
● Show the children how they can place the wolf card on the grid and explain that their task is then to program the robot to move in order to 'catch' the wolf.
● Each child in the group should be able to take a turn in both choosing where the wolf should be on the grid and programming the robot.

Differentiation
● Support: Less confident learners may benefit from simply moving the robot around the floor rather than using the mat and wolf cards. They may benefit from mixed-ability groupings or adult support when entering their instructions into the robot.
● Challenge: More confident learners will grasp the programming concepts quickly and can be encouraged to think about how they can program the robot using a sequence of instructions. They should program the instructions into the robot before pressing 'go'. They could also share this knowledge with their own and other groups.

Review
● Ask a few children to demonstrate what they have learned about using the robot. They will hopefully share how they can move the robot around the mat and enter a sequence of instructions before pressing 'go'.
● If the children have been working in groups, you could ask each group to demonstrate movement; for example, making the robots turn right or left, move forwards, move backwards and so on, when you give the instruction.

Curriculum objectives
● To understand what algorithms are, how they are implemented as programs on digital devices and that programs execute by following precise and unambiguous instructions.

Lesson objectives
● To give simple sequences of instructions to a programmable floor robot.
● To program a floor robot to follow the specific sequence of a story.
● To identify and correct errors in programs (debugging).

Expected outcomes
● Can program a floor robot with a sequence of instructions in order to achieve specific goals.
● Can debug a simple program.

Resources
Interactive activity 'Three little pigs' on the CD-ROM; floor robots; a robot mat; photocopiable page 129 'Three little pigs cards' (1); photocopiable page 130 'Three little pigs cards' (2); photocopiable page 131 'Disguises'; materials to create a wolf disguise for the robots

Sequencing stories and instructions

In this lesson, the children start to work with sequencing by programming their robot in a more structured way to move around the mat using sequences of instructions.

Introduction
● Ask for volunteers to demonstrate the basic operations of the floor robot used in Lesson 1, making sure to discuss how sequences can be programmed in before pressing 'go'; for example, moving forwards twice, then turning left and moving forwards again. You could use a robot mat and the 'wolf' card from photocopiable pages 129 and 130 'Three little pigs cards' (1) and (2) to demonstrate this if you wished, or simply move the robot around a large table or the floor.

Whole-class work
● Explain that in this lesson you will be using the 'Three Little Pigs' story as a theme and your robot will be helping you to tell the story.
● Using the interactive activity 'Three Little Pigs' on the CD-ROM as a class, sequence the story into the correct order (re-read the story first if required).
● Show the children the robots disguised as 'wolves'. The children could decorate the robots themselves. Alternatively, you could cut out the image from photocopiable page 131 'Disguises' and stick it on the robot.

Whole-class/group work
● As before, depending on how many robots you have, you may need to complete this activity as a whole class or split the class into groups.
● Give each group a robot mat and the 'house' cards from photocopiable pages 129 and 130 used in the introduction.
● The children should put the cards on three squares on the mat and then program the wolf to visit the houses in the correct order of the story.
● Encourage them to say the words from the story as they move their 'wolf' around: *Little pig, little pig, let me in!; Not by the hair on my chinny-chin-chin, I will not let you in!; Then I'll huff and puff and blow your house down.* Then the robot moves to the house to try to 'blow' it down.
● If you have the time, you could create houses from boxes to represent the straw, wood and brick houses. The first two would be knocked down by the robot and the brick house would stay standing.
● Encourage children to 'debug' their program, testing it out, finding errors and then correcting them.

Differentiation
● Support: Less confident learners may benefit from adult support in the group work and could focus on simply getting the robot to move to each of the houses in turn.
● Challenge: More confident learners will be able to sequence the instructions confidently and could add their own additions to the story sequence. For example, they could draw a picture of the chimney, put it in a chosen square and then program moving to this into their sequence.

Review
● Go through the story in order as a class, getting the children to demonstrate how they moved their robots to the right place at the correct time.
● Emphasise that they have been working with sequences – they have been sequencing the story and their programs in this lesson.
● Ask questions to probe their understanding of the debugging they have been doing, such as:
  ● *How did you check whether your robot went to the right place?*
  ● *What did you do if the wolf went to the wrong place?*
  ● *How did you correct it?*
  ● *How did you help each other to get the right sequence?*

Curriculum objectives
● To understand what algorithms are, how they are implemented as programs on digital devices and that programs execute by following precise and unambiguous instructions.

Lesson objectives
● To program a floor robot with devised sequences of instructions.
● To test and debug a programmed algorithm to achieve an intended goal.
● To be creative and experimental.

Expected outcomes
● Can program a floor robot with sequences of instructions.
● Can debug a program.

Resources
A 'robot mat'; photocopiable page 129 'Three little pigs cards' (1); photocopiable page 130 'Three little pigs cards' (2); photocopiable page 131 'Disguises'; floor robots; suitable music for the robots to 'dance' to; materials to create a pig disguise for the robot(s)

Floor robot dancing

In this lesson, the children build on the sequencing work completed in the previous lesson and program their robot to 'dance' to music. This will give them an opportunity to be creative and experiment with programming.

Introduction
● Explain to the children that the wolf has now gone. You could recap the point in the story where this happens.
● Tell them that the three little pigs are very happy and have decided to have a dance to celebrate!
● Show the children a robot that is disguised as a pig using photocopiable page 131 'Disguises' and explain that their job is to make up a dance routine for the pig. If you have three robots, this would fit the story very well, but it is not obligatory.

Whole-class work
● Put on the music you have chosen and discuss with the children how the pigs will be feeling and what sort of dance they might like to do.
● You could ask for volunteers to demonstrate the kind of dance they would do if they were happy.
● Ask for volunteers to program a few instructions into the robot so that everyone sees how the 'dancing' could work. You could show the children how the mat could be used for the pigs to dance around their houses.
● Explain that they will be creating their own dance for their pig.
● Their first task (if you have more than one robot) is to create the robot disguise, although you could choose to make these prior to the lesson if you want the children to get straight on to the dance.

Whole-class/group work
● Give each group a robot if possible and materials to make the disguise. The children could create a pig's tail and face using card, attaching it with sticky tack. Alternatively, you could cut out the image from photocopiable page 131 'Disguises' and stick it on the robot.
● Ask the children to work out the dance routine for their robot. At this stage, it is fine for them simply to experiment with different moves and come up with a sequence for a dance. Encourage the children to be as creative as possible, from a simple one forward, one back and turn, to more complex routines.
● You may wish to give each group a robot mat and the 'house' cards from photocopiable page 129 and 130 'Three little pigs cards' (1) and (2).

> ### Differentiation
> ● Support: Less confident learners could concentrate on creating one or two simple moves, which they repeat to create their dance sequence.
> ● Challenge: More confident learners will be able to create more complex dance sequences and you could, if possible, give them two robots with which to create some synchronised dancing.

Review
● Ask for volunteers to demonstrate their dances to the class. You may be able to view all of the dances the children have created for their robot.
● Ask questions to probe their understanding of the sequencing and debugging they have been doing, such as:
  ● What was your favourite dance move and why?
  ● How did you program that move into the robot?
  ● How did you check whether the move was correct?
  ● What did you do if it was wrong?
  ● How did you put your dance moves together in a sequence?
● Assess the children's progress through explanations of their dance routines.
● You could video or photograph the children's work for a display.

Curriculum objectives
● To understand what algorithms are, how they are implemented as programs on digital devices and that programs execute by following precise and unambiguous instructions.

Lesson objectives
● To plan an algorithm to allow a floor robot to reach a specific goal in the most efficient way.
● To program a floor robot with sequences of instructions to follow a planned path.
● To test and rewrite their algorithm as necessary to achieve a specific goal (debugging).
● To begin to understand how a floor robot executes an algorithm.

Expected outcomes
● Can plan, implement, test and debug an algorithm to achieve a specific goal.
● Can begin to understand that a computer program within a floor robot executes an algorithm.

Resources
A 'robot mat'; photocopiable page 132 'Little Red Riding Hood cards'; photocopiable page 133 'Maze planning'; photocopiable page 131 'Disguises'; floor robots; materials to create a Little Red Riding Hood disguise for the robot(s); materials to prepare a wolf disguise for the robot(s)

Programming a floor robot to follow a path

This lesson continues to encourage children to think creatively and they extend their confidence in working with a floor robot. Using a 'Little Red Riding Hood' theme, they also develop their understanding of programming their robot to implement algorithms that they have created.

Introduction
● Remind the children of the programming they have already completed with their robot, encouraging them to discuss the sequences of instructions they have programmed into their robot.
● Probe the children's knowledge and understanding that sequences of instructions are called 'algorithms' and that they have been programming their algorithms into their robots using the program inside the robot.

Whole-class work
● Explain that in this lesson they will be planning and creating algorithms to help Little Red Riding Hood to get to Grandma's house through a forest maze.
● Show the children the robot(s) disguised as Little Red Riding Hood. You could have the children decorate the robots themselves. Alternatively, cut out the image from photocopiable page 131 'Disguises' and stick it on the robot.
● Place Grandma's house and five to six trees from photocopiable page 132 'Little Red Riding Hood cards' on the robot mat to create a forest maze.
● As a class, work through the first few sequences of instructions to get the robot on its way to Grandma's house.

Whole-class/group work
● Give each group a copy of photocopiable page 133 'Maze planning'. Ask the children to use this to plan how they will create their maze with the trees and where Grandma's house should be.
● Once they have planned their maze, give them the robot mat and the cards from photocopiable page 132 'Little Red Riding Hood cards'. They should place the trees and Grandma's house onto the grid squares as in their design.
● The children then use their plan to work out the best route for Little Red Riding Hood to travel to reach Grandma's house. Emphasise that they are working out the best algorithm to program into their robot.
● Next, the children program their robot with the correct sequence of instructions to get to Grandma's house.
● Encourage children to 'debug' their algorithm and program, testing it out, finding errors and then correcting them.

Differentiation
● Support: Less confident learners could use fewer cards and create a simple maze route.
● Challenge: Encourage more confident learners to design a complex maze and position Grandma's house in different places around the maze that increase the challenge.

Review
● As a class, discuss how the children created their mazes and implemented them. It would be good for groups to try out other groups' mazes if possible.
● Discuss how they created the 'best' route for Little Red Riding Hood to reach Grandma's house. Ask: *How did you work out that was the best way to go? Why was that the best way to reach Grandma's house?*
● Reiterate that they worked out the best sequence of instructions needed to get to Grandma's house (this was their algorithm) and then the computer program in the robot was able to move the robot based on these instructions.
● Encourage the children to discuss how they debugged their algorithm and program. Ask: *How did you test if your algorithm was right? How did you change your algorithm to ensure that Little Red Riding Hood reached Grandma's house?*
● Keep their maze planning work to use in the next lesson.

Curriculum objectives
● To understand what algorithms are, how they are implemented as programs on digital devices and that programs execute by following precise and unambiguous instructions.

Lesson objectives
● To use problem-solving and logical thinking skills to plan the best algorithm for a robot to take to achieve a specific goal.
● To plan an algorithm to allow a floor robot to reach a specific goal in the most efficient way.
● To program two floor robots with sequences of instructions to follow a planned path.
● To test and rewrite algorithms as necessary to achieve their goal (debugging).
● To explain verbally how they chose the best algorithm and programmed their robot.

Expected outcomes
● Can use problem solving and logical thinking to program multiple floor robots, debugging them as necessary to follow a chosen path.
● Can explain how they wrote an algorithm and programmed a floor robot in simple terms.

Resources
A 'robot mat'; photocopiable page 132 'Little Red Riding Hood cards'; photocopiable page 131 'Disguises'; children's completed 'Maze planning' work from last lesson; floor robots; materials to create a Little Red Riding Hood disguise for the robot(s)

Programming multiple floor robots

In this lesson, the children build on the work they completed last lesson and develop further their understanding of planning algorithms and programming these into a floor robot to follow a path. They will be given two floor robots and use their problem-solving and logical thinking skills to work out the best route for the second robot to take.

Introduction
● Set up a maze to use as a demonstration with the Little Red Riding Hood robot halfway to Grandma's house.
● Remind the children how they planned their maze and the best route for Little Red Riding Hood to take through the maze to Grandma's house, and how they programmed this into their robot and debugged their algorithm to make sure that it worked.
● Bring out the wolf robot and explain that he has now spotted Little Red Riding Hood and is going to try to get to Grandma's house before her. Place the wolf on the mat in a different location to Little Red Riding Hood.

Whole-class work
● As a class work out the route that the wolf can take to Grandma's house, avoiding Little Red Riding Hood. You will need to consider this when setting up your mat prior to the lesson.
● Encourage the children to 'think like a wolf', as they predict the route Little Red Riding Hood will take, trying to avoid her and get to Grandma's house first. It will depend on how well your class grasped last week's activity as to how complex this should be.

Group work
● Give each group their 'Maze planning' work from the last lesson and ask the children to recreate their maze.
● Ask half of the group to program the best route for Little Red Riding Hood to get to Grandma's house.
● Give the second half of the group the wolf robot and ask them to program it to get to Grandma's house before Little Red Riding Hood, remembering that he has to make sure that Little Red Riding Hood does not see him!
● Once they have had a go, the whole group can work together to work out the best route for the wolf.
● They will probably have to make many adjustments to their route – remind them this debugging is an important part of programming. If there is no suitable second route through, they may even have to cut down some trees in their forest, or wait until Little Red Riding Hood has a nap and then sneak past!

Differentiation
● Support: Less confident learners may benefit from adult support and may find it helpful to focus on one of the robots only. They could plan and program simple routes, increasing the complexity as their confidence builds.
● Challenge: More confident learners can come up with creative ideas as to how the wolf can get to Grandma's house first. They could add further obstacles, such as 'dead ends' and the woodcutter to increase the challenge.

Review
● Pair up groups and ask them to demonstrate and explain to the other group how they found the best route for their wolf. This is an excellent opportunity to assess children's progress and you could video the children's explanations as evidence of progress.
● Encourage the children to use the correct language in their explanations, asking them questions such as: *Did the program follow your algorithm as you expected? How did you debug your algorithm?*

Curriculum objectives
● To understand what algorithms are, how they are implemented as programs on digital devices and that programs execute by following precise and unambiguous instructions.

Lesson objectives
● To be creative, experimental and work cooperatively with their peers.
● To use problem-solving and logical thinking skills to plan the best algorithm for a robot to take to follow a planned path in the most efficient way.
● To explain verbally how they chose the best algorithm and programmed their robot.
● To explain how they would change their approach in the future.

Expected outcomes
● Can confidently program a floor robot to follow a path in the most efficient way.
● Can use problem solving and logical thinking to quickly debug their algorithm.
● Can begin to evaluate their own work.

Resources
Floor robots complete with fairy-tale disguises (from previous lessons); selection of suitable obstacles that could be created from any objects such as building blocks; flags made from cards for start and end positions

Fairy tale robots obstacle race

In this lesson, the children start to consolidate the work they have completed during this chapter and work collectively to create a class obstacle course for the robots. They then write their algorithms and program the robots in an attempt to reach the end of the course first and be crowned the winner of the 'fairy-tale robots obstacle race'.

Introduction
● Explain to the children that the fairy-tale robots they have been using for the past five lessons are going to have an obstacle race and that they need to make the course for the robots to race around and through.
● Explain that once they have built the course, they will be in charge of devising algorithms for the robots and then programming them to see who will reach the end first and be crowned the winner.

Whole-class work
● Discuss how an obstacle race course can be created. Mark out a suitable area for each group and give out materials. If you have enough materials, you may prefer to ask groups to create their own mini course and then challenge other groups to complete it.
● As a class, build an obstacle course using the materials you have provided. Remind the children that they need to ensure that the course has enough space for the robots to fit round and through. It is helpful to keep the course relatively simple, at least for the first go.

Group/whole-class work
● Give each group a disguised robot from one of the previous lessons and give them some time to review the course and plan the best route for their robot.
● The children can plan their algorithm and program their robot with what they think is the best sequence of instructions to reach the finish line.
● Ask the children to choose the order in which they will debug their robot so that only one person from each group at a time is on the course. When that person has had their go, the next one will go up when it next needs to be debugged and so on.
● Depending on the course(s) you have built and the number of robots you have, you may wish to have a time-trial event with one robot on the course at a time, or you may wish to line the robots up and press 'go'.
● Crown the winning robot!

Differentiation
● Support: Less confident learners will benefit from mixed-ability groupings or adult support, particularly in debugging their algorithm and programming the robot when it is on the course.
● Challenge: Encourage more confident learners to think about how the course could be constructed to ensure the desired level of simplicity/complexity. They can be tasked with checking that the robots can fit through/round all the obstacles and should be able to create efficient algorithms and debug them confidently, helping others if required.

Review
● As a class, discuss why that robot was the winning one. The reasons that robot was the winner may differ greatly and be down to chance or an efficient use of time, but this discussion is very useful to have.
● You could discuss how the group came up with their algorithm and how they debugged it, encouraging the children to discuss within their groups and share how they could improve their own robot's performance in another race.
● You may also discuss why the obstacle course was or was not effective and how it could be improved.
● Assess the children's progress through their group work and review discussions.
● The race provides a good opportunity for videoing or photographing their work.

Curriculum objectives
● To understand what algorithms are, how they are implemented as programs on digital devices and that programs execute by following precise and unambiguous instructions

Lesson objectives
● To program a floor robot with devised sequences of instructions.
● To use problem-solving and logical thinking skills to plan the best algorithm for a robot to take to follow a planned path in the most efficient way.
● To test and debug a programmed algorithm to achieve an intended goal (debugging).
● To explain and demonstrate how they debugged their algorithm.

Expected outcomes
● Can program a floor robot efficiently with sequences of instructions.
● Can debug an algorithm to ensure a desired outcome is achieved.
● Can explain their programming and debugging process.

Resources
Photocopiable page 134 'Fairy tale cards' (1); photocopiable page 135 'Fairy tale cards' (2); photocopiable page 'Mini fairy tale map' from the CD-ROM; floor robots

Fairy tales: Assess and review

This lesson provides an opportunity to review the key learning points from the chapter. In small groups, children plan and write an algorithm for a specific purpose, program a floor robot to follow their sequence of instructions, test and debug their work and then explain how they have changed their algorithm after testing. Through assessment of the children's work in this and previous lessons, and teacher observation, you can undertake assessment and review aspects of the chapter and adjust future learning of the algorithms and programming topic as necessary.

Introduction
● Remind the children that throughout this chapter they have been creating algorithms and programming the floor robot to implement their algorithms.
● Explain that today they will work independently to write an algorithm for the floor robot to visit different points on a fairy-tale map. They will then program this into the robot and see how many different places they can visit. You may wish to pair the children up or for them to work in small groups depending on the number of floor robots and adult support available.
● Show the children the Fairy-tale map – this is the robot mat used in the previous lesson but with 'Fairy tale cards' (1) and (2) stuck on. Highlight to them the starting point and the different places they need to visit in order.
● Show them photocopiable page 'Mini fairy tale map' from the CD-ROM and explain to them that they should draw the best route and then write down their algorithm in the space as shown. You may wish to complete a further example as a class.

Independent work
● Give the children a copy of photocopiable page 'Mini fairy tale map' each and ask them to work independently.
● When they think they have found the best route and written their algorithm, they should program it into the robot(s) on the large map(s).
● They should then note where errors occur and change their algorithm accordingly and then test it out again.
● Once they think they have a fully correct algorithm, they should write it in the box provided.
● They can then explain either in writing or verbally how they have changed their algorithm after testing.

> **Differentiation**
> ● Support: You may wish to give less confident learners fewer places to visit on the map so they can write algorithms with fewer steps. They could also draw the route and leave out writing their algorithm task on the second 'Mini fairy tale map' activity.
> ● Challenge: More confident learners should be challenged to create the most efficient route and be asked to explain the debugging process in detail.

Review
● If you wish, you could demonstrate as a class the most efficient algorithm and the children could review their own work, identifying and sharing where they could make adjustments.
● Review children's progress through the outcomes of their independent work and adjust learning in the 'algorithms and programming' topic in Year 3 as appropriate.

Three little pigs cards (1)

Three little pigs cards (2)

■SCHOLASTIC
www.scholastic.co.uk

Disguises

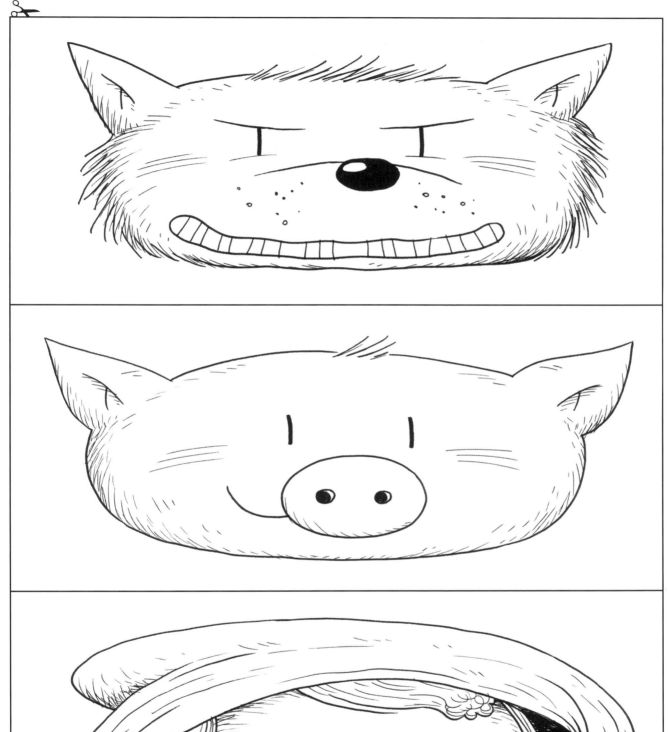

Little Red Riding Hood cards

I can put a story into the correct order.

How did you do?

PHOTOCOPIABLE

SCHOLASTIC
www.scholastic.co.uk

Maze planning

■ Draw your maze and position Grandma's house.

<table>
<tr><td></td><td></td><td></td><td></td></tr>
<tr><td></td><td></td><td></td><td></td></tr>
<tr><td></td><td></td><td></td><td></td></tr>
<tr><td></td><td></td><td></td><td></td></tr>
</table>

■ How will Little Red Riding Hood get to Grandma's house?
Draw the best route through the forest maze.

I can work out the best route to follow.
I can plan an algorithm.

How did you do?

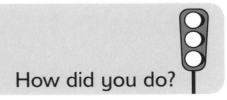

Fairy tale cards (1)

Fairy tale cards (2)

Zoos

This chapter builds on the previous learning about 'How computers work' from Year 1. The children recall their learning about the component parts, including the mouse, keyboard and screen. The learning is developed to consider inside the computer, revisiting the central processing unit (CPU) and introducing the memory and the hard drive. The children develop their knowledge of computers in everyday life outside of school. They use a zoo theme and zoo stories, to explore the parts of a zoo and consider the potential uses of technology. They imagine a future zoo and how technology could enable new experiences. Finally, they make analogies with maps of the zoo and the structure of computers.

Expected prior learning

● The children will have experienced naming the keyboard, mouse, screen and CPU from Year 1. They will be expected to remember the functions of those parts.
● From prior visits, reading and seeing zoos on television, the children should know about the main features and animals kept in zoos.
● They should know how to extract information from texts and websites.

Chapter at a glance

Subject area
• How computers work

National Curriculum objective
• To recognise common uses of information technology beyond school.

Week	Lesson objectives	Summary of activities	Expected outcomes
1	• To identify the main parts of a computer. • To name the main parts of a computer. • To describe the function of the main parts of a computer.	• Children name the parts and functions of the computer, for example, monitor/screen, mouse and keyboard. • They are introduced to a zoo theme by being asked about visits they may have had to zoos. • Children listen to the story Zoo by Anthony Browne and are encouraged to make predictions as the story progresses. • They ask questions about the story.	• Can name parts of the classroom computer. • Can describe how to use the keyboard, mouse and screen.
2	• To know that a computer follows instructions. • To explain the basic functions of the CPU. • To explain the basic function of the memory. • To describe a simple relationship between the parts of a computer.	• Children recall the story Zoo. • They remember that computers follow instructions called programs. • They create a set of instructions for a game of 'I-spy' in the car. • They learn that the computer contains a CPU and that it can be thought of as a computer's 'brain'. • Children describe that the CPU is where the instructions are followed and are introduced to the basic functions of memory through card games.	• Can identify that a computer follows instructions. • Can explain the basic function of the CPU and memory.

Week	Lesson objectives	Summary of activities	Expected outcomes
3	• To name a sound file format, for example .mp3. • To know that a sound file is stored on a digital device. • To name a video file format, for example .mov. • To know that a video file is stored on a digital device.	• Children go on a virtual zoo trip. • They identify animals and use voice recorders to record animal sounds. • They recall what a sound file format is and that it is stored on a digital device. • Using a video recorder they act out filming the animals. • They recall what a video file format is and that it is stored on a digital device.	• Can name a sound file format. • Can name a video file format.
4	• To explain the basic function of the hard drive. • To discuss that a hard drive stores data and form analogies with other data storage devices.	• Children are introduced to the basic function of the hard drive. • They remember the names of as many zoo animals as possible. • They name their favourite animals. • They research animals, collecting facts about them.	• Can explain the basic function of the hard drive.
5	• To name common uses of technology within school. • To name common uses of technology outside of school. • To explain why technology is useful in the local environment.	• Children think about the common uses of technology within the school environment. • They recall the virtual visit (or actual visit) to the zoo and think of the uses of technology there. • Children describe their own maps for an imaginary zoo. • They recall the uses of computers outside school, in the environment.	• Can recognise common uses of technology outside of school, for example, at the zoo. • Can recognise common uses of technology outside of school, for example, in the local environment.
6	• To name common uses of technology outside of school. • To predict future uses of technology outside of school.	• Children consider how technology could be used in future zoos. • They develop the map of their imaginary zoo adding examples of technology and its benefits.	• Can predict future uses of technology.
Assess and review	• To assess the half-term's work.	• Children recognise technology found in the zoo and its functions. • They name common uses of technology outside of school. • They explain why technology is useful in the local environment.	• Assess and review.

Overview of progression

● The children progress their knowledge of the parts of the computer, from the easier-to-observe keyboard, mouse and screen, to the inside components such as the CPU, memory and hard drive.
● They will consider the differences between standard desktop computers and tablet computers.
● Previously, the children have discussed computers in their school and immediate local environment. In this topic, they consider the use of computers and technology outside of school.

Creative context

● Linking to English, the children write about real-life events, such as going to the zoo and using maps. They develop their non-fiction writing to describe the functions of the parts of the computer and parts of the zoos.
● Using maps and positional language in the zoo visitor guide supports the teaching in the maths curriculum.
● Geography can be closely linked through identifying the local environment, the locations of zoos, the country origins of the animals and drawing maps.

Background knowledge

● The children will have knowledge of zoos from visits, books and television programmes. They will know a range of animals, though this should be developed through the lessons, as zoos look after rarer species.
● The children will have experienced computers and tablet computers in and out of school. As they develop their knowledge, the teaching needs to adapt to highlight new technologies.

Lesson objectives
● To identify the main parts of a computer.
● To name the main parts of a computer.
● To describe the function of the main parts of a computer.

Expected outcomes
● Can name parts of the classroom computer.
● Can describe how to use the keyboard, mouse and screen.

Resources
Zoo by Anthony Browne; interactive activity 'My computer (1)' on the CD-ROM; photocopiable page 145 'Computer parts – what do I do?'

What's my name?

This lesson offers an introduction to the 'How computers work' topic, building on the prior learning in Year 1 about the visible parts of the computer – keyboard, mouse and screen. It introduces the zoo theme, by recalling visits to the zoo and reading Anthony Browne's Zoo story.

Introduction

● Begin the lesson by playing a 'name' game. The children act out clues using an object and the others have to guess what it is. The aim of the game is to get them thinking about objects and their purpose; this is similar to naming parts of the computer and identifying their functions.
● Split the class into two teams. Each team thinks of five objects, for example a hammer, a camera, a can of drink, and writes each name on a piece of paper. The individual pieces of paper are folded and passed to the other team. Each team takes turns to select a player who will act out clues for the object (without saying its name). Give points for the number of correct guesses in two minutes. Review the game, asking the children to describe what that object does or what its function is – for example, a camera takes pictures.
● Gather the children around the classroom computer. Ask them if they remember the names of its parts. Select individuals to name the parts, for example, mouse, keyboard, screen or monitor and main computer or box. Some children may remember that the main part is the CPU.

Whole-class work

● Show the children photocopiable page 145 'Computer parts – what do I do?' Explain that they are going to add labels to the picture of the computer and then explain the function of the parts. This is a formative assessment task to see what they can remember and also to bring in their learning from home and other life experiences.

Independent work

● The children work individually to complete the photocopiable sheet.

Whole-class work

● Bring the class together and review the questions. Select children to explain the functions of each part. Focus on highlighting the 'input' and 'output' of information and also that there is a 'processing' of the instructions inside the computer.
● If possible, show a tablet computer and ask a child to demonstrate how to use it. Again, highlight the input (through the touchscreen), the output (through the same screen) and that the instruction happened inside the tablet.
● Computers are used in many public places, such as museums, shopping centres and even in zoos. A zoo theme will be used in this chapter, as a way of highlighting that computers are present in places that may be unexpected.
● Introduce the theme of zoos, by asking the children to recall their visits to the zoo and the sights they have seen there.
● Read the story Zoo. Encourage the children to make predictions as the story progresses. Ask simple comprehension questions about the story.

Differentiation
● Support: Less confident learners can complete the photocopiable sheet, though they may need adult support to write and add the vocabulary to their answers.
● Challenge: More confident learners can attempt to explain what is happening inside the computer, with the instructions.

Review

● Remind the children of the main points of the learning to name the parts of the computer and their functions. Use the interactive activity 'My computer (1)' on the CD-ROM to reinforce this.

Curriculum objectives
● To recognise common uses of information technology beyond school.

Lesson objectives
● To know that a computer follows instructions.
● To explain the basic functions of the CPU.
● To explain the basic function of the memory.
● To describe a simple relationship between the parts of a computer.

Expected outcomes
● Can name parts of the classroom computer.
● Can identify that a computer follows instructions.
● Can explain the basic function of the CPU and memory. can describe how to use the keyboard, mouse and screen.

Resources
Interactive activity 'Drag and drop animals' on the CD-ROM; photocopiable page 146 'Traffic jam memory cards'

Inside the box

This lesson develops the children's learning about parts of the computer, now focusing 'inside the box'. The children learn about the central processing unit (CPU) which was introduced in Year 1, and the computer's memory. The children play 'I-spy' and memory games to identify the instructions needed for a computer program. They make an analogy between a computer memory and our memory.

Introduction
● Start by reading the beginning of the *Zoo* story, including the part about being caught in a traffic jam.
● Remind the children of their work on algorithms. They have been covering many examples of using algorithms and they should know that computers follow algorithms or instructions precisely. They should also know that the instructions followed by a computer are called programs.

Whole-class work
● In the story, the family are involved in a traffic jam. Ask the children to think of when they have been on a long car journey or stuck in a traffic jam. What did they do? They may have played a game to pass the time.
● Using 'I-spy', as an example, discuss the instructions on how to play.

Paired work
● Ask the children to play 'I-spy' in pairs.
● Pausing their game, ask them to decide which instructions are essential.

Whole-class work
● Select pairs of children to give examples of the objects they chose during the game. Did they guess them? Now ask, *What are the instructions on how to play the game?*
● Collect the instructions together on a display board.
● Explain that a computer follows instructions too. It contains a CPU, which can be thought of as its 'brain'. The CPU is where the instructions are followed.
● Review the instructions that the children suggested for 'I-spy'. Ask: *Are they detailed enough for a computer to follow?*
● The next step is to introduce the concept of computer memory.
● Explain to the children that they are going to play a memory game called 'Traffic jam', using photocopiable page 146 'Traffic jam memory cards'.
● In this game, one child places the four cards in a random order, for example, black car, white van, grey lorry and motorbike. The cards are shown for ten seconds, before they are turned over. Then the second child has to remember the order, by placing their cards in the same order.

> **Differentiation**
> ● Support: Less confident learners could explain verbally how to play the games or give a demonstration.
> ● Challenge: More confident learners could write down rules for 'I-spy' and 'Traffic jam memory game'.

Review
● Ask the children if they could remember the order of the vehicles. Choose one child to demonstrate the game, showing how they remember the order.
● Explain that the computer has a memory, so that it can work on instructions straight away.
● Conclude by remembering the sequence that the animals come into the story. Use the interactive activity 'Drag and drop animals' on the CD-ROM to place the animals in the correct order.

We're all going to the zoo

A 'virtual' visit to the zoo enables the children to think about the animals in their zoo habitats. Using webcams, they observe creatures and then act out being that animal. Using sound recorders, they make animal noises and identify the sound file format. This is repeated, using video cameras to record them behaving like animals and, again, identifying the file format.

Introduction
● Start the lesson by saying *We're going to the zoo!* Explain that the children will be going on a virtual visit to the zoo. They will be using their imaginations and also live webcams in zoos.
● An actual school visit would be an excellent way of introducing the learning.

Whole-class work
● Explain that in the zoo there are webcams, which allow the live streaming of video from the zoo to their classroom.
● Using the Zoovue website (www.zoovue.com/) select different animals and zoos to visit. Can they find the animals from the *Zoo* story?

Group/paired work
● Ask the children to think of three animals. *What noises do they make when they are happy? ...sad? ...eating?*
● In small groups use the sound recorders to capture the noises.

Whole-class work
● Bring the class together and ask for example sound files for the animals. Transfer the sound file from the device to the computer.
● Tell the children that the sound file was stored on the device and now has been copied on to the computer. Play the sound file.
● Using the computer's file manager, it may be possible to see the sound file and its extension, for example .wav or .mp3.
● If possible, show the sound file extension. If not, tell the children that there are file formats for sounds and they will have heard of 'mp3 players'. Explain that an mp3 is a way of storing the sound information.

Group/paired work
● Ask the children to use the same three animals as before. *What actions do they make when they are happy? ...sad? ...eating?*
● In small groups, the children use the video recorders to record short videos of themselves acting like animals, capturing images and sound.

Whole-class work
● Bring the class together and ask for example video files for the animals. Transfer the video files from the device to the computer.
● Tell the children that the video file was stored on the device and now has been copied on to the computer. Play the video file.
● If possible, show the video file extension. If not, tell the children that there are file formats for videos, such as 'wmv', 'mov' or 'mp4'. Explain that an mp4 is a way of storing the video information.

> ### Differentiation
> ● Support: With help, less confident learners could record a short video to state where the videos are held and a common file format type.
> ● Challenge: More confident learners could identify several sound and video file formats by researching on the internet.

Review
● Ask: *Is an .mp3 a file format for sound or video? Is a .wmv a file format for sound or video?*

Curriculum objectives
● To recognise common uses of information technology beyond school.

Lesson objectives
● To explain the basic function of the hard drive.
● To discuss that a hard drive stores data and form analogies with other data storage devices.

Expected outcomes
● Can explain the basic function of the hard drive.

Resources
Photocopiable page 147 'How big?'; photocopiable page 148 'My animal facts'; hole punch; ringbinder file

Animal facts: where can we store the data?

This lesson offers an introduction to the computer hard drive. The children research different animals and create a fact file. The paper-based file is used to form an analogy with a computer hard drive, where the data can be stored and retrieved.

Introduction
● Start the lesson by asking, *Who can give me the name of a zoo animal?*
● Split the class into two teams and ask them to list as many zoo animals as they can. The team with most unique names will win (so if the other team has that animal in their list as well, it does not count towards the final score).
● Explain that the list of animals the children produced came from information stored in their brains. The list could be stored on paper also. The information on the list could be retrieved later. With a computer, the information is stored on a hard drive and retrieved when needed.

Whole-class work
● The children may have heard TV adverts where a laptop is advertised with a *750 gigabyte* or *2 terrabyte* hard drive. This is the size of the storage on the hard drive.
● Using photocopiable page 147 'How big?', the children compare the memory sizes of different items.
● Explain to the children that the size of the hard drive in home computers, is getting larger, every year. This can be attributed to the advancements in technology. Ask: *Do you think storage will continue to get bigger? Why do you think that?*

Group work
● In groups, the children select a favourite animal they are going to find more about. They then complete photocopiable page 148 'My animal facts'. The children could use books and leaflets about the animals or research using the internet.
● The Zoovue (www.zoovue.com/animals) website and Switchzoo website (www.switchzoo.com/animallist.htm) has facts about animals that the children could use for research.

> **Differentiation**
> ● Support: Less confident learners will need support to scaffold their writing and also to extract the information from the texts. Peers can support them as part of group work.
> ● Challenge: More confident learners could collect notes from the given websites and also search using keywords for further information online.

Review
● Select children to describe the facts that they have found in their groups.
● Collect the children's animal fact sheets. Hole-punch the sheets and place them into a ring binder file. Explain that all of the information is held in the file.
● Now, explain that the computer also stores information on its hard drive. This is an important part of the computer, which works with the CPU.

Curriculum objectives
● To recognise common uses of information technology beyond school.

Lesson objectives
● To name common uses of technology within school.
● To name common uses of technology outside of school.
● To explain why technology is useful in the local environment.

Expected outcomes
● Can recognise common uses of technology outside of school, for example, at the zoo.
● Can recognise common uses of technology outside of school, for example, in the local environment.

Resources
Interactive activity 'Zoo map' on the CD-ROM; photocopiable page 149 'My zoo'; photocopiable page 150 'Technology in my zoo'; *Zoo* by Anthony Browne

My new zoo

The children create an imaginary zoo and highlight where technology can be integrated. They begin by remembering uses of computers within school, such as the school office and the photocopier. They then think about the local environment and places they know, such as a supermarket. For the imaginary zoo, the children consider where technology could be useful.

Introduction
● To begin the lesson, remind the children about their lessons in Year 1. Ask: *Where do we find computers around our school?* They will recall obvious places, such as the computer room, the teacher's computer or the school office. Do they remember other places? Discuss the tills or cashless system in the dining hall or the device that scans the books in the library?
● Re-read *Zoo*. Ask the children to think where computers might appear in the story? For example, the car could have a satnav system, the entrance ticket office may have a till or a discount card scanner. The cafe may have a till and a computer to keep a track of sales on different days of the year (relating to the weather). The gift shop may have a database to keep track of the stock.
● In the different animal enclosures, computers may be used to control the different conditions. For example, in the reptile house, the animals need warmth and light – this will be carefully controlled and also monitored using technology. If it becomes too cold, an alarm may sound to alert the zoo keepers.

Whole-class work
● Explain that the children are going to design a map for their imaginary zoo. They can decide which animals will be included and where they are placed.
● Show examples of zoo maps:
    ● Edinburgh Zoo map www.edinburghzoo.org.uk/visiting/maps/
    ● Chester Zoo map www.chesterzoo.org/zoo-map
● Use the interactive activity 'Zoo map' to give an example of where the items could be located.

Group/paired work
● In groups or pairs the children plan their own zoo, using the interactive activity 'Zoo map' on the CD-ROM. Once they have had the opportunity to arrange the items, they can draw their map on photocopiable page 149 'My zoo'.
● The children can describe the facilities in their zoo, for example in the gift shop, using the till to pay for items or a photobooth to have their photograph taken with an animal. Using photocopiable page 150 'Technology in my zoo' they can add details about the location and the features.

> ### Differentiation
> ● Support: Less confident learners can use the interactive resource to plan their map. They may need support when transferring ideas to photocopiable page 149 'My zoo'.
> ● Challenge: More confident learners can plan a route guide to accompany the map, to direct visitors from one place to the next, with comments about the sights and animals present.

Review
● Select children to share their ideas for their zoo. Which animals will be present? How have they organised them? Where did they place the ticket office, café and gift shop?
● As a class, look at your example of the zoo, using the interactive activity. Where do the children think that technology will be used?
● Highlight that computers are all around us in school and the local environment around school. Ask: *Why are computers useful to us?*

Curriculum objectives
● To recognise common uses of information technology beyond school.

Lesson objectives
● To name common uses of technology outside of school.
● To predict future uses of technology outside of school.

Expected outcomes
● Can predict future uses of technology.

Resources
Interactive activity 'Zoo map' on the CD-ROM; photocopiable page 151 'Future zoo'

Zoo-ming into the future

Thinking of a zoo of the future, the children imagine what they could experience. They plan their future zoo and imagine where technology would be needed. Currently, zoos are using technology to enable visitors to access videos and more information. What could the future hold?

Introduction
● Start the lesson by reshowing from Lesson 5 the interactive activity 'Zoo map' on the CD-ROM. Ask: *Where did we think technology was being used?* Take answers from the children, then ask: *How does the technology help us?*
● Explain that technology is always changing. Ask the children to imagine the 'zoo of the future' – what would it be like?

Whole-class work
● Ask the children to name their senses – sight, sound, touch, taste and smell. New technology, such as 3D goggles, could enable the zoo visitor to see into the lions' lair or dive like a penguin. Where would the children like to see, using special goggles?
● Thinking about touch, ask them to imagine they could put on special gloves that would let them touch the dangerous animals. Which animals would they touch?

Group/paired work
● In small groups or pairs, children complete photocopiable page 151 'Future zoo'. They need to think of the main features and also explain their ideas.

Whole-class work
● Explain that robots are being used more in everyday lives, for example a robot vacuum cleaner, which can clean the carpets during the day while people are out of the house.
● Tell the children that robots are also used for repetitive jobs, such as manufacturing cars. Whereas humans would need sleep, food and breaks, the robots can keep going.
● Ask: *Would robots be useful in your future zoos? Where would they work? Why would you use a robot instead of a human?*

Differentiation
● Support: Less confident learners could draw their future zoo and add simple labels to show where they have included technology. They could verbally explain their ideas.
● Challenge: More confident learners could write about their future zoo, giving detailed explanations about the features and how technology would be integrated.

Review
● As a class, share examples of the children's ideas for the future zoo.
● As an example, discuss: *If the animals could be robots, the original 'real' ones could remain in the wild. Also, extinct creatures, such as the dodo or woolly mammoth could be brought back to life. Would this be a good use of technology?*
● Finally, ask the children for examples of technology within the school, the local environment and in other places such as zoos. Ask: *Why is the technology important to us?*

Curriculum objectives
● To recognise common uses of information technology beyond school.

Lesson objectives
● To name common uses of technology outside of school.
● To explain why technology is useful in the local environment.

Expected outcomes
● Can recognise common uses of technology outside of school, for example, in the local environment.

Resources
Interactive activity 'My computer (2)' on the CD-ROM; photocopiable page 'Technology around the zoo' from the CD-ROM; photocopiable page 'Technology around us' from the CD-ROM

Zoos: Assess and review

This lesson offers an opportunity to review the learning over the topic. The children revisit the learning about the use of technology and identify why it is useful in the different places in the zoo. They also consolidate earlier learning about the parts of the computer.

Introduction
● Start the review lesson by reminding the children of the zoo topic. They have thought about how technology is useful in the local environment and in the zoo examples.
● In this lesson, they will think about the technology used in the different areas of the zoo and highlight why it is useful. Ask:
    ● *Where is technology used around our school?*
    ● *Where is technology used around our local area?*

Whole-class work
● Display a zoo website, for example, Edinburgh Zoo 'Restaurants and facilities' page: www.edinburghzoo.org.uk/plan-your-visit/stage-1/restaurants-and-facilities
● Ask the children to think about how technology will be used in the different places.

Independent work
● The children use photocopiable page 'Technology around the zoo' from the CD-ROM to show their understanding of where the technology may be used, for example in the shop, with the till or in the reptile house, monitoring the environment.
● Following on from thinking about the zoo, the children can use photocopiable page 'Technology around us' to think about the use of technology in the shopping centre, the sports centre and the train station.

Whole-class work
● Remind the class that at the beginning of the topic they were thinking about the parts of a computer, before they continued to focus on the use of technology around them.
● Either as a class or in pairs, allow the children time to discuss the parts of the computer and remember the function for each part.
● Review the learning about the computer by sharing the interactive activity 'My computer (2)', on the CD-ROM which shows the inside of the main box, containing a CPU, memory and a hard drive. Explain that this is a very simple model and that these parts are very important for the computer.

Differentiation
● Support: Less confident learners could use photocopiable sheet 'Technology around the zoo' to simply recall examples that have been studied in the lessons.
● Challenge: More confident learners could describe the use of technology at the shopping centre, sports centre and train station and may volunteer further information.

Review
● As a class, share examples of the use of technology in the zoo. Ask:
    ● *Where is technology used in places, such as zoos?*
    ● *Why is technology useful to us?*
● Explain that the use of technology is growing rapidly and that it will become even more integrated into their lives as they grow older.

Computer parts: what do I do?

■ Label the parts of the computer and say what each part does.

What do I do?

What do I do?

What do I do?

What do I do?

I can label the parts of a computer and say what
each part does.

How did you do?

Traffic jam memory cards

PHOTOCOPIABLE

SCHOLASTIC
www.scholastic.co.uk

How big?

■ Information is stored digitally on a computer hard drive.

Size is measured in bytes, one byte being the amount of information needed to encode a single character of text.

1 kilobyte (kB) is 1000 bytes (B).

1000 kB is 1 megabyte (MB).

1000 MB is 1 gigabyte (GB).

1000 GB is 1 terabyte (TB).

■ Draw lines to match the items to the most likely sizes:

Item	Possible file size
A short word-processed document	5 MB
A digital photo	4 GB
A feature-length, high-definition film	1 TB
All of the data on a computer hard drive	50 kB

I can explain that information is stored on a hard drive.
I can explain that the size of the information stored is measured in bytes.

How did you do?

My animal facts

My animal's name is:

Here is a drawing of my animal:

Fact 1	
Fact 2	
Fact 3	
Fact 4	
Fact 5	

I can research facts about an animal.

How did you do?

PHOTOCOPIABLE

My zoo

■ Draw animals on your zoo map.
■ Add an entrance, a ticket office, a cafe and a gift shop.
■ Where would you need computers?

I can design my own zoo map.

How did you do?

Technology in my zoo

■ Would technology be used in a zoo gift shop?

1. Draw what you would have in your gift shop.

[blank box]

2. What would you use a computer for in the gift shop?

_____

_____

_____

■ Would technology be used in a zoo cafe?

1. Draw what you would have in your cafe.

[blank box]

2. What would you use a computer for in the café?

_____

_____

I can recognise where technology is used in a
zoo and what it does.

How did you do?

PHOTOCOPIABLE   **SCHOLASTIC**
www.scholastic.co.uk

Future zoo

■ What would the zoo look like in the future?

■ Think about your senses – seeing, touching, hearing, tasting and smelling.

1. What would you be able to see? How could technology help?

_____

_____

2. What would you be able to touch? How could technology help?

_____

_____

3. What would you be able to hear? How could technology help?

_____

_____

4. What would you be able to taste? How could technology help?

_____

_____

5. What would you be able to smell? How could technology help?

_____

_____

I can imagine how technology might help us in the future.

How did you do?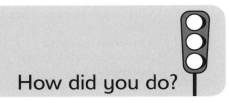

Ourselves

This chapter uses *Funnybones* by Janet and Allan Ahlberg to focus on how we communicate with others. Thinking about communication online and offline, the children discuss using technology safely and respectfully. The lessons build on the learning from Year 1 about personal information, avatars, story sequencing and working collaboratively. The children work together face-to-face and using online tools, so they can learn about the differences in their communication methods. The technology can enable collaboration, so children need to recognise how they can use it effectively.

Expected prior learning

● The children will remember creating avatars to represent themselves and also about personal information. They will have used camera and sound recorder tools in earlier topics. Through the algorithms topics, they will have sequenced stories into the correct order.

Chapter at a glance

Subject area
• Communication

National Curriculum objective
• Children should be taught to use technology safely and respectfully, keeping personal information private; identify where to go for help and support when they have concerns about material on the internet.

Week	Lesson objectives	Summary of activities	Expected outcomes
1	• To list what makes a 'good' friend. • To identify how 'good' friends communicate through role-play. • To discuss methods of communication that are face-to-face. • To identify what to do when a friend upsets them – tell someone. • To discuss people who are not friends that they might meet online.	• Children read the story *Funnybones* and discuss the big and little skeleton's friendship. • They discuss the language in the story that repeats 'dark dark'. • They discuss how we communicate face-to-face and act out a role play of the skeletons planning an outing. • The skeletons are planning to scare people – the children discuss what they should do if someone upsets them. • They talk about online communication and how they can meet friends and also to be aware of people who scare others.	• Can identify the traits of friends that they know and online friends. • Can identify aspects of appropriate behaviour online.
2	• To discuss friends they meet in-person and online. • To know that an avatar is a picture to represent a person online. • To know that an avatar is a way of protecting identity online.	• Children re-read *Funnybones* imagining they were going to interview the skeletons. • They discuss what questions they would ask. • Children role play being a news reporter interviewing the skeletons using a sound recorder. • They discuss the appearance of the skeletons and the children are reminded of the avatars they drew in Year 1. They draw themselves as avatar skeletons.	• Can protect their identity online by not using their full name. • Can protect their identity online by choosing an avatar.
3	• To collaborate, face-to-face, to create a story. • To discuss non-verbal communication (for example, facial expressions).	• The children fix the dog skeleton. • They sequence the story. • While creating the story they think about non-verbal communication, for example, facial expression.	• Can collaborate to create a story.

■SCHOLASTIC

Week	Lesson objectives	Summary of activities	Expected outcomes
4	• To collaborate, using online tools, to create a story. • To discuss the differences between collaborating when face-to-face and when online.	• Following on from the previous lesson, the children create a story online using an online 'sticky note' style website. They also upload an image of themselves acting part of the story. • As a class, the children sequence the story and highlight the difference between collaborating face-to-face and being online.	• Can collaborate online to create a story.
5	• To discuss taking turns when collaborating online and offline. • To respect the views of others.	• Children recall the senses and consider which ones they use when face-to-face and when online. • They read a passage from Funnybones and stop to imagine what they can see, hear, touch, and so on at various points. • Children are reminded about taking turns in games and link this to behaviour online. • They use video conferencing to record a conversation.	• Can explain how to collaborate respectfully.
6	• To link to the learning on algorithms and precise instructions. • To explain how comments can be misunderstood when online compared with face-to-face.	• Linking to the algorithms topic, children create a sequence of instructions about communication. • Children re-read Funnybones, and discuss how the skeletons frighten each other. This is used to reinforce how important it is to communicate clearly as sometimes information can be misunderstood.	• Can understand the need for clear communication, when collaborating online.
Assess and review	• To assess the half-term's work.	• Capturing images and sounds to create a Funnybones story about using the computer to communicate.	• Assess and review.

Overview of progression
● The children progress their knowledge and experience of sequencing stories, with a focus on collaboration. Throughout the lessons, they identify the differences between collaborating face-to-face and when online.
● They use new online tools to create their stories, uploading images and adding text. They experience the collaborative nature of web 2.0 tools.

Creative context
● The lessons link closely to the English curriculum, using the story to focus on sequencing the main features, building fluency and confidence in reading. The children write for different purposes and record questions for an interview in a news report. They use speaking and listening skills to work collaboratively.
● Linking to the maths curriculum, as the children reconstruct the skeleton bodies they use mathematical vocabulary to describe position, direction and movement.
● In science, the children study the skeleton in Year 3; however, they will recognise the main features of the body at this stage.

Background knowledge
● The children will have knowledge of skeletons being scary from events such as Halloween. They will know the main parts of the body and be able to arrange the parts into the correct place.
● From previous lessons, the children will know how to use the camera and sound recorder. They should also recognise the correct file types.
● The children will have used the mouse to drag and drop items on the computer when arranging stories into the correct order, so their sequencing skills will be developed with a new context.

An introduction to Ourselves and the *Funnybones* stories

This lesson offers an introduction to the topic of 'Ourselves' and uses the story *Funnybones*. This story forms the basis of this chapter, which focuses on communication when face-to-face and when online.

Introduction
● Introduce the lesson by asking: *What do you know about skeletons?* The children may associate skeletons with Halloween and scary stories. Ask who has got a skeleton. Respond to the children's answers before asking them to feel their own skulls, arm bones and leg bones.
● Play the game 'Heads, shoulders, knees and toes' to reinforce the names of the body parts.

Whole-class work
● Explain that today they will be learning about ourselves and how we communicate with each other. To help with this, the class will be reading the *Funnybones* story, which is about three skeletons.
● Read the first page as an introduction. Re-read, asking the children to join in saying 'dark, dark'. Introduce the three characters – big, little and dog skeleton. What do the children predict will happen in the story?
● Read the whole story, then ask: *How do we know the skeletons are friends?* The children might suggest because they live together, spend time together, play together or laugh together. Explain that they communicate with each other in a friendly way.

Paired work
● Tell the children that they have bones in their faces – can they feel them? Re-read the introduction and ask the children to place their hand on their cheeks as they say 'dark dark' – can they feel their faces moving? Now, in pairs, ask them to face their partner, and watch their faces as they say the words. They will be role playing the parts of the skeletons, so they can imagine what their bones look like and feel like.
● Ask the children to act out the skeletons planning their night out, using the photocopiable page 161 '*Funnybones* script'. They should say. *What shall we do tonight? Let's take the dog for a walk... and frighten somebody! Good idea! Woof!* Then, they act out climbing the stairs and going out of a door.

> **Differentiation**
> ● Support: Less confident learners may need support to read the script.
> ● Challenge; More confident learners can improvise their own script.

Review
● Bring the class together and select different pairs to act out the scene. Select three children to ask whether they think the skeletons are friendly. (They are friendly to each other, but in the story, they are looking to go and frighten somebody – does that make them friendly?)
● Use photocopiable page 162 'Friendly or unfriendly?' to list examples of friendly and unfriendly behaviour.
● Remind the children about their lessons in Year 1, where they thought about communication when face-to-face and also when online, for example, sending a text, an email or using video communication, such as Skype or FaceTime.
● Conclude the lesson by saying that sometimes people can be friendly and sometimes not friendly and that this is the same when online too.

Curriculum objectives
● To use technology safely and respectfully, keeping personal information private; identify where to go for help and support when they have concerns about material on the internet.

Lesson objectives
● To discuss friends they meet in-person and online.
● To know that an avatar is a picture to represent a person online.
● To know that an avatar is a way of protecting identity online.

Expected outcomes
● Can protect their identity online by not using their full name.
● Can protect their identity online by choosing an avatar.

Resources
Photocopiable page 163 'My skeleton avatar'; photocopiable page 164 'Skeleton questions'; sound recorder

Skeletons in the news

The skeletons in the story are worthy of making the news, so in this lesson, the children will be news presenters. They will interview skeletons to find out about them. They will use sound recorders to capture the interview questions and answers, in their role play. This lesson also revisits the learning in Year 1 about online profiles and avatars.

Introduction
● Re-read the *Funnybones* story again. Pause on different pages to ask, *What question could you ask the skeletons?* For example: *Why does the big skeleton always say 'Good idea'? Where have they come from? Are there any other skeletons in the town?* Write the questions down so that the children can view them.
● Using photocopiable page 164 'Skeleton questions', the children write their own questions for each of the skeletons in the story.

Whole-class work
● Explain that they are going to be news reporters, interviewing the skeletons. Where have they seen news reporters before? For example, on the television or working for newspapers. Using a sound recorder, they will ask a question each for the big, little and dog skeleton.

Group work
● In small groups of four, the children assume the roles of news reporter, big, little and dog skeleton. The news reporter asks a question of each character, in turn, then they respond with an answer. The children can use the questions they have created using photocopiable page 164 'Skeleton questions'.
● Using a voice or sound recorder, the news reporter can record the questions and answers.

Differentiation
● Support: Less confident learners may need support to construct their answers to the questions and in empathising with the characters.
● Challenge: More confident learners could assume the role of the news reporter and ask more questions of the characters.

Review
● Bring the class together and select groups to either act out their interviews or to playback an example question and answer, using the sound recorders.
● For the news reports, the newspaper or TV programme might use a photograph of the people involved. Online news websites also use photographs in the same way. Show the CBBC Newsround website as an example: www. bbc.co.uk/newsround/
● Remind the children that, sometimes, they may not want to use their full name or photograph, for example, when communicating online they may use their first name and an avatar.
● Ask the children to draw an avatar of themselves as skeletons (using photocopiable page 163 'My skeleton avatar').

Curriculum objectives
● To use technology safely and respectfully, keeping personal information private; identify where to go for help and support when they have concerns about material on the internet.

Lesson objectives
● To collaborate, face-to-face, to create a story.
● To discuss non-verbal communication (for example, facial expressions).

Expected outcomes
● Can collaborate to create a story.

Resources
Interactive activity 'Funnybones story' on the CD-ROM; photocopiable page 165 'Skeleton bones (1)'; photocopiable page 166 'Skeleton bones (2)'; digital camera; sticky tack

Making stories together

Focusing on collaboration, the children create a story based on the *Funnybones* text. They collaborate to repair the skeleton dog, focusing on the instructional language used. They sequence the story, before acting out the scenes in groups, using digital cameras to record the process. The class then collaborates to retell the story.

Introduction
● Begin the lesson by re-reading the section of the *Funnybones* story, where the dog skeleton has fallen apart and the skeletons try to put it back together again.
● Using the parts from photocopiable page 165 'Skeleton bones (1)' and photocopiable page 166 'Skeleton bones (2)', give the 8 pieces to 8 different children. Ask the children to try one at a time to stick their piece on a display board. Can they collaborate to put the dog back together?

Whole-class work
● Explain that clear communication is needed. Take one of the pieces of dog bone and ask a child to describe its shape. Now give the piece to a child and ask another to direct them to place it back on the skeleton – this time, they will create a new creature, by placing it in a different place on the body.
● What sort of words did they use? For example, 'turn it round', 'upside down', 'near the head', 'clockwise'.

Paired work
● In pairs, using the interactive activity 'Funnybones story' on the CD-ROM the children drag and drop the story into place. However, one child will sit behind another, so that the first child is operating the computer and the second is behind giving instructions, so clear communication is needed. The first child is not allowed to turn to face the second and the second cannot point at the screen, they can only use words to describe what to do.

Differentiation
● Support: Less confident learners may need peer or adult support to order the story into the correct sequence.
● Challenge: More confident learners could sequence the story and write down the instructional words they use.

Review
● As a class, review the story sequence. Did they manage to get it into the correct order?
● How easy or difficult was it for the first child operating the computer?
● Did they struggle to understand the other child because they could not see their face?
● How was it for the second child, with no pointing and using only words to describe what they wanted?
● Conclude the lesson by restating that clear communication is needed and that we often communicate through our facial expressions when face-to-face.

Curriculum objectives
● To use technology safely and respectfully, keeping personal information private; identify where to go for help and support when they have concerns about material on the internet.

Lesson objectives
● To collaborate, using online tools, to create a story.
● To discuss the differences between collaborating when face-to-face and when online.

Expected outcomes
● Can collaborate online to create a story.

Resources
● Interactive activity 'Funnybones story' on the CD-ROM; digital camera; drywipe boards

Collaborating online to tell our story

Following on from the previous lesson, the children consider the differences between communication when face-to-face and when they are online. In groups, the children act out six scenes from the story and capture them using a digital camera. Using an online tool, the class see that they can add digital sticky notes on to a website and so sequence their version of the story.

Introduction
● Remind the children of the previous lesson where they put the dog skeleton together and sequenced the story by using clear communication. Explain that today they will create a reconstruction of the story by acting out the scenes and uploading the images to an online collaboration web tool.
● Prior to the lesson, check that the website http://padlet.com can be accessed. This is an online 'sticky note' style website. You can add a new 'sticky note' to the online wall, in the same way a sticky note could be placed on the wall in the classroom. Advantages of the online tool are that it is more permanent and can last longer than a classroom display, more than one person can access it at a time and it can be accessed from home, as well as school.
● From the Padlet website, select 'Build a wall' then select 'Modify wall', then 'Address'. A new name for the wall's address can be added. For example, use the school name and 'funnybones', for example, if the school name was 'Fairfield school', then http://padlet.com/wall/fairfieldfunnybones
● Prior to the lesson, practise adding a new note by double-clicking on the wall. Try typing into the note, to see the text appear. Now try uploading a photograph, by selecting the 'Upload a file' symbol on the note.

Whole-class work
● Explain that the children will act out six scenes each from the story (shown in interactive activity 'Funnybones story' on the CD-ROM). They will pose for a camera image and the images will be put together into a story.

Group work
● Place the children into six small groups. Allocate a scene from the interactive activity to each group. Allow them to plan and act out the scene, before capturing images with a digital camera.
● Visit each group with one camera to collect the six images.

Differentiation
● Support: Less confident learners may need peer or adult support to remember the story and to act out their role.
● Challenge: More confident learners could write speech bubbles on A4 paper or drywipe boards, to hold next to their mouths in the photographs.

Review
● Before bringing the class together, upload the six images to six separate notes.
● As a class, ask each group to show the acting of their scene. Now the scenes need to be put in order. Using the online wall, ask the children to order the scenes.
● Explain to the class that they could have each added their image on to a new note from different computers and even from different countries.
● Demonstrate adding an image to the shared wall, by using a different computer in the classroom. On the main display screen, the browser may need to be refreshed (reloaded) if the image does not appear straightaway.
● (**Note:** the Privacy settings for the Padlet wall can be changed to stop anyone else finding or posting on the wall. From the 'cog' symbol on the right-hand menu, select the 'padlock' image and change the settings.)

Curriculum objectives
● To use technology safely and respectfully, keeping personal information private; identify where to go for help and support when they have concerns about material on the internet.

Lesson objectives
● To discuss taking turns when collaborating on and offline.
● To respect the views of others.

Expected outcomes
● Can explain how to collaborate respectfully.

Resources
Photocopiable page 167 'Our senses'; video communication tool, if available (for example Skype or FaceTime); *Funnybones* by Janet and Allan Ahlberg

Our senses

This lesson considers the children's senses. They think about what they see, hear, touch, smell and taste, in different situations. Using the *Funnybones* story, they imagine what the skeletons can sense during the story. This continues as they think about their senses when communicating face-to-face. When thinking about sharing online, children realise the importance of taking turns when replying to each other, using video communication.

Introduction
● Start the lesson by asking, *What are our senses?* The children should know sight, hearing, taste, touch and smell, but may need prompting and clues to help them remember. Ask them to think about the room they are in now. Ask: *What can you see? What can you hear? What can you touch?* Now invite them to imagine they are in the school dining hall. Ask: *What can you smell? What can you taste?*
● Using photocopiable page 167 'Our senses', ask the children to label the senses onto the body outline.
● Read the *Funnybones* story and stop to allow the children to describe what the skeletons can see, hear, smell or touch.

Whole-class work
● Explain that they are going to play the 'Yes/no' game – one person asks questions and the other person is not allowed to say either 'yes' or 'no' in their reply. Demonstrate this to the class by choosing one child at a time.

Paired work
● In pairs, the children play the 'Yes/no' game. After several tries, stop the children and now ask them to think about their senses again. Ask: *What could you see when playing the game?* (The other child's face) *What could you hear?* (The other child and background noise)

Whole-class work
● As a class, explain that when communicating online, we need to take turns. If possible, organise for a Skype or FaceTime call to the class computer or tablet (or even a your own phone). Show how the person on the video call needs to listen to the others talking, before responding.
● If a video call is not possible, acting out a telephone call in the classroom will exemplify turn-taking.
● Using the video communication tool or when acting the telephone call, play the 'Yes/no' game again, but this time, do not let them answer. Jump in with another question, so that they do not get a turn.
● Emphasise the importance of turn-taking, in order to play the game properly.

> **Differentiation**
> ● Support: Less confident learners could see whether they can answer three questions, without saying 'yes' or 'no'.
> ● Challenge: More confident learners could give examples of other games where turn-taking is important.

Review
● Remind the children that when communicating online, we need to take turns. During the video call, the people needed to listen, before responding.
● Also highlight, if the people disagreed while having a conversation, that they should still take turns and listen to the other person's view.
● Finally, remind the children that they were thinking about the senses. How is it different communicating when they can see and hear someone online to only being able to hear them?

■ SCHOLASTIC

Curriculum objectives
● To use technology safely and respectfully, keeping personal information private; identify where to go for help and support when they have concerns about material on the internet.

Lesson objectives
● To link to the learning on algorithms and precise instructions.
● To explain how comments can be misunderstood when online compared with face-to-face.

Expected outcomes
● Can understand the need for clear communication, when collaborating online.

Resources
Photocopiable page 'How do I look after my animal?' from the CD-ROM; photocopiable page 'Do you understand?' from the CD-ROM; *Funnybones* by Janet and Allan Ahlberg

Looking after skeleton animals

Linking to the algorithms topics, in this lesson the children create a list of instructions about clear communication. The children play games to emphasise the need to take turns and listen to each other. Re-reading the *Funnybones* story, the skeletons decide to frighten other people, but eventually they end up frightening each other. The children remember that sometimes people can be unkind face-to-face and also when online. The lesson reinforces the need for clear communication to avoid being misunderstood.

Introduction
● Remind the children of the previous lessons and how they have focused on clear communication, sometimes using technology such as cameras, voice recorders and online tools.
● Link their learning to the algorithms and programming lessons, where precise instructions are needed. In this lesson, they are going to write instructions about looking after an animal.

Whole-class work
● Explain that the *Funnybones* story followed a sequence. In the story, the skeletons arrive in the zoo and play with the skeleton zoo animals. Can they recognise the different animals?
● Explain that they are going to contact the zoo keepers in other countries to ask how to look after the animals.
● Using photocopiable page 'How do I look after my animal?' on the CD-ROM, show how to write a question on the letter and pass it to another child to answer. The child writes a response on the paper and passes it back.

Paired work
● In pairs, the children use photocopiable page 'How do I look after my animal?'. One child writes a question and the other writes the answer.

Whole-class work
● Highlight to the children that they needed to take turns to send the instructions and ask the questions. Ask for two children to read their example instructions.
● Using the photocopiable page 'Do you understand?' from the CD-ROM, the children look at when messages are sent online and whether they can be clearly understood. Read one example and ask the children to explain what they think it means.
● Allow the children to work in small groups to read the messages and interpret what they think the messages mean on the photocopiable sheet.
● Bring the class together and ask each group to read the message and then explain what they thought it meant. This can be followed by the question, *Was it a clear message?*

Differentiation
● Support: Less confident learners may need support structuring questions and answers.
● Challenge: More confident learners could invent their own animals and animal names and foods.

Review
● Ask the children to state instructions for clear and precise communication.
● List their ideas, writing them on a display board. Can they be prioritised, based upon a class vote?
● Re-reading the *Funnybones* story, the skeletons frighten each other. Mention that sometimes people are not always kind and that this can be the same online, as well as when face-to-face.
● Explain that sometimes comments can be misunderstood, so clear communication is required.

Curriculum objectives
● To use technology safely and respectfully, keeping personal information private; identify where to go for help and support when they have concerns about material on the internet.

Lesson objectives
● To collaborate, face-to-face, to create a story.
● To discuss the differences between collaborating when face-to-face and when online.

Expected outcomes
● Can collaborate to create a story.
● Can understand the need for clear communication, when collaborating online.

Resources
Digital camera; photocopiable page 'What happens next?' from the CD-ROM

Ourselves: Assess and review

This lesson offers an opportunity to review the learning in the chapter, assessing whether the children can collaborate to create a story and whether they can remember how to communicate clearly. They create a new *Funnybones* story, combining the scenes from each group. They then review their learning about communication when face-to-face and when online.

Introduction
● Explain that the *Funnybones* book is one in a series of books about the skeletons. Other titles are: *The Ghost Train, Bumps in the Night* and *Skeleton Crew*.
● Explain that the children are going to collaborate to write a new Funnybones story about the skeletons.
● Each group will act out an instruction to communicate clearly.

Whole-class work
● Choose four children, who will be used to demonstrate the activity. Ask them to pretend that they are the skeletons in the cellar. They decide to go out and do something.
● The children will decide what happens next. For example, they go up the stairs out of the cellar to play football. Children act out the next scene.

Group work
● Organise the children into six groups. Let them have time to plan their story using the photocopiable page 'What happens next?' from the CD-ROM and practise acting it out. Using a digital camera, the children capture images of the scenes in their story. Can the children collaborate in their groups to create a story?

Differentiation
● Support: Less confident learners may need support to plan their story and with their acting out of the scenes.
● Challenge: More confident learners could plan the next scene and write speech bubbles on the photocopiable sheet. They could also think about stage directions, such as, *The skeletons creep slowly from the left to the right of the scene.*

Review
● Bring the class back together and ask each group to present their story.
● Each event happens on each of the days of the week.
● Read the opening words, *On Monday, the skeletons decided to go out and do something. They went up the stairs and...* Then the children act out their scene.
● Next you read, *On Tuesday, the skeletons decided to go out and do something. They went up the stairs and...* Then the next group performs.
● Repeat for Wednesday, Thursday, Friday and Saturday.
● Then explain that On Sunday, the skeletons decided to use the computer to send a message to their friend. Ask:
    ● *What do the skeletons need to remember when communicating with other people online?*
    ● *What could be a difference between communicating face-to-face and online?*
● Conclude the lesson by reading the final page from the *Funnybones* book.

Funnybones script

The big skeleton sat up and scratched his skull.

Big skeleton: What shall we do tonight?
Little skeleton: Let's take the dog for a walk …
                   and frighten somebody.
Big skeleton: Good idea!
Dog skeleton: Woof!

So, the big skeleton, little skeleton and the dog skeleton went up the stairs out of the dark dark cellar.

I can act out a script.

How did you do?

Friendly or unfriendly?

■ Can you list some examples of being friendly and being unfriendly?

Friendly ☺	Unfriendly ☹

■ Can you think of an example of someone being friendly online?

_____

_____

■ Can you think of an example of someone being unfriendly online?

_____

_____

I can make a list of friendly or unfriendly actions.

How did you do?

PHOTOCOPIABLE

SCHOLASTIC
www.scholastic.co.uk

My skeleton avatar

My skeleton's first name is: _____

■ Draw your skeleton avatar in the box.

I can draw an avatar.

How did you do?

Skeleton questions

■ Write two questions for each skeleton.

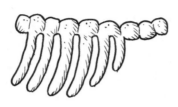  

Questions for big skeleton:

1. _____

_____

2. _____

_____

Questions for little skeleton:

1. _____

_____

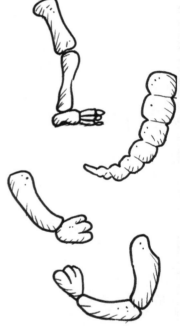

2. _____

_____

Questions for dog skeleton:

1. _____

_____

2. _____

_____

I can write interview questions.

Skeleton bones (1)

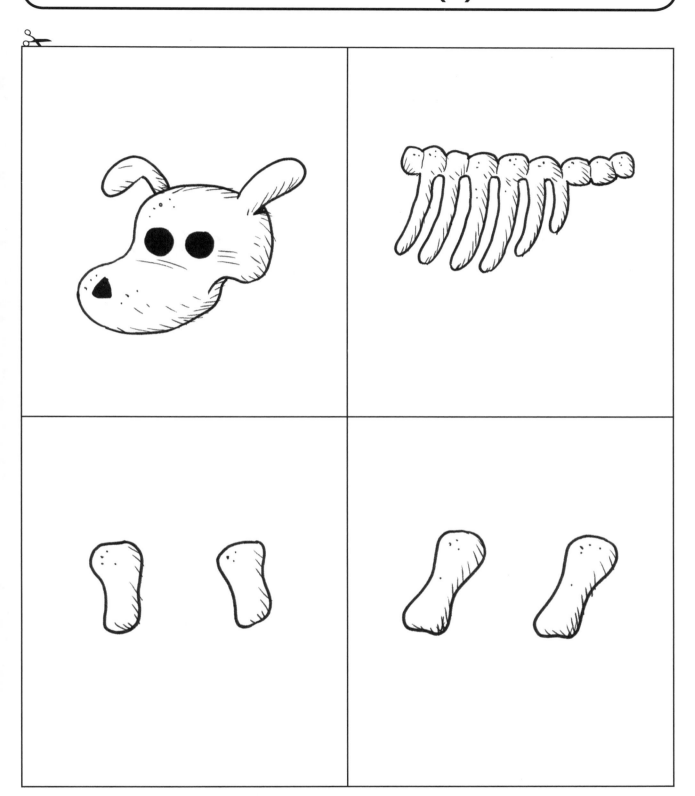

Name: _____   Date: _____

Skeleton bones (2)

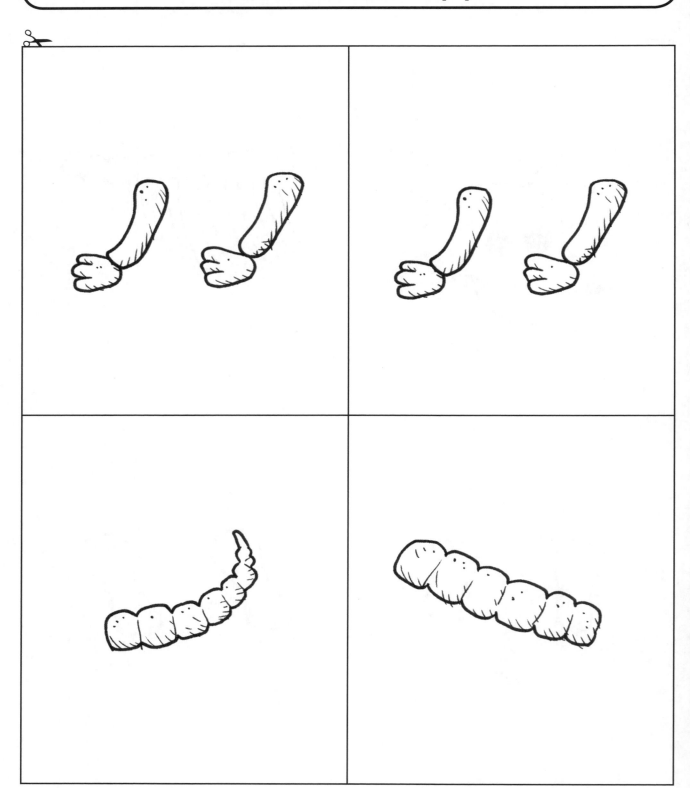

PHOTOCOPIABLE

Our senses

■ Draw your face on the body and add labels for your five senses.

I can recognise the five senses

How did you do?
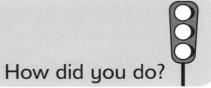

Habitats

This chapter builds on children's learning in Year 1, Autumn 1 in which a dinosaur theme was used to introduce the children to organising and sorting data. In this chapter they will re-familiarise themselves with organising and storing digital content, in the form of data. They are introduced to databases for the first time, as they find out how branching databases can be used to organise data. They collect their own data and display the results using charts to analyse their data in simple ways.

Expected prior learning

• The children will have experience of different types of animals and where they live. They will be able to understand that there are different types of insects and animals and that they live in different places. From work completed in previous chapters, they will also know and be able to name the different types of data and understand that data can be collected and displayed using tally sheets and charts.

Chapter at a glance

Subject area
• Data and information

National Curriculum objective
• To use technology purposefully to create and organise digital content.

Week	Lesson objectives	Summary of activities	Expected outcomes
1	• To identify the basic data types of image, video, audio and text. • To ask and answer simple questions about data in order to identify different minibeasts and their microhabitats. • To organise digital content in simple ways.	• Children are reminded of different basic data types. • They match minibeasts to their correct microhabitat.	• Can describe and use basic types of data. • Can use technology to organise digital content.
2	• To organise data into groups according to simple rules. • To sort the data according to specific attributes.	• Children identify similarities and differences between microhabitats. • They sort and categorise microhabitats in different ways.	• Can categorise data sets into groups. • Can sort data according to specified criteria.
3	• To know what a branching database is and how it can be used. • To understand that a branching database can be created from a series of 'yes' and 'no' questions. • To be able to search a branching database to identify specific items and attributes. • To modify and extend a branching database.	• Children are introduced to how a branching database works. • They complete a drag-and-drop whole-class activity. • In a paired activity they stick animals in the right place according to branching database. • They add to the branching database with another animal, or question and animal if able.	• Can categorise data sets into groups. • Can understand how a branching database works.
4	• To plan a simple branching database with accuracy. • To create a simple branching database. • To add additional questions and answers to a branching database. • To work with others to improve their work.	• Children create their own simple branching database by adding text, images and additional questions to a template. • They swap their database with others to check accuracy and suggest and make improvements.	• Can categorise data sets into groups. • Can create a simple branching database.
5	• To design a simple tally sheet for data collection. • To collect data from relevant people using a tally sheet. • To organise data in simple ways. • To draw simple initial conclusions from the data collected.	• Children design a tally sheet collectively to determine in which habitat they would like to live. • They collect data using their tally sheet. • They draw simple conclusions based on the data collected.	• Can collect data using a tally sheet. • Can organise collected data in an effective way.

Week	Lesson objectives	Summary of activities	Expected outcomes
6	• To understand that data can be displayed graphically and this can make data easier to interpret. • To know what a block graph is. • To display data they have collected using a simple block graph. • To draw conclusions from their data by analysing their block graph.	• Children create simple block graphs from collected data. • They analyse block graphs using a series of questions. • They discuss how using graphs can help to analyse data.	• Can create digital block graphs to display data in graphical ways. • Can analyse block graphs effectively.
Assess and review	• To assess the half-term's work.	• Children complete a 'rainforest branching database' activity in which text and images are dragged into the correct places, then answer questions about the completed database. • They create and analyse a 'minibeasts block graph'.	• Assess and review.

Overview of progression

● Throughout the lessons the children build upon their knowledge of sorting, collecting, manipulating, organising, displaying and analysing data. They begin by ordering the data in different ways before moving on to using branching databases to understand that data can be categorised into different groups. They then collect, display and analyse their own data, which develops their understanding of how data can be used.

● Organising the data using tally charts and block charts helps the children to understand that data can be represented in different ways and that charts can help them to see more clearly what the data is telling them. They will build on this knowledge and understanding in future years when they learn about how data is used by computers and humans.

Creative context

● The lessons have strong links to the mathematics curriculum with children collecting data using tally sheets, displaying data using block charts and analysing it in simple ways. The computing lessons should also enhance the children's learning in English as they build their literacy skills when reading and writing.

● This 'Habitats' topic has strong links to the science curriculum as children consolidate their knowledge of where animals live and the differences between habitats.

Background knowledge

● The children may have knowledge of habitats from work completed in science. However, even if they do not, they will be familiar with the concept of animals living in different places. From the work completed in previous chapters, they will know the difference between images, text, video and audio, although they are reminded of this key vocabulary in the first lesson.

● Collecting data using a tally chart and then representing their data in a block chart builds on the work completed in Year 1. However, you will need to assess the children's capability to understand the charts and may feel that using pictograms is more helpful for some children.

Curriculum objectives
● To use technology purposefully to create and organise digital content.

Lesson objectives
● To identify the basic data types of image, video, audio and text.
● To ask and answer simple questions about data in order to identify different minibeasts and their micro-habitats.
● To organise digital content in simple ways.

Expected outcomes
● Can describe basic types of data.
● Can use technology to organise digital content.

Resources
Interactive activity 'Which type of data?' on the CD-ROM; media resource 'Which microhabitat?' on the CD-ROM; interactive activity 'Which minibeast lives here? on the CD-ROM'; photocopiable page 177 'True or false cards'

Organising digital content

This introductory lesson reminds the children of how digital content, in data form, can be stored in different formats and organised in different ways. The children will initially be identifying different types of data before sorting minibeasts into their different microhabitats to set the scene for their learning in this chapter.

Introduction
● Show the children the interactive activity 'Which type of data?' on the CD-ROM.
● Ask the children to name the different types of data shown and encourage them to use the key vocabulary of 'image', 'text', 'audio' and 'video', which they are reminded of in this activity.

Whole-class work
● Explain that they are going to be using the topic of habitats for the work in this chapter and ensure that all the children understand that a habitat is a place where an animal or a plant lives.
● Explain that they are going to be starting with microhabitats, or a small area in which 'minibeasts', or invertebrates live.
● Display the media resource 'Which microhabitat?' on the CD-ROM on the whiteboard and work as a class to identify the microhabitat of each minibeast shown.

Paired/independent work
● Ask the children to access the interactive activity 'Which minibeast lives here?' on the CD-ROM and explain that they need to match the correct minibeast to the correct microhabitat in the first exercise.
● The second task of this activity asks the children to drag and drop the correct definition to the type of data displayed.

Differentiation
● Support: Mixed-ability pairings may be useful for the 'Which minibeast lives here?' activity and less confident learners may benefit from adult help in remembering the different types of data together with the different habitats.
● Challenge: More confident learners can use the internet to find images of minibeasts and their habitats.

Review
● Give the children photocopiable page 177 'True or false cards' and explain that they should show the card they think is correct as you make statements about the work they have been doing; for example: *A dragonfly lives under a log. An ant's microhabitat is usually under a stone. An image can be heard. Text usually has pictures on it.*
● Review the children's progress through their discussions and the outcomes of the 'Which minibeast lives here?' activity.

Lesson objectives
● To organise and categorise data into groups according to simple rules.
● To sort the data according to specific attributes.

Expected outcomes
● Can categorise data sets into groups.
● Can understand how a branching database works.

Resources
Interactive activity 'Which habitat?' on the CD-ROM; photocopiable page 178 'Habitat cards (1)'; photocopiable page 179 'Habitat cards (2)'; photocopiable page 180 'Sorting habitats'; media resource 'Which minibeast lives here?' on the CD-ROM (optional)

Sorting and categorising data and information

In this lesson, the children will be sorting and categorising data in different ways. First, they identify similarities and differences between microhabitats before looking at different habitats and sorting and categorising them in different ways. These activities will provide the basis for the next lesson, in which they will be introduced to branching databases.

Introduction
● Recap the last lesson with the children, discussing with them what they now know about minibeasts and their habitats. Ask questions to elicit responses around how microhabitats are similar and how they are different, which helps to introduce this lesson's focus. For example: *Is that microhabitat dry or damp? Is that minibeasts' microhabitat on land or in water?*
● You could display the results of the media resource 'Which minibeast lives here?' on the CD-ROM from the previous lesson to stimulate discussion if you wish.

Whole-class work
● Explain to the children that you are now going to look at habitats of larger animals too.
● Work through the interactive activity 'Which habitat?' on the CD-ROM on the board, identifying the habitats and which animals live in them.
● Encourage the children to think about the different ways the habitats are similar and different. For example: *Is this habitat warm or wet? What do you think the weather is like in this habitat?*

Group/paired work
● Explain to the children that they are going to be sorting habitats in different ways. Give each group a set of the eight cards from photocopiable pages 178 and 179 'Habitat cards (1) and (2)'. Ask them to sort the habitats in order of size, from the smallest to the largest habitat.
● Give the children photocopiable page 180 'Sorting habitats' and, using their habitat cards, they should sort their habitats into different groups; for example those that are warm/cold, wet/dry, underground/overground, and so on.

> **Differentiation**
> ● Support: Mixed-ability pairings or groupings may be useful for less confident learners, who may also benefit from support when sorting their habitats into different groups.
> ● Challenge: More confident learners could devise their own additional categories in which to sort their habitats and share these with their group, who can then sort their habitats accordingly.

Review
● As a class, discuss how the children sorted their habitats and what type of categorisation was most difficult or easiest. Discuss how they identified which habitat belonged in which group. Pose questions that will encourage the children to think about what this means. For example: *Are there more cold habitats than warm? Are most habitats dry or wet?*
● Review the children's progress through their discussions and outcomes of the 'habitat cards' activities and class discussion.

Curriculum objectives
● To use technology purposefully to create and organise digital content.

Lesson objectives
● To know what a branching database is and how it can be used.
● To understand that a branching database can be created from a series of 'yes' and 'no' questions.
● To be able to search a branching database to identify specific items and attributes.
● To modify and extend a branching database.

Expected outcomes
● Can categorise data sets into groups.
● Can understand how a branching database works.

Resources
Interactive activity 'Which animal am I?' on the CD-ROM; photocopiable page 181 'Animal branching database'; photocopiable page 182 'Animal branching database questions'

Searching a branching database

In this lesson, the children learn how to search and use a branching database in order to identify animals and their habitats. This introduces them to the idea of using a branching database and how 'yes' and 'no' questions can be used to sort and identify data. They will then be able to use their knowledge and understanding in future lessons when they create their own branching database.

Introduction
● Remind the children that in the last lesson they were sorting their habitats in different ways.
● Explain that in this lesson they are going to be learning another way of sorting habitats and introduce them to the term 'branching database'.

Whole-class work
● Work through the interactive activity 'Which animal am I?' on the CD-ROM together, highlighting that they need to find out which animal lives in which habitat. Emphasise the 'yes and no' questions and ensure they understand that the questions lead either to another question or to the answer.

Independent/paired work
● Explain that the children will now be using a branching database to find out which animals live in which habitats.
● Give out photocopiable page 181 'Animal branching database' and page 182 'Branching database questions'.
● Explain to the children that they should follow the branching database and then answer the questions. Work through the first one together as an example.

Differentiation
● Support: Less confident learners may need further adult support in searching the database, or mixed-ability pairings may be useful. They can be given one or two questions only on which to focus if needed. They may find it useful to use the 'habitat cards' from the previous lesson.
● Challenge: More confident learners could add to the branching database, adding another question(s) to distinguish further between habitats. For example, they could add the question *Are there lots of trees in this habitat?* to distinguish between woodland and farm, and add a suitable image of an animal they know that lives in woodland.

Review
● Use 'who am I' questions to assess their understanding of using the database. For example, *I live in a small, wet place; where do I live and who am I?* If you find many of the children are finding searching the database difficult, spend more time working through it together.
● The children's progress can be assessed through the outcomes of the animal branching database activity and class discussion.

Curriculum objectives
• To use technology purposefully to create and organise digital content.

Lesson objectives
• To plan a simple branching database with accuracy.
• To create a simple branching database.
• To add additional questions and answers to a branching database.
• To work with others to improve their work.

Expected outcomes
• Can categorise data sets into groups.
• Can create a simple branching database.

Resources
Interactive activity 'UK animal habitats branching database' from the CD-ROM; photocopiable page 183 'Branching database template'; photocopiable page 181 'Animal branching database (optional)

Creating a branching database

In this lesson, the children develop their understanding of branching databases further. They create their own simple branching database using a paper template, add to it if appropriate to their ability and understanding and work collaboratively to check and improve their work.

Introduction
• Remind the children that in the last lesson they looked at branching databases and how these worked by answering a series of questions to discover which animal lived in which habitat. You could show them photocopiable page 181 'Animal branching database' from the last lesson to prompt discussion, as a recapping tool, and to go over any misunderstandings from the last lesson.
• Explain that in this lesson they will be creating their own branching database using a template.

Whole-class work
• Show children the interactive activity 'UK animal habitats branching database' on the CD-ROM and go through the yes/no questions together methodically as a class.
• Explain that they will be undertaking a similar activity, looking at animals that live in the UK, but with different habitats and animals.

Group/paired work
• Give out photocopiable page 183 'Branching database template' and explain that the children need to follow the questions in the database and fill in the text and image gaps.
• Highlight the blank boxes on the photocopiable sheet and explain that this is where they can add their own question(s) to the branching database. They need to think of two other animals and a question that would distinguish these from each other.
• Whether or not you choose to use this last element of the activity will depend on how confident the children are with using and creating their branching database.

Differentiation
• Support: Less confident learners may need further support with following the template and putting the right animals in the right places.
• Challenge: More confident learners will be able to think of additional questions confidently and could create further elements to their branching database.

Review
• Ask the pairs or groups to swap databases with each other and check each other's databases to ensure they work and that the animals and questions are in the correct positions.
• Children should particularly check that they can follow the additional questions that have been added and share any changes to the other group's work they think should be made.
• As a class, you could use this as an opportunity to discuss the importance of checking for accuracy and that really you are 'debugging' each other's work, which they are familiar with from the algorithms and programming modules.

Curriculum objectives
● To use technology purposefully to create and organise digital content.

Lesson objectives
● To design a simple tally sheet for data collection.
● To collect data from relevant people using a tally sheet.
● To organise data in simple ways.
● To draw simple initial conclusions from the data collected.

Expected outcomes
● Can collect data using a tally sheet.
● Can organise collected data in an effective way.

Resources
Photocopiable page 'Habitat tally sheet template' from the CD-ROM

Collecting and organising data

In this lesson, the children collectively design a tally sheet to collect data on which habitat their classmates would like to live in. They then collect their data before drawing simple conclusions from them. The data will be manipulated and analysed further in the next lesson.

Introduction
● Explain to the children that they are now going to be finding out in which habitat they would like to live.
● You can make this fun and encourage discussion by asking them to share what they would have to wear to survive, where they would sleep, live, and so on.

Whole-class work
● Discuss with the children how they are going to find out in which habitat most of the class would like to live.
● If they do not suggest it themselves, explain that a tally sheet will allow them to put a mark next to each habitat and that these marks can then be counted and the most popular habitat found.
● Working on the board, ask the children to collectively design a tally sheet. Ask: *Where would the names of the habitats go? Where would you record the tallies? Where would you total them up?*
● Once you are happy with the tally sheet, the children should copy it on to a piece of paper, or you can give out the photocopiable page 'Habitat tally sheet template' from the CD-ROM in which they can fill in the habitats. This may be useful if you are short of time or for less confident learners.
● Ask children questions to probe their understanding, for example: *Who should we collect the data from if we are trying to find out in which habitat our class would like to live?*

Independent/paired work
● Make sure that the children are clear about how to record each tally and then ask them to ask each other and, if possible, children in other classes too.
● Once they have asked everyone, they should count up how many tallies they have and write these numbers down in the total column.
● They should then work out which are the top five habitats according to their data.
● You might wish to add some structure to this activity; for example, giving children the letter A and B. They pair up and share favourite habitats, then As only move round the room sequentially, or you may want to ask them to ask ten people only.

Differentiation
● Support: Less confident learners may benefit from mixed-ability pairings or further support in putting their tallies in the right place and writing the numbers down.
● Challenge: More confident learners could write a list of the habitats in order from most to least popular to determine their 'top five'.

Review
● As a class, discuss the results of the initial counting of the data. Ask: *Are they all the same? What could be a reason for differences in your totals?* (They asked different people, people may have given a different answer.)
● Explain that in the next lesson they will be entering their data into a table and using the table to create a graph to display the data they have collected so they can analyse it further.
● Monitor the children's progress during the tally collection activity and their ability to draw simple conclusions from the data during the class review.

Curriculum objectives
● To use technology purposefully to create and organise digital content.

Lesson objectives
● To understand that data can be displayed graphically and this can make data easier to interpret.
● To know what a block graph is.
● To display data they have collected using a simple block graph.
● To draw conclusions from their data by analysing their block graph.

Expected outcomes
● Can create digital block graphs to display data in graphical ways.
● Can analyse block graphs effectively.

Resources
Media resource 'Block graph' on the CD-ROM; interactive activity 'My block graph' on the CD-ROM; completed tally sheets from previous lesson; photocopiable page 'Analysing my block graph' from the CD-ROM

Displaying and analysing data

Following on from the last lesson, the children will now enter the data they have collected into a template and then create simple graphs to allow them to display the data and analyse it easily.

Introduction
● Explain to the children that today they are going to be using the data they collected in their tally sheets and displaying them using a block graph which will help them to see clearly which the most popular habitats are.
● Tell them that first of all you will show them what a block graph is so they can see for themselves how useful a block graph is when analysing data.

Whole-class work
● Display the media resource 'Block graph' on the CD-ROM and ask the children what they think it is representing (it shows favourite animals). Ask the children questions to analyse the data in simple ways. For example:
    ● *Which animal is the most popular?*
    ● *Which animal is the least popular?*
    ● *How many children said that a polar bear was their favourite animal?*
● Discuss why displaying the data in this way can make it easier to understand.

Independent/paired work
● Ask the children to access the interactive activity 'My block graph' on the CD-ROM and show them how they can enter the results from their tally collection sheet to generate the block graph.
● Give them photocopiable page 'Analysing my block graph' from the CD-ROM and ask them to answer the questions.

Differentiation
● Support: Less confident learners may benefit from mixed-ability pairings or further adult support in creating and analysing their block graph.
● Challenge: More confident learners will be able to analyse their graph with ease. They should be encouraged to think about why this might be a more/less effective way of analysing data than just counting the numbers. They can write this on the back of their photocopiable sheet.

Review
● As a class discuss which habitats were the most popular places in which to live. You could come up with a top five. Discuss how the block graphs helped to analyse the data by asking questions such as: *Was it easier to tell which habitats were most popular by looking at the block graph rather than just the numbers? Why was this?*
● Assess the children's progress by assessing their block graph and the answers to the 'Analysing my block graph' activity.
● You could print off the block graphs and use them as display material.

Curriculum objectives
● To use technology purposefully to create and organise digital content.

Lesson objectives
● To be able to search a branching database to identify specific items and attributes.
● To plan a branching database.
● To create a branching database.
● To analyse a block graph.

Expected outcomes
● Can categorise data sets into groups.
● Can use a branching database effectively.
● Can create an accurate branching database.
● Can analyse data in simple and useful ways.

Resources
Interactive activity 'Habitats and minibeasts' on the CD-ROM

Habitats: Assess and review

This lesson allows children to demonstrate the learning they have developed in this chapter. They are asked to complete two drag-and-drop activities to show their understanding of how to create a branching database and how to create a block graph and are asked a number of questions about each. You may wish to allocate the tasks to the children or ask them to complete both, depending on your assessment of their learning so far in this chapter.

Introduction
● Remind the children that throughout this chapter they have been learning about how data can be collected, sorted, organised, displayed and analysed.
● Explain that in this lesson they will be given two tasks – one focusing on branching databases and one on block graphs (or you may give them a choice or allocate tasks to them, or indeed give all your children the same task, according to your professional judgement).

Independent work
● The children should work through the task(s) on the interactive activity 'Habitats and minibeasts' on the CD-ROM as independently as possible.
● On screens 1 and 2: 'Rainforest branching database' children drag and drop the correct animals into the correct positions and then answer the question.
● On screens 3, 4 and 5: 'Minibeasts block graph' children follow the instructions to create a graph and then answer the questions about the graph.

Differentiation
● Support: You may wish to allocate specific tasks to children, particularly less confident learners, and learners may need more adult help to complete their task.
● Challenge: More confident learners should be able to complete both tasks to a high standard and with full independence.

Review
● Go through some of the completed tasks, correcting any misconceptions.
● Review the children's progress through the outcomes of their independent work and adjust learning in the next chapter as appropriate.

■SCHOLASTIC

True or false cards

True

False

Habitat cards (1)

Rainforest

Ocean

Woodland

Farm

Name: _____   Date: _____

Habitat cards (2)

Arctic tundra

Pond

Grassland

Desert

Sorting habitats

■ Using the habitat cards, sort your habitats into different groups.
■ Answer the questions below.

1. How many habitats are warm or hot?

_____

2. How many habitats have trees?

_____

3. Which habitats are wet?

_____

_____

4. Which habitats can be found in the UK?

_____

_____

5. Which habitats are open spaces?

_____

_____

6. Can you sort the habitats in other ways?

_____

_____

_____

I can sort habitats.

How did you do?

■SCHOLASTIC
www.scholastic.co.uk

Animal branching database

■ Use the branching database below to answer the questions you are given.

Do I live in a hot place?

NO → Do I live in a wet place?

    NO → I live on a farm

    YES → Do I live in a large, icy place?

        NO → I live in a pond

        YES → I live in the Arctic

YES → Do I live in a wet place?

    NO → Do I live in a sandy place?

        NO → I live in grassland

        YES → I live in the desert

    YES → I live in the Rainforest

I can use a branching database.

How did you do?

Animal branching database questions

■ Use your animal branching database to answer the questions below.

1. Which habitat is hot and wet?

_____

2. Who lives in the hot and wet habitat?

_____

3. Who lives in a dry, sandy place?

_____

4. Which habitat is cold, wet and icy?

_____

5. Who lives in the cold, wet and icy habitat?

_____

6. Who lives in the cold, dry habitat?

_____

I can use a branching database to answer questions.

How did you do?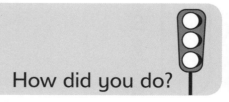

PHOTOCOPIABLE

Branching database template

■ Complete the branching database below by adding text and images in the boxes.

Do I live on a farm?

YES

Do I have horns

YES

NO

NO

Do I live in woodland?

YES

NO

YES

NO

YES

NO

I can use a branching database.

How did you do?

Pirates

Arrrrr! Yo-ho-ho! This chapter engages the children in a pirate theme to consider e-safety. They will consider their personal information and how they present themselves in person and when communicating through technology. The lessons build on the learning from the Year 1 'Sea and coast' and the Year 2 'Ourselves' topics, focusing on who they consider to be a friend and what pieces of treasured information should be shared. Work in this area reinforces the message that if they find content or have contact with someone that makes them concerned, then they know where to get help.

Expected prior learning

- The children will have learned about communication when face-to-face and online. They should know that they need to be kind when talking in person and that the same rules apply when online.
- They know about keeping personal information safe and being careful how they share information. Using the pirate theme, this is reinforced in the lessons.
- The children have been taught that if they find content or have contact with someone online that upsets them, they should tell someone trusted. This message is repeated in these lessons.

Chapter at a glance

Subject area
• E-safety

National Curriculum objective
• To use technology safely and respectfully, keeping personal information private; identify where to go for help and support when they have concerns about content or contact on the internet or other online technologies.

Week	Lesson objectives	Summary of activities	Expected outcomes
1	• To understand how to behave positively with others when face-to-face and online.	• Children are introduced to the pirate theme for the e-safety lessons, by sharing a range of pirate stories. • Children recall what they know about pirate stories. • They identify the common features of pirate characters. • Children consider how to be respectful towards other people's information.	• Can explain how to be respectful towards other people's information.
2	• To discuss methods of communication that are face-to-face. • To discuss methods of communication that are not face-to-face (for example, letters, postcards, email, a social network site). • To discuss friends they meet in-person and online.	• Children discuss how pirates talk. • They look at the differences between spoken and written language. • Children discuss methods of communication that are not face-to-face. • They create a pirate postcard to send to another pirate friend. • They consider electronic communication. • They discuss the friends the children might meet in person and online.	• Can verbally communicate information with another child.
3	• To understand how to behave positively with others when face-to-face and online.	• Children write a ship's log for an imaginary list of events. • They are introduced to blogging as a way of communicating digitally. • They role play adding comments as feedback to the blog posts, focusing on behaving positively with others.	• Can use technology to communicate basic information.

Week	Lesson objectives	Summary of activities	Expected outcomes
4	• To identify what to do when a friend upsets them – tell someone. • To discuss people who are not friends, who they might meet online. • To form the link that online friends should behave kindly and if they upset you, tell someone.	• Children listen to a simple version of *Treasure Island*. • Children identify what to do when a friend upsets them – tell someone. • They form the link that friends should behave kindly, whether face-to-face or online.	• Can explain where to go for help and support when they have concerns about content on digital devices.
5	• To know who to go to for help and support when they have concerns about content on the internet.	• Children are introduced to a 'Treasure maps' theme, and they think about the good and bad features of using the internet. • They identify a route to follow to find someone who can offer help and support.	• Can explain where to go for help and support when they have concerns about content on the internet.
6	• To begin to understand how to stay safe when online.	• Children watch a safety pirate story. • They identify the characters, setting and plot. • In groups, they act out the story, which has the main message of 'Who can you tell?'	• Can explain where to go for help and support when they have concerns about content or contact on the internet.
Assess and review	• Assess and review	• Children create a pirate character. • They use an interactive activity to dress up a character and complete a character profile. • Children consolidate their learning about being kind face-to-face and online. • They know 'who to tell' when having concerns about content or contact on the internet.	• Assess and review

Overview of progression
● Throughout this chapter, the learning is consolidated from Year 1 and from earlier in Year 2. The children progress their knowledge of other channels of communication online, for example Facebook and online games.
● They will learn more about online safety through other e-safety materials provided in schools from the 'Childnet' e-safety providers, so giving a joined-up message about being safe and also enjoying being online.

Creative context
● The lessons link to the English curriculum, considering the phonetic spelling of pirate talk and how it sounds. The children use adjectives to describe their pirates and also identify the common features of pirate stories.
● For maths, they use treasure maps, with numbered squares, reinforcing the sequence of numbers and counting. They use directional language to help find the treasure hiding in the school.
● Linking to geography, the pirate theme enables learning about maps and different parts of the world. For history, the children could investigate online to find out about real pirates and see whether these match their storybook impression.

Background knowledge
● In Year 2, the children are developing their understanding of the world around them and also the online world. They may not be using email or social media, but many children will be familiar with going online and searching the web. It is important, therefore, that they understand the benefits of going online and also how to stay safe.
● Using technology respectfully is important, because while the children can see and read body language when face-to-face, they cannot do so when communicating by text online. They need to know that the same rules apply to communicating online in a kind and friendly manner.
● Reinforcing the message from Year 1 and into Year 3, the children need to know who to go to for help and support, if they find content or have contact that makes them uncomfortable.

Curriculum objectives
● To use technology safely and respectfully, keeping personal information private; identify where to go for help and support when they have concerns about content or contact on the internet or other online technologies.

Lesson objectives
● To understand how to behave positively with others when face-to-face and online.

Expected outcomes
● Can explain how to be respectful towards other people's information.

Resources
Photocopiable page 193 'Information treasure'; pirate artefacts (optional)

Yo-ho-ho! Pirates!

This lesson introduces the pirates theme, which will help to teach the children about e-safety. They read pirate stories and share what they know about storybook pirates. This will help them to identify the common features of pirates and lead to thinking about being respectful of other people's information.

Introduction
● To set the scene, you could dress the classroom with pirate artefacts, for example eye patch, Jolly Roger flags, treasure. You could play an a clip from an appropriate pirate movie.
● Play the 'Pirate game': http://education.scholastic.co.uk/resources/4048

Whole-class work
● Explain to the children that they will be learning about pirates and about being safe when online.
● Ask the children to name famous pirate stories they have read. Examples could be *Captain Flynn and the Pirate Dinosaurs, The Night Pirates, The Pirate Crunchers* and *Pirate School*. Can they recall what happened in the stories?
● Choose one pirate story and read it with the class. Can the children remember the name of the pirate? What did the pirate look like? What did the pirate say? What did the pirate do?
● What were the common features of the pirate stories? List the features on a display board.

Group/paired work
● In pairs, give the children photocopiable page 193 'Information treasure'. Sharing one sheet, they add their personal information to the spaces in the coins such as name, age, date of birth, address, favourite band, favourite sports person. They then cut out the coins and the treasure box.
● Ask the children to imagine being online on the computer and sending messages to someone they have not met face-to-face.
● They should look at each of the coins and decide whether it is information they should treasure and keep private or whether they could share it.
● If they think the information should be treasured, place it on top of the treasure box picture; if it can be shared, they give it to their partner.

Whole-class work
● Ask the class to bring the coins that were shared. Which coins have been shared? Can the children explain why? From previous lessons, they should remember not to share their full name, address, or date of birth. They may be able to justify sharing information about hobbies or bands they like, but not, for example, *I like football and play at Langley Park on Saturday mornings.*
● After discussing the responses, remind the children that they must keep personal information private.

Differentiation
● Support: Less confident learners may need help remembering and writing their personal information, such as address and date of birth.
● Challenge: More confident learners could justify each piece of information to explain why it should be kept private or could be shared.

Review
● Conclude the lesson by thinking about being respectful. For example, if one of the children stated they liked the band One Direction, did other children who don't like the band laugh at them or tease them?
● Explain to the children that they need to respect others and their information, whether they are face-to-face or online. This prepares the children for teaching about cyberbullying in the following years' lessons.

■SCHOLASTIC

Curriculum objectives
● To use technology safely and respectfully, keeping personal information private; identify where to go for help and support when they have concerns about content or contact on the internet or other online technologies.

Lesson objectives
● To discuss methods of communication that are face-to-face.
● To discuss methods of communication that are not face-to-face (for example, letters, postcards, email, a social network site).
● To discuss friends they meet in-person and online.

Expected outcomes
● Can verbally communicate information with another child.

Resources
Photocopiable page 194 'Pirate postcard'; drywipe boards

Talking like a pirate

Some children may enjoy talking like pirates, so in this lesson they communicate with each other using accents. They compare the phonetic sounds and the written words. They then send pirate postcards, comparing face-to-face communication with communication over a distance. Finally, they consider friends they meet in-person and online.

Introduction
● Begin the lesson by welcoming the children by talking like a pirate. *Arrr-harrr, me hearties, today we are going to talk like pirates.*
● Explain that they must talk and write like pirates for the whole lesson!

Whole-class work
● Ask one of the children for an example sentence of a pirate speaking. Ask the children to write the words on drywipe boards. Can they spell out the words phonetically?
● Ask: *Do the words look different to the way they are spelt?* For example, *Me hearties* might be written *Mee hartees.*
● Explain that they can speak to communicate face-to-face (in pirate), but they could also write the message and pass it to each other. Imagine they are online on the computer and ask, *How could you send the message?* Examples could be email, a message board, a social network site.
● Tell the children that they are going to send a 'pirate postcard' to one of their friends.

Paired work
● Give each child a copy of photocopiable page 194 'Pirate postcard'. They complete the picture before attempting to write like a pirate in the message box.
● In the message box, ask the children to write a short description of their postcard's picture in pirate language.
● When complete, the children swap postcards with a partner, who then reads the message.

Differentiation
● Support: Less confident learners could draw the picture and complete one sentence in phonetic pirate language.
● Challenge: More confident learners could add more adjectives to describe their scene.

Review
● As a class, ask the children to read out their postcards, can they be understood without looking at the picture?
● Explain that today they have been communicating face-to-face. If a friend from the class moved to a different part of the world, they could communicate online, to continue their friendship. However, explain that they may make friends with people who they have not met in person. As always, remind the children to be friendly and kind, while being careful with their personal information.

Curriculum objectives
● To use technology safely and respectfully, keeping personal information private; identify where to go for help and support when they have concerns about content or contact on the internet or other online technologies.

Lesson objectives
● To understand how to behave positively with others when face-to-face and online.

Expected outcomes
● Can use technology to communicate basic information.

Resources
Photocopiable page 195 'Pirate names'; photocopiable page 196 'Captain's log'

Captain's log

In this lesson, the children choose pirate names and write about their life on board a ship. They write a ship's log for one day – the log has a beginning, middle and end. The log is compared with a digital log called a 'blog'. The children then make comments about each other's work. Are they being kind?

Introduction

● All pirates have exciting names. Start the lesson by asking the children to name pirates they know from stories. Can they invent a new name? For example, 'Long John Silver' could be changed to 'Wild Harry Gold'. Can they see a pattern? (Beginning with an adjective, then a more familiar name and ending with a colour.)
● Using photocopiable page 195 'Pirate names', let the children experiment with different pirate names and choose one. You could cut the names up beforehand and get children to pick names from a hat, or just allow children to see all of the names and choose themselves.

Whole-class work

● Explain to the children that they are going to pretend to be the pirate captain (using their new name). They will write the ship's log – recording the events on board, like a diary.
● Ask them to think of a typical pirate day. What would happen at the start of the day? What would happen in the middle and at the end?

Paired work

● Using photocopiable page 196 'Captain's log', ask the children to think about the start of the day and write a sentence to describe it. For example, *I woke up and there was my parrot on my bed. 'Get up, time for breakfast,' he said.*
● They now write a sentence for the middle of the day. For example, *We robbed a big ship, full of treasure.*
● Finally, they now write a sentence for the end of the day, for example, *I fell fast asleep, hugging all my treasure.*

> **Differentiation**
> ● Support: Less confident learners may need support with writing their sentences, adding punctuation and adjectives.
> ● Challenge: More confident learners could write more than one sentence for each part of the day. They could add more adjectives to give a better description of their day.

Whole-class work

● Ask the children to read their captain's logs. Do they record what happened during the day? Are they exciting? How could they improve their stories?
● The logs could be more detailed by adding more descriptions to the beginning, middle and end. Also, they could add more events in between.
● Explain that they have created a diary for one day, and that they could continue writing each day and that would be a record of life on board ship.
● Explain that there are digital logs too. A 'blog' is a digital way of recording what is happening and what the pirates may be thinking. Tell them that the word 'blog' is short for a 'web log'.

Review

● Conclude the lesson, by asking one child to read their captain's log. Ask another child to give a comment. Did they like it? What did they like?
● Once they have commented, ask, *Was the comment kind?*
● The technique of 'two stars and a wish' could be used, where children give two positive comments and a wish for how the other child could make their log better. This prepares the children for work in the following years about blogging, comments and being kind.

Curriculum objectives
● To use technology safely and respectfully, keeping personal information private; identify where to go for help and support when they have concerns about content or contact on the internet or other online technologies.

Lesson objectives
● To identify what to do when a friend upsets them – tell someone.
● To discuss people who are not friends, who they might meet online.
● To form the link that online friends should behave kindly and if they upset you, tell someone.

Expected outcomes
● Can explain where to go for help and support when they have concerns about content on digital devices.

Resources
Simple version of *Treasure Island*; photocopiable page 197 'The black spot'; large piece of paper

The black spot!

In the story of *Treasure Island*, the captain is given the black spot. This upsets him, as his crew no longer want him to be their leader. The children think about when their friends upset them. Who can they tell? This forms the link between friends they talk with in person and online. If someone upsets them online, they should tell someone trusted.

Introduction
● Start by reading a simple version of *Treasure Island*. In the story, Long John Silver was given *the black spot*; this means he has lost the support of his crew and they do not want him to be their captain.

Whole-class work
● Ask the children whether they have ever played a game with friends and one of them has said, *I don't want to play with you anymore!*
● Explain that they are going to act out a play. Select two children to pretend to be playing a game in the school yard. They are going to mime their actions and not speak. First, they have to pretend to fall out. Second, one shouts at the other and they begin to cry. Finally, the upset child goes to the teacher and explains what has happened.

Paired work
● In pairs, the children act out the play themselves. They could change the scenario, for example, playing a video game together, playing football or playing with a toy.
● Using photocopiable page 197 'The black spot', the children write down all of the words they might feel, for example, *sad, lonely, let down, hurt*.

> ### Differentiation
> ● Support: Less confident learners could write their words on the photocopiable sheet 'The black spot' and may need support to think of examples.
> ● Challenge: More confident learners could use a dictionary to check the spellings of the words they have used. They could organise the words alphabetically.

Review
● As a class, ask the children to gather together the words they have written about their feelings. On a large piece of paper, draw a black circle in the middle. Taking one word from each child (even if their word is repeated, add it to the paper) write the words in a spiral, going from the edge of the black spot outwards.
● Tell the children that their friends can make them feel very upset. Who can the children go to when they are upset? Reinforce that they can go to their teacher, parent or a trusted adult.
● Explain that they can become friends again.
● Finally, make the link to communicating online. Friends can make them upset by their words when online and so the same action should happen – tell someone!

Curriculum objectives
● To use technology safely and respectfully, keeping personal information private; identify where to go for help and support when they have concerns about content or contact on the internet or other online technologies.

Lesson objectives
● To know who to go to for help and support when they have concerns about content on the internet.

Expected outcomes
● Can explain where to go for help and support when they have concerns about content on the internet.

Resources
Photocopiable page 198 'Treasure map'; coins or shiny objects; dice; large piece of paper

Treasure map

The children search for pirate treasure in this lesson. Using an imaginary map, they play a game to navigate the good points and the bad points of searching online. They think about the issues that arise, reinforcing that they know who to go to for help, if they have concerns about what they find online.

Introduction
● Start the lesson with a 'Hunt the thimble' style game, by hiding plastic coins or other shiny objects around the classroom. The children search the room and collect the coins. Allow ten minutes for them to search, before bringing the class back together.
● Explain that there is another treasure hidden in the room and that there is a map to show where it is located.
● If possible, before the lesson, hide an object in the school field or playground. If this is not possible, hide it in the room.
● Draw a simple map on the board or a large sheet of paper to show that 'X marks the spot' of the treasure. Select a pair of children to search for it, while the others watch or help to guide.

Whole-class work
● Explain that the children are going to make their own treasure maps game. Display photocopiable page 198 'Treasure map'. Demonstrate how to play the game 'Good and bad online', that is, roll the dice and move along the numbered squares.

Paired work
● In pairs, the children use the photocopiable sheet 'Treasure map' to navigate the online 'high seas'. Let them play it at least twice, before pausing and asking them questions about the places that they visit in the game.

Differentiation
● Support: Less confident learners could play the game but may need adult or peer support to read the labels and prompting questions to understand whether it is a good or bad feature of the web.
● Challenge: More confident learners could read the labels for the good and bad points on the treasure map and invent new hazards and good points to add.

Review
● Bring the class together and select individual children to explain the good features of the web they encountered. Now, select other children to explain the bad features.
● Draw a simple map on the board or a large piece of paper. Ask them to imagine that this map helps them find help.
● Building on the previous learning, ask the children to state who should they go to, if they are worried by content they find on the web. They may suggest a teacher, parent, carer, head teacher or teaching assistant.
● Write the names of these trusted adults on the map (for example, *Teacher – Mrs White*) and draw lines to represent paths to each of the people's names.
● Re-ask the question, *Who should you go to if you are worried about something you find online?* Then follow the paths and say the names of the people.
● Finally, give a positive message to say that there is a treasure of new knowledge and learning to be found online. It is important to focus on the good points, yet leave children with a clear understanding of what to do if they encounter a bad point on the web.

Tell me a pirate story

The lesson focuses on retelling a story, by recording facts through note taking and then writing the story. The children watch a video from the 'Childnet' safety resources. This has a pirate theme and focuses on being safe online. The children collaborate to remember the main features, before watching it again to make notes. Using this information, they write the story. They then write their own story with a pirate theme.

Curriculum objectives
● To use technology safely and respectfully, keeping personal information private; identify where to go for help and support when they have concerns about content or contact on the internet or other online technologies.

Lesson objectives
● To begin to understand how to stay safe when online.

Expected outcomes
● Can explain where to go for help and support when they have concerns about content or contact on the internet.

Resources
Simple version of *Treasure Island*; photocopiable page 199 'My pirate story'; drywipe boards

Introduction
● Start the lesson by re-reading the simple version of *Treasure Island*. Ask: *How many facts about the story can you remember? Who are the main characters? Where is it set? What happens in the story's plot?*
● Explain that if they make notes, they may be able to remember more. Also, if they were to work together as a class, then maybe even more facts would be collected.

Whole-class work
● Explain that they are going to watch a short video. The resource is part of the 'Childnet' series of lessons on safety and features a pirate girl called Kara. In the video, she encounters people not being kind online.
● Watch the video with the class (www.childnet.com/resources/the-adventures-of-kara-winston-and-the-smart-crew/chapter4)
● Can they name the main characters, the setting and the plot?
● Using drywipe boards or paper, ask the children to write one note about the story that no one has mentioned already. Replay the video to allow them to see it and make their note.
● Select children to share their notes and record them on the board. Can they see they are gathering more information?

Pair work
● In pairs, ask the children to think of a new story featuring the characters from the video. In their story, someone should share a picture of them that they would not want to be placed online.
● Once they have practised acting their story, they can use photocopiable page 199 'My pirate story' to write their own story.

> ### Differentiation
> ● Support: Less confident learners can include a simple beginning, middle and end.
> ● Challenge: More confident learners can extend their stories, using speech marks and punctuation.

Review
● As a class, select pairs to act out their story and then read their version of it.
● Ask another child to remember a fact about the story that has been performed. Then ask another child to give another fact.
● Finally, conclude the lesson by reminding the children that in the video and in their stories, they have always been told that, if someone upsets them online or if they find material that concerns them, they should tell someone. Also, they should be able to name the trusted person that they would tell.

Curriculum objectives
● To begin to understand how to stay safe when online.

Lesson objectives
● To begin to understand how to stay safe when online.

Expected outcomes
● Can explain where to go for help and support when they have concerns about content or contact on the internet.

Resources
Interactive activity 'Pirate dress up' on the CD-ROM; photocopiable page 'The pirate king' from the CD-ROM; photocopiable page 'Pirate king questions' from the CD-ROM

Pirates: Assess and review

The lesson reviews the learning from previous lessons about online profiles and sharing information. The children think about a 'pirate king' character and which pieces of information they could share. They remember, if someone or something online upsets them, they should tell someone they trust.

Introduction
● Start the lesson by dressing up a child in pirate clothes similar to the stories that have been read. Explain that this is the pirate king.
● The children could ask the dressed-up child questions that they answer in the style of the pirate. For example: *How old are you? Where do you sail? What is the name of your ship?*
● Demonstrate the interactive activity 'Pirate dress up' on the CD-ROM.

Paired work
● In pairs, the children use the interactive activity to choose clothes for the pirate to wear. Can they give the pirate a name and personal details?
● Using photocopiable page 'The pirate king' from the CD-ROM, they complete the character profile for their pirate.

Whole-class work
● Bring the class together and ask three children to share the details about their pirate king.
● Explain that the pirate king is very moody and sometimes can be nice and sometimes can be nasty.
● On photocopiable page 'Pirate king questions' from the CD-ROM, the pirate king has a friendly face for his avatar. Ask the children, *Do you think he is kind and friendly?* Highlight to the children that just because someone's avatar is friendly, does not mean they are actually kind or friendly. They may use a friendly picture to trick children into thinking they are nice.

Paired work
● In pairs, the children use photocopiable page 'Pirate king questions' to act out the roles of the pirate king and themselves online. One child pretends to be the pirate king and asks the questions, the other child considers which pieces of information to share. For example, they should guard information about their full name, photos, postal or email addresses, school information, mobile or home telephone numbers and details of places they like to go.
● When listening to the conversations between the children, ensure that they are considering which information to share. They need to be careful, but there will be some information that they can share. For example, if asked *Do you play football?* it is OK to say 'yes', but they should not then say *I play football after school on Thursday at the Queen Street Park.*

> ### Differentiation
> ● Support: Less confident learners may need support in reading the questions and considering which pieces of information to share.
> ● Challenge: More confident learners could create further questions for the pirate king to ask about personal information.

Review
● Choose a child to play being the pirate king and another child themselves.
● Up to this point the pirate king has been nice, having a conversation and asking questions. For the final question, the pirate king turns nasty and demands that they answer the question.
● What should the child do? The children should be able to say that they would tell someone and then name a trusted adult, to whom they would go.

Information treasure

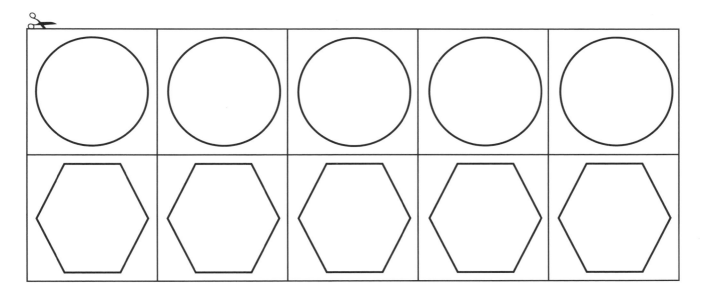

Name: _____   Date: _____

Pirate postcard

■ Draw and write your pirate postcard.

_____

_____

_____

_____

_____

_____

_____

I can write a pirate postcard.

How did you do?

PHOTOCOPIABLE

SCHOLASTIC
www.scholastic.co.uk

Pirate names

■ Make your own pirate name. Choose one of the first names and one of the last names and put your own name in the middle.

First names:

✂

Clever	Lucky	Speedy	Captain	Strong
Happy	Funny	Scary	Deadly	Sleepy

Last names:

✂

Bronze	Gold	Black	Silver	Redbeard
Seagull	Sparrow	Swan	Blackbeard	Hook

My pirate name is: _____

I can choose my own pirate name.

How did you do?

Captain's log

■ Write your own captain's log.

_____

_____

_____

_____

_____

_____

_____

_____

_____

_____

_____

_____

_____

_____

_____

I can write a captain's log.

How did you do?

PHOTOCOPIABLE

■SCHOLASTIC
www.scholastic.co.uk

The black spot

■ Write words in the boxes. The words should describe how you might feel if someone was unkind to you.

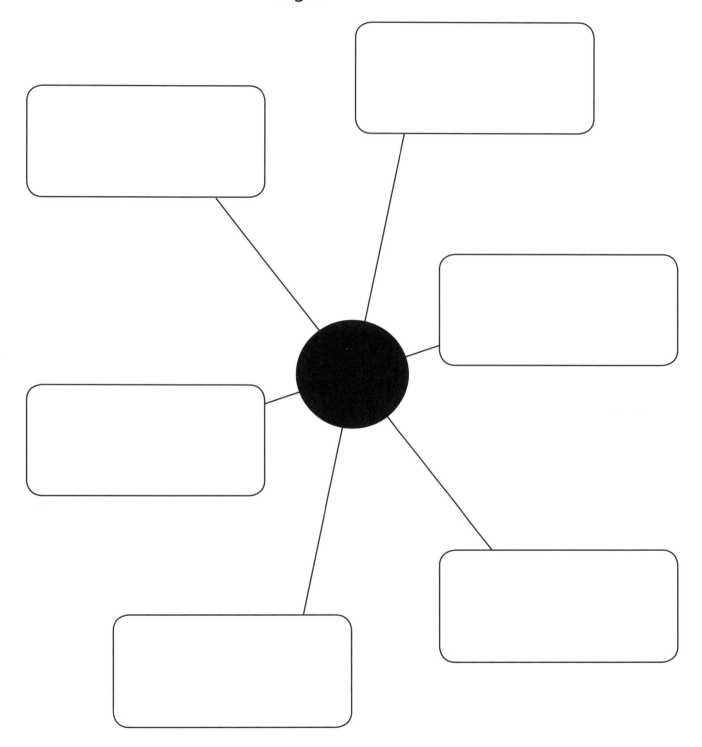

I can write words to describe how I feel.

How did you do?

PHOTOCOPIABLE

Treasure map

■ Play the game 'Good and bad online'.

Use a dice to play the game. If you land on something good about being online, move forward two squares. If you land on something bad about being online, move back one square.

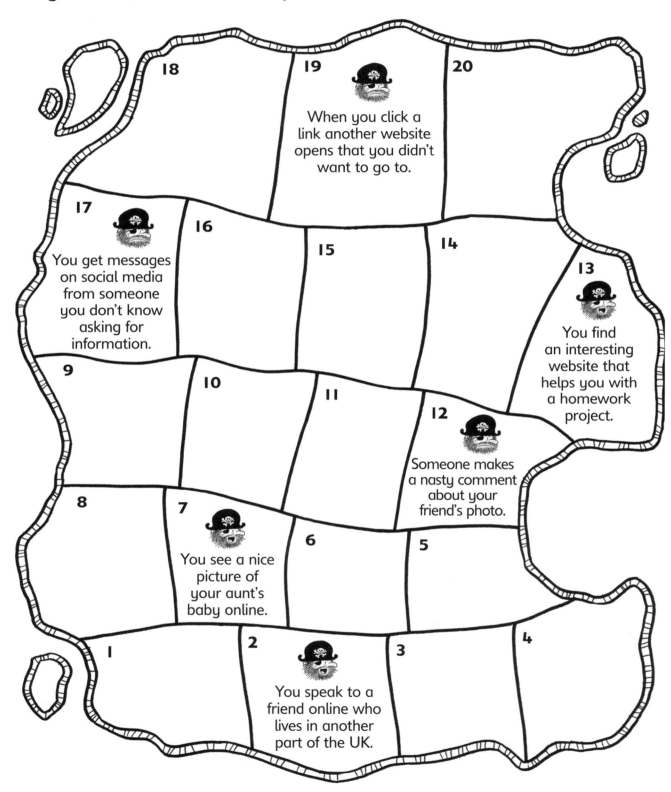

PHOTOCOPIABLE

My pirate story

■ Write your pirate story below.

Notes:

```



```

Beginning:

```



```

Middle:

```



```

End:

```



```

■ If you feel upset, who should you tell?

I can write a pirate story.

How did you do?

Year 1 Autumn 1: Dinosaurs

Overview

● In the lessons, the children have been introduced to different dinosaurs, through images and text. They have identified the types of data presented and explored using it. When using a tablet computer, it is possible for the children to collect their own images and add text. They could even add audio to their pictures or pretend to make the sounds of the dinosaurs.

Resources

● A picture collage app, such as 'PicCollage' on the iPad (free)

Lesson activities

● Using a picture collage app, the children place images together on one screen. Before they begin making their collage, they may need to collect images to use.

● Using 'Safe Search', they could search for dinosaur images. You may prompt the children by displaying the names of dinosaurs for them to copy into the search window.

● Once selected, the children need to save the images on to the tablet, then add them to the collage.

● The children can resize and rearrange the images and then add text to name the images and add facts.

● The objective of the lesson is to recognise the different types of data, so this should be reinforced throughout.

Saving images on the iPad

1. Use 'Safe Search' (http://primaryschoolict.com/), to locate images of dinosaurs.

2. Once the desired image is onscreen, carefully press and hold on the image.

3. After a short delay, the option box appears, with options to 'Save image' or 'Copy'.

4. Select 'Save image' and the image will be found in the camera roll of the 'Photos' app.

Using 'PicCollage' on the iPad

1. Open the app and tap the screen to create a new collage.

2. Tap anywhere to add a photo. From the menu, select 'Add photos' and then 'Camera roll'.

3. Select the photos to add, then press the tick button.

4. Drag and arrange the images, using two fingers to shrink, stretch and rotate them.

5. Select the '+' button at the bottom of the screen to add more photos or text, to label the dinosaur and to add facts.

Year 1 Autumn 2: Traditional stories

Overview

● The children have been learning to sequence events into the correct order. They have been playing games, such as, 'Simon says', and thinking about everyday tasks that involve instructions. For example, getting dressed in the morning follows a sequence. Can they identify the steps in the sequence and write precise instructions for another child to follow?

Resources

● A presentation app, such as, 'Keynote' on the iPad (free with new iPads)

Lesson activities

● The children consider getting dressed to go outside on a snowy morning. They need to think about which clothes to wear. Using the camera on the tablet, they work in pairs or small groups to take photos of different winter clothes. Can they identify the correct order for putting them on? For example, socks must go on before wellies, gloves must go on after wellies and after coat. The images can be added to a presentation app, such as, 'Keynote' on the iPad. The children then drag the images into the correct order. View all the presentations as a class.

Using the 'Keynote' app on the iPad

1. Open the 'Keynote' app.

2. Select the 'Create presentation' slide.

3. Choose a simple style (black, white or gradient).

4. Double tap on the main title and add the children's names.

5. Select the '+' on the bottom left-hand side to add a slide.

6. Choose the style of one large image on a slide.

7. Once added, select the '+' on the bottom right-hand side of the slide.

8. Select the image of getting dressed from the camera roll, to replace the image.

9. To rearrange the slides, drag a thumbnail of a slide (the small picture on the left) to the correct position in the sequence.

10. On completion, view presentation, by selecting the arrow (top right-hand side).

Year 1 Spring 1: Computers in everyday life (1)

Overview

- The children have been learning about the computer and its component parts. They have been finding out about the functions of the different parts and recognising that not all computers look the same. They will have seen desktop computers, which can have a separate screen, keyboard and mouse, but they will also know that laptops have a built-in screen and integrated keyboard and touchpad. Now, when considering the tablet computer, they need to be able to recognise the parts, even though they are even more integrated.

Resources

- Emoji or emoticons, a built-in feature of most tablets

Lesson activities

- The children use the camera to collect images of computers in the school and their parts, keyboard, mouse and screen.
- Ask the children about inputs and outputs.
  - *How do you input words into a desktop computer?* (Using a separate keyboard)
  - *How do you input words into tablet computer?* (Using an onscreen keyboard)
  - *How do you input instructions by controlling what happens on the screen?* (Using a mouse on the desktop computer; using a finger on a touchscreen on the tablet)
  - *How does the computer output information?* (On the screen on the desktop computer; also on the screen on the tablet, yet this is also an input device)
- To practise writing on the tablet, the children can write an 'emoji' story. Emoji, or emoticons, are emotional icons, such as smiley faces, used in messages. The children can write a short story about their holidays, replacing words with emoji symbols.

Using Emoji symbols on the iPad

1. On the iPad, select the 'Settings' icon.

2. Tap 'Settings', then 'General', then 'Keyboard'. Tap 'Keyboards'.

3. Tap 'Add New Keyboard'. Locate and tap 'Emoji'.

4. Using 'Notes' or another word processing app, touch the screen to bring up the keyboard.

5. Select the globe icon to start the emoji keyboard.

Year 1 Spring 1: Computers in everyday life (2)

Overview

- The children have been recognising where computers are used around the school. Using the mobile tablet devices, they can collect photographs of these computers to share with the class. They then identify the functions of the computers, for example, a computer in the school photocopier controls the copying and printing.

Resources

- 'TinyTap' app (free)

Lesson activities

- The children use the tablet devices to collect photographs of the computers in school. They may work in a small group of four, taking turns to take the photographs. Once collected, they can discuss what each computer does. This could be displayed for the class to see and the children can explain their thinking.
- Alternatively, an app could be used to match the function of the computer to the picture. The 'TinyTap' app on the iPad enables pictures to be added and then matched with text, audio or images.

Using the 'TinyTap' app on the iPad

1. Open the 'TinyTap' app. Select 'Create +'.

2. Select 'Import image' then 'Albums'.

3. Select all of the images required (no more than two per page).

4. Select 'Add activity' then 'Create a sound board'.

5. The children draw around a part of the picture corresponding to the computer and record their voices, explaining what it is and where it is found in the school.

6. You could create other activities, such as 'Ask a question', 'Cut a shape puzzle' and 'Say something'.

Year 1 Spring 2: Plants and animals

Overview

● The children have been learning about instructions and sequencing, preparing for their programming lessons in Year 2. To reinforce the learning, there are many apps that allow selection and sequencing. For example, on the iPad, the 'Sorting Machine' app gives a number of scenarios, where the children sort the objects in different ways – smallest to tallest, highest to lowest and so on.

Resources

● 'Sorting Machine' app on the iPad (free, with in-app purchases for higher levels)

Lesson activities

● Ask three children to stand at the front of the class. Can they sort themselves from the tallest to the smallest, then the smallest to the tallest? Allow them the opportunity to try to sort themselves without help from the class. Now choose four children and ask one of them to be the 'sorter'.

The sorter organises the other three children into height order. Ask: *Was this quicker? Why would it be different?* Explain that, when working as a group, sometimes it is good to organise themselves and sometimes it is good to have a leader.

● Explain that they are going to be sorting using a simple app. On the iPad, the 'Sorting Machine' app is a good example.

Using the 'Sorting machine' app on the iPad

1. Open the 'Sorting Machine' app.

2. Select 'Start' and level '1'.

3. The task is explained on the screen, for example lowest to highest character.

4. Drag the objects into the correct order.

5. Select the blue circular button with the tick to continue to the next activity.

Year 1 Summer 1: *Handa's Surprise* (1)

Overview

● In the *Handa's Surprise* lessons, the children experience capturing still images, voice recordings and video. The tablet can carry out these tasks and as it is mobile and integrated, images and audio can be combined easily.

● Using the tablet's camera, the children take photos of themselves, acting out the story. Once captured, the images can be manipulated. On the iPad, the 'Photos' app allows the images to be rotated and cropped, which helps to improve the presentation.

Resources

● Camera and 'Photos' app (part of the iPad tools), 'AirDrop' (part of the iPad tools)

Lesson activities

● In Lesson 2, the children act out the *Handa's Surprise* story and use a camera to capture the scenes. By using the tablet's camera, they can take images of themselves setting off on their journey and meeting the monkey. Then using the 'Crop' tool, they could ensure that characters are in the scene and remove unwanted space.

● In Lessons 3 and 4, the children record audio to capture the sounds of the animals, play instruments and also narrate the story. They can carry this out using the video-recording feature of the camera. The camera could be facing an image from the story while recording. The aim is to focus on the audio during these lessons. However, in Lesson 5, videoing the story is the main focus. The children can re-enact the story and capture it using the video tool.

● In the concluding lesson, the class comes together to tell the whole story. With the iPad, the children can combine their stories using 'AirDrop'. You could play the videos one after the other.

Using the 'Photos' app on the iPad

1. Once an image has been captured, select the 'Photos' app (usually found on the Home screen).

2. Select the image, so that it fills the screen.

3. Select 'Edit' (top right-hand corner of the screen).

4. From the bottom of the screen, the 'Crop' tool can be selected.

5. Drag the corners of the image to focus in on the subject.

6. When ready, select 'Crop' (top right-hand side). A new image is saved.

Sharing videos between iPads

1. Switch on the 'AirDrop' feature (drag a finger up, from the bottom of the screen, select 'AirDrop' then 'Everyone').

2. Open the 'Photos' app and select the image or video.

3. Select the share icon (bottom left-hand side – the icon is a rectangle, with an arrow pointing upwards).

4. All iPads that are available will appear in the list. Select the teacher's iPad and the image or video will be sent.

5. On the teacher's iPad, accept the incoming image or video and it will be saved in the camera roll in 'Photos'.

Year 1 Summer 1: *Handa's Surprise* (2)

Overview

● The concluding lesson in the *Handa's Surprise* chapter involves combining the children's videos to create the retelling of the whole story. As seen in the earlier lesson advice, you can simply view the videos one after the other. However, using a movie editor, they can be combined into one video.

● A movie editor is a tool for combining still images, videos, music and narration. In this lesson, it allows the combined video clips to be placed into one video and narration of the story added, with background music – giving a more complete feel to the movie.

Resources

● 'iMovie' app (free with new iPads)

Lesson activities

● In the lesson, the children role-played the story in sections and then combined the clips to create the whole story. Using a tablet and video app, such as 'iMovie', the clips can be added in order.

● The children act out their scenes consecutively and then you can use your tablet to record the action. Afterwards, display the video on the large screen and ask the children to play percussion instruments to respond to the action.

● Finally, add the narration as a separate track. This allows practice and rehearsal for the narrators, with the ability to re-record smaller sections to improve the quality.

Using the 'iMovie' app on the iPad

1. Combine the videos from the class iPads on to the teacher's iPad (using 'AirDrop').

2. Open the 'iMovie' app, from 'Projects' select the '+' at the top right-hand side.

3. Select 'Movie' on the 'New Project' screen, then select 'Simple' and 'Create Movie'.

4. Touch the first movie clip to add in the 'Video browser' on the top right-hand side.

5. Select the downwards arrow to insert the movie clip into the main movie.

6. Repeat for each movie clip in order.

7. Rewind the main movie to the beginning, by swiping it to the right.

8. Select the microphone symbol (on the bottom right-hand side) to add narration.

9. If necessary, remove the background audio on the video clip (tap the movie in the timeline, select 'Audio' and slide the volume to zero).

Year 1 Summer 2: Sea and coast

Overview

● The children have been using analogies about being good friends when online and when face-to-face. In the English lessons, the children will be writing stories and illustrating them with drawings. Using a tablet computer enables them to add photographs they take themselves or images collected from the internet. Also, they can add videos and audio, enhancing the experience further.

Resources

● 'Book Creator' app (free – only one book)

Lesson activities

● Using a book creation app on the tablet, such as 'Book Creator' on the iPad, the children draft out their story. For example, they could put a simple text note on each page to say what they plan to do. This plan could be created on paper first. For children who find writing or typing difficult, they could record their voices on each page, explaining what they plan to do.

● Next, they begin to add text, pictures and background sounds, such as seagulls and waves crashing on the shore. An easy starting story would be to retell part of *The Lighthouse Keeper's Lunch*. Then they create their own version, by changing the menu to contain their favourite food.

Using the 'Book Creator' app on the iPad

1. Once the children have read the story, open the 'Book Creator' app.

2. Add a new book by clicking '+' then 'New book'.

3. Select 'Portrait'.

4. Using the book, show them the front cover – it has a title, author name and a picture.

5. Ask the children to add a title and their name to the front cover, by selecting '+' then 'Add text'.

6. Once added, the text can be modified by selecting the text (surrounded by a blue rectangle), then the 'i' on the top right-hand side.

7. Images can be added in a similar way. Select '+' then 'Photos' and 'Camera roll'.

Saving images from websites

8. Once an image has been found, press and hold the finger on the image.

9. After a short delay, a new menu will say 'Save image' or 'Copy'.

10. Select 'Save image' and it will go into the camera roll.

11. From the camera roll, the image can imported into 'Book Creator'.

Year 2 Autumn I: *Oliver's Vegetables* (I)

Overview

● The children have been introduced to simple flowcharts to represent a sequence of instructions. They will recognise the simple flowchart shapes, an extended oval for start and stop, a rhombus (or they may say diamond shape) for a decision and a rectangle for a process or 'doing something'. By using simple examples, such as getting dressed, they can see how the instructions can be represented in the flowchart form.

● Many presentation tools on tablet computers have the ability to add the flowchart shape and add text to these. The children can draft their instructions and then see if they can create their flowcharts.

Resources

● A presentation app, such as 'Keynote' on the iPad (free with new iPads)

Lesson activities

● Ask the children about cleaning their teeth. What is the first step? Using a new, clean toothbrush and toothpaste, ask one of the children to pretend to brush their teeth. Did they guess the first step correctly? Continue by identifying each step and writing it on a display, so they can all see it. Once finished, remind the children about using flowcharts.

● Draw a start shape on the board, then write the first step in words. Which shape should they place around it? A rectangle is a process, such as 'Put toothpaste on the brush'. If it is a decision such as, 'Is there toothpaste on the brush – yes or no?' then use the diamond or rhombus shape. Model the process for the children and then demonstrate how to use the app to add shapes and text.

Using the 'Keynote' app on the iPad

1. Open the 'Keynote' app.

2. Select 'Create presentation'.

3. Choose the white theme.

4. On the new slide, add the title 'Brushing my teeth'.

5. Add a blank slide by selecting '+' on the bottom left-hand side.

6. From the icons on the top right-hand side, select '+' and a menu will appear. There are five boxes along the top of the menu.

7. Select the square (far right-hand icon). This is the shapes menu and the different flowchart shapes can be tapped to add them to the slide.

8. Once a shape is on the slide, double tap to add text.

9. From the same menu, you can add lines to join the shapes together.

Year 2 Autumn I: *Oliver's Vegetables* (2)

Overview

● The children are learning about sequences, algorithms and programming, using the *Oliver's Vegetables* theme. Patterns are a key concept here. Using the camera on a tablet, they can collect images of patterns around the classroom, the school buildings, school vegetable patch, the playground or field, and maybe visit the local area. They can then create a book to organise the images.

Resources

● 'Book Creator' app (free – only one book)

Lesson activities

● Allow the children time to explore different areas and capture images of patterns. Once these images have been collected (such as brick work, carpets, wooden floors) the children can combine them into a book. Using the 'Book Creator' app on the iPad, the images can be added, one image per page. The children can then use the pen tool to annotate the pictures, showing where the patterns repeat and also add audio clips to explain why they like the pattern.

Using the 'Book Creator' app on the iPad

1. The images can either be collected prior to using the app or can be added directly into the book.

2. To add an image, select the '+' then 'Photos'.

3. Select 'Camera roll' and choose an image.

4. Alternatively, the children can select '+' then 'Camera' and an image can be added directly onto the page.

5. To annotate, select '+' then 'Pen', in order to draw on the image.

6. The children could add sound to the page too, to explain why they like or dislike the pattern. Select '+' then 'Add sound'. Press 'Start recording' and speak clearly.

7. Press the stop button and it asks if you would like to use this recording. Select 'Yes'.

Year 2 Autumn 2: Fairy tales (1)

Overview

● As the children develop their skills in using algorithms and precise instructions, there are many game apps that are useful for exemplifying sequences. For example, in 'Angry Birds', the children have to identify the properties of the birds, decide upon a plan to complete the challenge and then execute it accurately.

● Other apps allow onscreen objects to be controlled using simple instructions. For example, on the iPad the 'Bee-Bot' app simulation using the Bee-Bot programmable toy. So, the children can experience using the real toy and the simulated world. There are two 'Bee-Bot' apps, the first is free and the second, 'Bee-Bot Pyramid', has a small cost, though it has more developed programming tasks.

Resources

● 'Bee-Bot' app (free)

Lesson activities

● If you have the Bee-Bot floor robot, the children can complete many challenges. They can create a maze using blocks or books as obstacles, then program the Bee-Bot to move through them.

Using a stopwatch, they could time how long each child or small group takes to get through the challenges. To complement this, they could design a scoring system, for example, the fastest team gets 10 points, second fastest 9 points.

● Moving onto the tablet, the children could play an onscreen maze game, such as the 'Bee-Bot' app on the iPad. Ask them what the differences are between using the real Bee-Bot and using the onscreen one.

Using the 'Bee-Bot' app on the iPad

1. Open the app and select 'Back' to exit the advert for the 'Pyramid' game.

2. Select 'Play' and game '1'.

3. The instructions explain 'Get Bee-Bot to the flower'. Press 'Start'.

4. Using the direct arrows, press the forward button once, then 'Go'.

5. If the time is in the top three fastest for completing the game, then add your name.

6. Select 'Menu' to select the next game.

7. The game builds in complexity as the games progress, up to game 36.

Year 2 Autumn 2: Fairy tales (2)

Overview

● There are other apps that can progress the children's skills and understanding of programming. These apps are being targeted as programming apps for children, for example, 'Kodable' on the iPad, uses a progression of learning by introducing new commands, variables and repeats, as the children complete each level.

Resources

● 'Kodable' app (free)

Lesson activities

● Using a programming game app, such as 'Kodable' on the iPad, the children can complete each level to get the furry character from the left side of the screen to the right. It is very similar to using the direction commands in the 'Bee-Bot' app, though it introduces new concepts, such as repeats. The children could work individually or in pairs to attempt each level. At the end of the lesson, invite children to explain to the class their thinking and strategy when completing levels.

Using the 'Kodable' app on the iPad

1. Open the 'Kodable' app and watch the introductory movie.

2. Select 'I'm a kid', then 'Play' and then level '1'.

3. The first level begins with '1, 2, 3 Roll!' and select game 1.

4. The tutorial guides the children through the task of dragging the arrows across into the program boxes and then playing the game.

5. The player moves on to the next level and the programs slowly become more complex.

Year 2 Spring 1: Zoos

Overview
● In this chapter, the children are learning about zoos and how computers work. They will have recalled visiting zoos and seeing the animals and also some of the features of the layout of the zoos. The focus of this learning is to think about where computers are used in the local environment, so they will have identified computers being used in the shopping tills in the zoo cafe, ticket office and gift shop. In this lesson, the children will consider how computers can be used for monitoring the animals.

Resources
● 'Switch Zoo' app (free)

Lesson activities
● The children are going to create a new species of animal for the zoo. On the tablet computers, there are apps that enable the creatures to be mixed up, such as 'Switch Zoo' on the iPad. If an app is not available, they could draw their animal and photograph it.
● Once the new animal has been created, ask the children to think about its habitat. Does it like water? Does it need to be warm? Does is like bright lights?

Once they have decided on the new animal's favourite conditions, they can consider how that could be monitored by a computer. For example, if it likes a warm room, then they need a temperature sensor to measure how warm the room is. If it likes water, they might need a water height sensor to make sure a bowl is filled with new water each day. Explain that computers can measure these conditions all day long and not get bored or need a break for food or sleep, like humans would do.

Using the 'Switch Zoo' app on the iPad
1. Open the 'Switch Zoo' app.
2. The children select the head, legs and body for their animal.
3. The app mixes the bodies and blends them together.
4. Allow children time to experiment and then think of a name for their new creation.
5. Now in pairs, ask them to describe to their partner, what type of habitat the new creature would need. For example, hot, cold, wet, dry, smooth ground or rocky.

Year 2 Spring 2: Ourselves

Overview
● Using the *Funnybones* story, the children have been thinking about communication and being kind when face-to-face and online. There are many animated avatar apps that can be used to bring a photograph or drawing to life. The children then have the opportunity to 'put words into their mouths'. Are they going to be kind?

Resources
● 'Morfo' app (free – can create, but not save videos)

Lesson activities
● Using an avatar creation app, such as 'Morfo' on the iPad, the children can animate a face. The first step is to find a picture to use. They can take a photo of themselves or a friend. They could draw a picture of the *Funnybones* character's head and animate it. Often it is very powerful to use a celebrity or famous person from history, to animate. For example, they could use Neil Armstrong to say his famous words when he landed on the moon. The children can create their avatars and then plan the words they will say. Are they being kind and behaving the same as they would when face-to-face?

Using the 'Morfo' app on the iPad
1. Once a picture has been chosen, open the 'Morfo' app.
2. Select 'Create' then 'Touch here to choose a photo'. It is important that the person in the photo is facing directly at the camera, in order for the animation to work well.
3. Choose the photo, then select 'Done'.
4. Pinch and stretch the white outline, to fit it onto the photo face, then select 'Done'.
5. Move the eyes, nose and mouth to fit, by dragging, pinching and stretching, then select 'Finish'.
6. A voice recording can be added by selecting 'Record', then 'Start'.
7. Play back the recording to see the face talk.
8. Select 'Share' to keep the video. In the free version, the animation can be created, but not kept. In the paid version, the video can be added to the camera roll and used in other apps, such as, 'Book Creator'.

■SCHOLASTIC

Year 2 Summer 1: Habitats

Overview

- The children have been learning about handling data and information. To help organise their thinking they can use 'mind mapping' apps that follow the flowchart style. This reinforces the learning in the algorithms and programming lessons. To further develop the learning, the children can create branching databases or tree-diagrams to create an animal identification key.

Resources

- 'Kidspiration maps lite' app (free)

Lesson activities

- Begin the lesson by playing the game 'Guess who?' The teacher selects three children from the class and thinks of one child, without saying which one. The children need to create questions to guess who it is, for example: *Do they have brown hair?* Once they have played the game, ask another child to take the role of the chooser and answer the questions.
- Using a simple mind-mapping app, such as 'Kidspiration maps lite' on the iPad, the children think of their questions to identify an animal.

They choose three different animals. In the 'Kidspiration maps lite' app, they can swap the boxes for a graphical image of an animal. Once complete, they try out the key with a partner. To begin the lesson, it may be useful to give a model example for the children to copy.

Using the 'Kidspiration maps lite' app on the iPad

1. Open the 'Kidspiration maps lite' app.

2. Select 'Create diagram'.

3. In the first oval on the screen, it says 'Main idea'. Add the first question to separate the animals, for example: *Does it have a tail?*

4. Select the yellow arrow to add another oval. Type 'Yes' then select the first oval and add another oval. In here, type 'No'.

5. The second question can be added, which continues to separate the animals.

6. From the menu at the top, select the yellow picture frame to display the icons menus.

7. Add an oval and then double tap on an animal icon picture to replace it with the picture.

Year 2 Summer 2: Pirates

Overview

- Arrrrgh, me hearties! Using the pirate theme, the children have been learning about communication. The way pirates communicate can be in a theatrical pirate voice and using pirate phrases. The children may have many experiences of this style through reading books and seeing films. They can recreate a pirate story using different animation apps. One example is the 'Toontastic Jr. Pirates Puppet Theater' app. It structures the story through a beginning, middle and end series of animations.

Resources

- 'Toontastic Jr. Pirates Puppet Theater' app (free)

Lesson activities

- The children can read and retell their favourite pirate stories. What are the names of the characters? What are the common features of the stories? What happened at the beginning, middle and end of the story? Using an app, such as 'Toontastic Jr. Pirates Theater', the children can create a story by dragging the characters around the screen and speaking the words (in a pirate style). They complete the beginning, middle and end before sharing their story with the class. Did the structure of beginning, middle and end help them create the story? Did they communicate the story clearly?

Using the 'Toontastic Jr. Pirate Theater' app on the iPad

1. Open the 'Toontastic Jr. Pirate Theater' app and watch the introductory movie.

2. Select 'Beginning', 'Middle' and 'End'.

3. Select 'Next' and the story begins. Watch the movie, then it will count down to begin recording.

4. Move the characters by dragging and speaking clearly. The children could work in pairs to play different characters. Then press 'Stop'.

5. Choose the theme music, then progress to recording the middle and then the end.

6. Add a title and a 'Directed by' name.

7. Watch the movie that has been created.